DEWEY

&

the DILEMMA of RACE

An Intellectual History, 1895–1922

DEWEY

&

the DILEMMA *of* RACE

An Intellectual History, 1895–1922

Thomas D. Fallace

Foreword by Robert Westbrook

Teachers College, Columbia University
New York and London

Published by Teachers College Press, 1234 Amsterdam Avenue, New York, NY 10027

Portions of Chapter 2 were adapted from the following: "John Dewey and the Savage Mind: Uniting Anthropological, Psychological, and Pedagogical Thought, 1894–1902," *Journal of the History of the Behavioral Sciences, 44*(4) (2008), pp. 335–350, copyright © Wiley-Blackwell; and "Repeating the Race Experience: John Dewey and the History Curriculum at the University of Chicago Laboratory School," *Curriculum Inquiry, 39*(3) (June 2009), pp. 381–405, copyright © Wiley-Blackwell.

Portions of Chapter 3 were adapted from the following: "The Mind at Every Stage Has Its Own Logic: John Dewey as Genetic Psychologist," *Educational Theory, 60*(2), (April 2010), pp. 129–146. Reprinted with permission.

Library of Congress Cataloging-in-Publication Data

Fallace, Thomas D. (Thomas Daniel)
  Dewey and the dilemma of race : an intellectual history, 1895–1922 / Thomas D. Fallace ; foreword by Robert Westbrook.
    p. cm.
  Includes bibliographical references and index.
  ISBN 978-0-8077-5164-0 (pbk.)—ISBN 978-0-8077-5165-7 (hardcover)
  1. Dewey, John, 1859–1952. 2. African Americans—Education. 3. Race relations. 4. Education—Philosophy. I. Title.
  LB875.D5F36 2011
  370.89—dc22

                                                              2010030550

ISBN 978-0-8077-5164-0 (paperback)
ISBN 978-0-8077-5165-7 (hardcover)

Printed on acid-free paper
Manufactured in the United States of America

18 17 16 15 14 13 12 11   8 7 6 5 4 3 2 1

CONTENTS

FOREWORD

One of the perennial tasks of the intellectual historian, one that sometimes we undertake with a certain glee, is to remind our readers that their philosophical heroes were not Olympian gods but historical human beings. Their work bears the marks of their moments. Even those who stood against the dominant currents of thought in their time were affected by them, sometimes far more than we would like to acknowledge.

When intellectual historians reveal that the marks of time that thinkers bear clash with the reigning moral or political convictions of our era, we inevitably pause to reassess the usefulness of these thinkers. Martin Heidegger, for example, was a Nazi; much more of a Nazi than we once thought. Some now contend that his thinking was thoroughly infused and tainted by a perspective that inclined Heidegger to embrace Hitler's regime, rendering his philosophy useless, even dangerous, for contemporary readers. Others have argued his Nazism was incidental to his revolutionary overcoming of the Western philosophical tradition, which remains a fruitful, instructive, and enduring work of genius. In any case, very few can now responsibly read Heidegger without wariness.

John Dewey was not, of course, a Nazi. But he was, as Thomas Fallace makes abundantly clear, wedded for the first 30 years of his long career to a "genetic psychology" and a linear evolutionary historicism that will trouble anyone eager to appropriate his philosophy. Yet Dewey was convinced of the injustice of racial discrimination and cultural imperialism.

Dewey, Fallace demonstrates, held that "ontology recapitulates phylogeny"—that is, he was wedded to "the idea that the mind developed through distinct stages of growth, which either analogously or biologically retraced the intellectual history of the human race." The child, at the outset, thought like a savage, and the savage was the child of modernity. "Like most of his contemporaries," Fallace writes, "Dewey suggested that native, primitive, and aboriginal societies did not merely represent different or alternative forms of living (or social occupations, as Dewey called them), but instead they represented earlier forms of living that modern, civilized culture had moved beyond." Cultural history was singular; its development was linear and teleological; and the modern West was the mature, "higher" successor to the immature, "lower" forms of human society, including the immigrant, Native American, and African American regions of the American social landscape.

Fallace is a first-rate intellectual historian who carefully reconstructs the milieu of early twentieth-century American academic psychology and social science generally, and places Dewey firmly within it. He is careful to emphasize that within the frame of genetic psychology and linear evolutionary historicism there was room for considerable debate, and that Dewey was a moderate who rejected biological racism, claims of inherent (as opposed to situational) racial or cultural inferiority, and permanent inequalities. Fallace also acknowledges that it is he, not Dewey himself, who works out conjecturally the most troubling logic of Dewey's thinking, particularly when it comes to the matters of racial discrimination. Nonetheless, he concludes, "ethnocentrism was built into Dewey's early pedagogy and philosophy; it was part of its weight-bearing structure."

What rescues Fallace's account from the annoying, anachronistic finger-pointing all too common in this sort of argument is the evidence he offers of how difficult it would have been for Dewey to stand outside this dominant theoretical frame, as well as his account of the work of early twentieth-century contemporaries such as Franz Boas and W.E.B. Du Bois. Finally, he shows that Dewey found his way, albeit slowly and awkwardly, to this "cultural pluralist" perspective in the 1920s, and in so doing tied the power of other elements of his thinking to the possibility of alternative modernities at home and abroad.

This book is likely to most trouble the waters among educational reformers because the Dewey they look to for inspiration is largely the Dewey of the period Fallace considers—the author of *The School and Society, The Child and the Curriculum,* and *Democracy and Education,* and the founder of the Dewey School at the University of Chicago. Insofar as ethnocentrism is part of the "weight-bearing structure" of Dewey's thinking in these years--and it is here that I suspect debates over Fallace's arguments will center--those for whom Dewey is a lodestar face some difficult labor of reconstruction. Happily for them, and the readers of this book, "Reconstructing Dewey" has a decidedly Deweyan ring to it.

—*Robert Westbrook*

ACKNOWLEDGMENTS

THE RESEARCH FOR this book began with a Jepson fellowship from the University of Mary Washington. I thank the University of Mary Washington for the course release time. My original intention for this project was to write a book tracing the various and conflicting ways in which Dewey's ideas were used by educational reformers throughout the twentieth century. As I was preparing for this project, I could not find an adequate intellectual history tracing the development of Dewey's educational ideas, so I thought that I would try to write one myself. Since I was not trained as a philosopher and am relatively new to Dewey studies, the encouragement and feedback of more established scholars meant a great deal. I thank Eric Bredo, Eric Gable, Elizabeth Branch Dyson, and Johann Neem for ideas and context related to the manuscript. Robert Westbrook and Michael Eldridge were kind enough to read portions of the manuscript and provide encouragement and useful advice at crucial points in the writing process. Jim Garrison read almost the entire manuscript and not only suggested additional essays by Dewey that I needed to address, but challenged my ideas and helped me clarify my arguments throughout. He is a true scholar whose intellectual rigor and curiosity were an inspiration. I thank David Hicks for putting me in touch with Jim. I thank my beautiful wife, Victoria Fantozzi, for finding the time to read portions of the manuscript, while writing her own dissertation and caring for our son, Quinten. I also thank my student, Lindsay D'Adamo, for providing some timely and careful proofreading.

Portions of Chapter 2 appeared as "Repeating the Race Experience: John Dewey and the History Curriculum at the University of Chicago Laboratory School," *Curriculum Inquiry* 39(3) (June 2009), 381–405, and "John Dewey and the Savage Mind: Uniting Anthropological, Psychological, and Pedagogical Thought, 1894–1902," *The Journal of the History of Behavioral Sciences,* 44(4) (Fall 2008), 335–350. I thank Blackwell Publishing, Wiley-Blackwell Publishing, and the Ontario Institute for Studies in Education for permission to use this material. Portions of Chapter 3 appeared as "The Mind at Every Stage Has Its Own Logic: John Dewey as Genetic Psychologist,"

Educational Theory (April 2010), 60(2), 129–146. I again thank Blackwell Publishing for permission to use this material. I thank Brian Ellerbeck, Meg Hartmann, and the editorial staff at Teachers College Press for their support and ideas.

The Historical Dewey
and the Savage Mind

JOHN DEWEY IS the most studied educational philosopher of the twentieth century. So why do we need yet another book about him? Is there really anything new to be said? I certainly did not think so a few years ago when I began reading through Dewey's major works like *School and Society, How We Think*, and *Democracy and Education*. Despite the difficulty of Dewey's dense prose and the complexity of his ideas, I certainly got the gist of what he was saying. He wanted to break down divisions between theory and practice, thought and action, the child and the curriculum. He believed in hands-on activities, cooperative learning, making material immediately relevant for students, treating teachers as professionals, and reconstructing society through democratic means. I supplemented these readings with the biographies of Dewey by George Dykhuizen, Robert Westbrook, Steven Rockefeller, and Alan Ryan; the classic accounts of progressive education by Lawrence Cremin and Herbert Kliebard; and the award-winning account of the emergence of pragmatism by Louis Menand.[1] Armed with my hard-earned knowledge of Dewey's ideas, I was now ready to cite him in my scholarly work. By reading Dewey and appreciating his significance, I believed that I had successfully completed an important rite of passage into the profession of serious educational theory and research. I, like many educators, appreciated Dewey's insight and wisdom and read him as if he were speaking to me in the present.

During these readings, however, a few words that appeared in Dewey's educational work dozens of times perplexed me. Dewey kept making references to "the savage" and "primitive." For example, in *School and Society* Dewey wrote: "Many anthropologists have told us there are certain identities in the child's interests with those of primitive life. . . . There is a sort of natural recurrence of the child mind to the typical activities of primitive peoples."[2] Elsewhere Dewey argued that the content and form of past cultures "absolutely must be transmitted to the succeeding and immature generation if social life itself is not to relapse into barbarism and then into savagery."[3] As Dewey asserted in *How We Think*, were it not for education, "the story of civilization would be writ in water, and each generation would have laboriously to make for itself, if it could, its way out of savagery."[4] In *Schools of To-Morrow* Dewey praises a school where the student "learns to handle materials which lie at the foundations of civilization in much the same way that primitive people used them, because this way is suited to the degree of skill and understanding he has reached."[5] Likewise, in *Democracy and Education* Dewey explained that students should understand that "the entire advance of humanity from savagery to civilization has been dependent upon intellectual discoveries and inventions."[6] Again, in *The Dewey School* former University of Chicago laboratory schoolteachers Katherine Camp Mayhew and Alice Camp Edwards explained how "it could be said with truth that the fundamental interests of a child at this stage of growth and of a savage are the same: food, comfort, shelter. . . . It could be said that the child is like the savage in ability but not in capability."[7] Dozens of other references to "the savage," "primitive," and "barbarian" appear throughout Dewey's early and middle works. In 1902 he even wrote an essay specifically addressing the "savage mind," which William James praised in a letter to Dewey, calling it "humane" and "full of veracious psychological imagination." James encouraged Dewey to "keep up that line of study."[8]

To find out exactly what Dewey meant by "the savage" and why it kept appearing in his most popular and influential works on education, I began to read more about evolutionary theories of mind and behavior at the turn of the century and how the disciplines of history, psychology, sociology, anthropology, and even education were all working under an evolutionary paradigm that coordinated the psychological growth of the child with the sociological development of the human race.[9] This confirmed that Dewey's references to "the savage" situated him squarely in the intellectual world of the late nineteenth century, not our own. Today, educators no longer refer to "savages" and "primitives" when discussing pedagogy because by the First World War most psychologists abandoned the view that the intellectual ability and culture of the "savage" man corresponded with that of the young child. However, at the end of the nineteenth century almost every social scientist subscribed to some form of this view. Not only did most social scientists believe that the mind of the child corresponded with the mind of primitive man, but they believed that "savages" still walked the earth in the form of primitive tribes and cultures, representing earlier and abandoned forms of human social development. In addition, most believed that Native Americans and African Americans represented these earlier "primitive" forms. For example, Thomas Jesse Jones, a respected sociologist and head of the Hampton Institute in Virginia, argued in 1908 that reformers needed to be patient with the social progress of the American minorities he was teaching because Indians and Negroes had "suddenly been transferred from an earlier form of society into a later one without the necessary time of preparation."[10] Likewise, the most popular history textbook in America, David Saville Muzzey's *An American History,* insisted in 1911 that the "negroes are as a race, far, perhaps centuries behind whites in civilization."[11] Although Dewey did not agree specifically with these scholars, his ideas were, nevertheless, embedded in a similar set of cultural beliefs.

For example, in a letter he wrote to Clara Mitchell in 1895 outlining his plan for his laboratory school, Dewey explained how a "child's interest in present forms of living" should "lead him back to social groups organized in that way [for example]—hunting and fishing to the Indians." As Dewey explained, "This is geography as well as history because practically all stages of civilization are *now* presented somewhere on earth's surface [emphasis in original]."[12] Again, in *School and Society* Dewey argued that geography "presents the earth as the enduring home of the occupations of man."[13] In other words, like most of his contemporaries, Dewey suggested that native, primitive, and aboriginal societies did not merely represent different or alternative forms of living (or social occupations, as Dewey called them), but instead represented earlier forms of living that modern, civilized culture had moved beyond. Like his contemporaries, he believed that these social stages could be coordinated with the psychological development of the child. The earlier "stages of civilization" to which Dewey referred all happened to be represented by non-European, non-White societies. In fact, students at the Dewey School were specifically led to reach these ethnocentric conclusions. As Dewey School teacher Lauren Runyon taught her students, "In getting land from the Indians the same methods were used that have prevailed through the ages when a people with superior weapons and brains, in sufficient number, meet an inferior people."[14] In other words, according to Runyon, who taught under Dewey's supervision, members of more technologically advanced cultures were not merely different, but inherently superior to less advanced cultures. In another sample activity from the Dewey School—revealing the linear, ethnocentric scheme underlying the entire curriculum—students were instructed to "compare the American rivers with those of Africa, the Indians with the Negroes, and the degree of civilization of tribes in America with that of other peoples he has studied."[15] Through such comparisons, the Dewey School students were to arrive at the conclusion that modern, civilized society had surpassed the primitive Indian and Negro ones in a process of linear cultural development.

Despite the potentially provocative implications of Dewey's views, this book is not intended to be an exposé of his early racial and cultural orientation. Rather, I hope to historicize Dewey by placing him in his own intellectual and cultural context—that is, I hope to capture Dewey's original meaning by estranging him from the educational debates of our own time.

Specifically, I trace how the historical Dewey, like most of his contemporaries, struggled with a major dilemma of how to reconcile evolution, pedagogy, democracy, and race. The Darwinian theory of evolution suggested that knowledge was dynamic, fluid, and adaptive—it did not contain any latent, static, or essential potentials of the present or future world. Many proponents of the "new education" and the "new psychology" underlying the pedagogy that emerged in the 1890s fully accepted versions of this evolutionary view. But how to construct a theory of learning that was appropriate for a democratic form of living in which the alleged "winners," "losers," and "left-behinds" of evolution had to work and live together was a major challenge. At first Dewey created a linear, ethnocentric curriculum at the famous Dewey School that pointed to Western civilization as the cultural end point of all human progress. But pragmatism was a self-correcting theory of knowledge, and so by the First World War Dewey had reconstructed his orientation into what we now call the *cultural pluralist view*—the idea that cultures represent different ways of making sense of the world that do not necessarily move toward a single, generic type. In fact, by 1916 Dewey had realized that a plurality of cultures was a necessity for democratic living and intellectual growth. This shift was accompanied by an equally significant philosophical recognition of the significance of interaction in actualizing potentials. For example, in a 1922 essay on race prejudice Dewey called for an "international and interracial mind" reflecting "the adjustment of different types of culture to one another."[16] The same year, in an essay on individuality, equality, and superiority, Dewey remarked, "Inferior races are inferior because their successes lie in different directions, though possibly more artistic and civilized than our own."[17] This was a significant recognition that all cultures could not be subsumed within a single linear, hierarchical scheme as the curriculum at the Dewey School implied. However, despite Dewey's evolving views, an uncomfortable fact still remains: While Dewey was at the University of Chicago and beyond—when he did the majority of his writing on education—Dewey subscribed to his own version of the ethnocentric theory of correspondence that the psychological development of the child aligned with the sociological development of the race. That is, ethnocentrism was built right into Dewey's early pedagogy and philosophy; it was part of its weight-bearing structure.

LINEAR HISTORICISM AND GENETIC PSYCHOLOGY

So how do you write about Dewey's views on race during a period in which he did not explicitly address it? To do so, my inquiry reflects two historiographical assumptions. The first is that certain words used by Dewey and his collaborators, such as *savage, barbarian,* and *primitive,* reveal underlying beliefs about how the world was viewed by most nineteenth-century and early-twentieth-century social scientists. Particularly, I examined the secondary literature on how Dewey's use of the term *savage* represented an unspoken set of intellectual assumptions we no longer hold.[18] I then used this to arrive at a more nuanced interpretations of his educational, social, and cultural writings. As intellectual historian Thomas Kuhn suggests, "When reading the works of an important thinker, look first for the apparent absurdities in the text and ask yourself how a sensible person could have written them. When you find an answer . . . when these passages make sense, then you may find that the more central passages, ones you previously thought you understood, have changed their meaning."[19] Using Dewey's use of the term *savage* as a window into the intellectual world of the 1890s, I argue that Dewey framed his pre-1916 educational, social, and cultural thought in linear historicist and genetic psychological terms. Understanding this can allow us to uncover his racial views.

The second assumption is that unless he specifically noted otherwise (such as with his pointed critiques of the culture epoch theory, the transmission of acquired characteristics, and latent potentials), Dewey accepted the language and ideas of his peers and collaborators. In fact, such an approach aligned perfectly with Dewey's own philosophy. As Dewey explained in 1916, "In general it can be said that things we take for granted without inquiry or reflection are just the things which determine our conscious thinking. . . . And these habitudes which lie below the level of reflection are just those which have been formed in the constant give and take of relationships with others."[20] Thus Dewey's use of the term *savage* represented a set of ethnocentric ideas that existed "below the level of reflection," revealing the "habitudes" that he and his peers took for granted in their "give and take with one another." Therefore, I assume that Dewey employed the term *savage* because he knew it had meaning for his contemporaries and that, unless he explicitly stated otherwise, Dewey accepted the use of the term by his contemporaries, colleagues, and collaborators.

To understand fully Dewey's views of culture between the years 1894 and 1916, one must appreciate that Dewey viewed the world in historicist and genetic psychological terms. As a historicist, Dewey related all knowledge to prior knowledge; and as a genetic psychologist, he considered all knowledge as having incorporative contextual meanings organized through distinct psychological stages of consciousness. Dewey was part of a larger intellectual movement portrayed by historian Morton White as the revolt against formalism, which included an allegiance to "historicism" and "cultural organism." As White explains, *historicism* is the attempt to explain facts by reference to earlier facts, and *cultural organism* is the attempt to find explanations for certain phenomenon in social sciences other than the one that is primarily under investigation.[21] In both cases, the explanation of a phenomenon is approached in its contingent, developmental relationship to the broader social and historical context, instead of in reference to some external (and/or eternal) entity, essence, law, or truth.

Nineteenth-century historicism, however, came with ethnocentric baggage. In his controversial book *Provincializing Europe*, South Asian historian Dipesh Chakrabarty directly targets the ethnocentrism inherent in linear historicist views of progress such as Dewey's. Chakrabarty explains: "Historicism is what made modernity . . . not simply global but rather as something that became global over time, by originating in one place (Europe) and then spreading outside it. . . . Historicism thus posited historical time as a measure of the cultural distance (at least in institutional development) that was assumed to exist between the West and non-West."[22] Such a view inherently relegated non-Western cultures, including African, South Asian, East Asian, and Native American cultures, as previous steps toward the industrialized West—a "not yet" view of historical development that was used to colonize and suppress expressions of cultural autonomy by non-Western cultures in the United States and abroad. Linear historicism, according to Chakrabarty, "legitimated the idea of civilization" at a time when European ideologies and lifestyles were being imposed upon the "undeveloped" during the age of imperialism. While Dewey did not directly support imperialistic policies nor believe in the biological and psychical inferiority of any racial groups, his historicist approach to knowledge and education nevertheless conceived of culture in historicist terms and thereby related non-Western cultures to earlier steps toward the West.

By genetic psychologist, I mean that Dewey believed that human evolution involved intellectual growth, that this growth occurred through linear, universal psychological stages, and that each stage incorporated the prior one. He outlined these stages throughout the early and middle parts of his career, and understanding these stages can help explain the organization of his classic books like *How We Think* and *Democracy and Education*. Both of these works, I will argue, represent Dewey's transition from the linear historicism of the 1890s to his more mature work following the First World War, which was more concerned with cultural interactionism and the aesthetics of experience—ideas that led him away from the ethnocentric implications of his linear historicism and genetic psychology. By 1916 Dewey began referring to cultures in the plural and appreciated the necessity of a pluralistic social environment for the realization of potentials.

DEWEY, EVOLUTION, AND RACE

So what exactly did Dewey believe about evolution, education, democracy, and race? First, it is important to point out that throughout his career, Dewey rejected the inherent, latent, or predetermined inferiority of any racial or cultural group. For Dewey, all humans, regardless of race, were psychically equal. In addition, Dewey rejected the then-popular theory of the inheritance of acquired characteristics known as neo-Lamarckianism, which was used to ascribe biological superiority to Whites. He also rejected the then-popular imitation-suggestion theory of French sociologist Gabriel Tarde,[23] who argued that societies passively imitated one another, leading to distinct cultural types. For Dewey, humans were not born to achieve any necessary end nor were they biologically or sociologically predestined to fulfill any cultural role or level. Instead, humans developed through interactions mediated by their social environment. However, prior to 1916 Dewey believed that the degree of civilization contained in this mediating environment—arranged hierarchically and coordinated with the psychological stages of the child—determined whether one would develop to be savage or civilized. Consequently, those who were denied access to this civilized, scientific, democratic degree of culture were stuck in an earlier form. All of these earlier cultural groups happened to be non-White. In fact, in Dewey's *Ethics* textbook, co-authored with James Tufts, these earlier groups were identified specifically as "the so-called totem group, which is found among North American Indians, Africans and Australians, and was perhaps the early form of Semitic groups."[24]

After 1916 Dewey began to focus more on the significance of plurality in the environment as a necessity for actualizing potentials. Dubbed an "infinite pluralist" by his peer Scudder Klyce,[25] Dewey appreciated the necessity of preserving cultural difference and became more humble about the desire of non-Western cultures to be Westernized in prescribed ways. He revised his philosophical approach to make the preservation of cultural difference a necessity for actualizing the potentials of the individual and the society. After 1916 the linear historicist aspects of his work became less important, and the genetic psychological aspects of his work dropped out altogether. His pedagogy became less historical and more presentist, his philosophy became less psychological and more anthropological, and his views of evolution and race became less linear and more pluralist. As a result, he reconstructed his views into a form more palatable to twenty-first-century readers.

OVERVIEW OF THE BOOK

In the tradition of intellectual history I approach Dewey's views on evolution, education, democracy, and race as thinking rather than thought. This means that rather than imposing a present-day interpretive framework that would have been foreign to Dewey or ironing out the inconsistencies in his thought with his later works, I reconstructed his views using the ideas and language of the period in which he lived and wrote. I accept that Dewey struggled to make sense of his world by working with the intellectual tools of his own time as they emerged incrementally without knowledge of later developments. In Chapter 1, "Teaching Philosophy via Pedagogy," I trace how the contemporary events and influential figures of Chicago in the mid-1890s reinforced Dewey's emerging pragmatic beliefs, leading him toward a more social and historicist view of education. Based on this vision, he launched a laboratory school, coauthored a textbook on teaching mathematics, and challenged the leading educators of the day, William Torrey Harris and the American Herbartians. Chapter 2, "Repeating the Race Experience," explores how and why Dewey set up his curriculum at the famous University of Chicago laboratory school as an inquiry-based, linear historical reenactment of the social occupations of the human race. The ideas he formulated at his lab school found their biggest audience with the publication of the *Child and the Curriculum* and *School and Society*, both of which made direct reference to his linear historicism and genetic psychology. Chapter 3, "The Mind at Every Stage Has Its Own Logic," outlines Dewey's stages of psychological and sociological growth and how these provide insight into his evolutionary theory of ethics as well as allow for a genetic psychological reading of Dewey's classic *How We Think*. Chapter 4, "The Observable World Is a Democracy," traces Dewey's evolving thoughts on democracy and education in the context of the emerging behaviorist psychology, with special focus on the debate over the role of vocational education. I argue that the curricula described in the *Schools of To-Morrow* were specifically selected to demonstrate how vocational and academic content could be combined through a historicist pedagogy. Chapter 5, "The American Nation is Interracial and International in Its Makeup," places Dewey's thoughts on race and culture in the context of other scholars. Dewey rejected neo-Lamarckianism and believed in the psychical equivalence of all races, but prior to 1916 his linear historicism prevented him from reaching the cultural pluralist position of scholars such as W. E. B. Du Bois and Franz Boas. Chapter 6, "Mutual Adjustment to One Another," focuses on how the rise of social psychology, Dewey's trip to China and Japan, and his realization of the significance of a plural environment for actualizing potentials led Dewey to revise the ethnocentric historicism of the Dewey School curriculum and adopt his later, culturally pluralist views. Chapter 7, "The Environment Is Many, Not One," explores the arrival of this pluralist-interactionist view and how it played a central role his 1922 book *Human Nature and Conduct*, which sought to bring together Dewey's ideas on evolution, education, democracy, and race. As a result, Dewey's *historicism* evolved from what Chakrabarty defined as a linear "measure of the cultural distance" from the West to what Richard Rorty defined as the insistence that "historical circumstance goes all the way down—that is there is nothing 'beneath' socialization or prior to history which is definatory of the human."[26] Thus Dewey's historicism moved from a philosophy of linear development to a philosophy of interactional, pluralist redescription.

Ultimately, this book has two major objectives. The first is to resituate the historical Dewey in the thoughts and issues of his own time. In doing so, I question whether educators of the present can or should rip Dewey's early and middle ideas from the context that engendered them and apply them to current educational problems, issues, and agendas without explicitly recognizing that they are doing so. A major component of Dewey's pragmatism was that all knowledge was context-bound; it served a purpose in a particular situation and its usefulness was dependent upon that context. So it may be against the spirit of Dewey to take the solutions he worked out a century ago and apply them directly to the educational problems of the present. The second objective is to inspire a deeper appreciation for the complexity, intensity, and rigor of Dewey's arguments during a time when intellectuals were coming to terms with the repercussions of Darwin's theory of evolution and its applicability to human and social development. Dewey's linear historicism solved—at least temporarily—a number of philosophical, psychological, ethical, biological, pedagogical, and sociological problems of his day. So, ultimately, I want readers to have a somewhat contradictory experience upon reading this book: I hope they gain even greater appreciation for Dewey's genius and originality, but walk away less certain about whether his ideas are still applicable to the educational problems of the present.

Chapter 1

TEACHING PHILOSOPHY VIA PEDAGOGY

I N NOVEMBER 1894 John Dewey wrote a letter to his wife Alice explaining his recent visit to a local normal school for training teachers in Chicago where he had recently delivered some lectures on pedagogy. He was frustrated to discover that they had not accurately implemented the psychological principles he had outlined. "I guess I learned more psychology from their illustrations than they did from my principles," he reflected, "I think I'm in a fair way to becoming an educational crank; I sometimes think I will drop teaching philosophy and teach it via pedagogy." Dewey concluded that to bring about meaningful educational reform, lecturing and textbook-writing would not be effective; he would need to establish his own laboratory school. In the letter he envisioned what such a school would look like, "a school where some actual and literal constructive activity shall be the centre and source of the whole thing, and from which the work should always be in two directions—one the social bearings of that constructive industry, the other that contact with nature which supplies it with its materials."[1] An effective education, he later argued, required the child to relearn the lessons of the race in a manner that corresponded with how this development originally took place.

DEWEY'S ARRIVAL IN CHICAGO

Dewey was raised in Vermont as an evangelical Congregationalist. He remained a member of the church and worked with Christian organizations through his early career at the University of Michigan and the University of Minnesota. The German philosopher Georg Wilhelm Friedrich Hegel heavily influenced Dewey's earliest mentors, including H. A. P. Torrey, William T. Harris, and especially George Sylvester Morris. As a result, Dewey was initially attracted to Hegel's idealism because it accorded well with his religious faith and philosophical influences.[2] "Hegel's synthesis of subject and object, matter and spirit, the divine and the human, was," Dewey recalled, "no mere intellectual formula; it operated as an immense release, a liberation."[3] Dewey retained elements of his Hegelian idealism—especially notions of organicism and historicism—at the University of Chicago and beyond because the theory brought a sense of divine unity, which he so ardently sought, to the rapidly transforming modern world around him. *Organicism* was the belief that all knowledge was related and, therefore, should not be artificially segregated into disciplines. *Historicism* was the belief that the nature of a thing lied in its history, not its essence.

However, while in college and while earning his doctorate at Johns Hopkins University, Dewey was confronted with another major intellectual current of the time—*scientific positivism*. Sociologists such as Auguste Comte and Herbert Spencer refuted that there was any spiritual or divine force guiding society. Drawing inspiration from Isaac Newton's laws of physics and later Charles Darwin's theory of natural selection, the positivists argued that the world was governed by transcendent biological and natural laws—laws that were indifferent to human cognition.[4] Both the Hegelian and positivist views were historicist because both theories posited that the best way to study anything was to trace its historical development, and they both challenged the Aristotelian concept that entities had a predetermined "essence" in the intellectual realm that could be discovered independent of the experience of the physical world. Instead, the empirical reality of history was the key to discovering knowledge. In other words, both camps agreed that to understand any entity, one had to trace how it came into being. Dewey agreed.

When Dewey arrived in Chicago in 1894 he was 34 years old and had three children. Through his published work he had established himself as an up-and-coming scholar in philosophy. However, besides a couple of short essays addressing the college curriculum, he had shown little interest in elementary education up to that point. This would change rapidly in 1894 because as part of Dewey's appointment at the University of Chicago he was expected to take the lead in the newly established department of pedagogy. Dewey was attracted by the opportunity to find a practical application for his philosophical ideas. Within 2 years he would not only establish an influential laboratory school, but he would also author numerous essays and two major works on pedagogy, *The Psychology of Number and Its Application to Methods of Teaching Arithmetic* (with James McLellan) and *Interest in Relation to the Training of the Will*, introducing him to a national audience thirsty for applications of the "new psychology" and "new education."

THE NEW PSYCHOLOGY

The "new psychology" referred to the emerging findings based on empirical observation and scientific study. In opposition to what had come before, which was mainly philosophical speculation, the new psychologists struggled with how to apply the biological ideas of Darwin and the results of scientific experimentation to the development of the human mind. The new psychology began with Wilhelm Wundt's empirical studies of the faculty of attention. However, many psychologists rejected Wundt's Kantian dualistic distinctions between mind and matter and instead searched for purely biological explanations of mental states and evolution. Dewey subscribed early on to what we would now call *genetic psychology*—the idea that the mind developed through distinct stages of growth, which either analogously or biologically retraced the intellectual history of the human race. Genetic psychology was only one possible organizational scheme for the findings of new psychology, but it was the most influential approach in the United States in the 1890s. In one form or another, leading American scholars such as G. Stanley Hall, Charles Hubbard Judd, James Mark Baldwin, Lester F. Ward, Thorstein Veblen, and even, to a large degree, William T. Harris based their learning theories on historicist and genetic theories of race and culture. Dewey did not agree fully with any of these scholars. Instead, he had his own interpretation of how evolution applied to the development of mind and society.

By the 1890s psychologists in Germany, Britain, and the United States were divided into three groups based on this issue of the exact mechanism for psychic evolution. Ernst Haeckel, originator of the biogenetic law that ontogeny recapitulates phylogeny, considered both natural selection and the transmission of acquired characteristics as contributors to psychic evolution. Others, such as Wundt, barely recognized natural selection at all and instead (in accordance with Kant and Hegel) considered human will as the driving force behind evolution. Ultra-Darwinians like August Weismann drew upon his empirical research to disregard the inheritance of acquired characteristics altogether. Weismann had conducted an experiment in which he had cut off the tails of laboratory mice only to observe that their offspring did not end up inheriting the acquired characteristic of a shorter or cut tail.[5] Despite Weissman's experiment, many psychologists interested in pedagogy in some way subscribed to schemes that accepted the inheritance of acquired characteristics because if learning in the lifetime of the individual was not passed on to the offspring, then education could not be considered a major force of social reform and generational improvement.[6] For example, the theories of child-centered pedagogue G. Stanley Hall and social welfare advocate Lester F. Ward were both based on the assumption that acquired traits were biologically passed on.[7] This belief was referred to as "neo-Lamarckianism" because

Lamarck had first theorized on the significance of the transmission of acquired characteristics to evolution. In addition, many neo-Lamarckian reformers were social Christians who subscribed to religious-based social amelioration of class conflict. Unlike Darwinism, the doctrine of the transmission of acquired characteristics recognized a direction and purpose to social evolution and thereby allowed for divine guidance and intervention. Dewey never subscribed to neo-Lamarckianism—that is, to biological transmission of acquired characteristics—but he obviously believed in the acquired powers of social environment and education to shape the individual. For Dewey, it was culture, not biology, that passed along acquired traits.

To collect data for their genetic, evolutionary, and historicist themes, most anthropologists, sociologists, and psychologists employed the comparative method. This involved studying present-day premodern cultures for what they revealed about the laws of social development, as well as studying the biological impulses and instincts of children for what they revealed about psychical growth. Since researchers could not go back in time, the empirical data for these evolutionary laws had to come from these two sources: child study and ethnology. As G. Stanley Hall outlined in his explanation of the influence of anthropology on psychology, "the origin of language, character, temperament, will probably never have any solution unless they are found in the study of infancy, the growth of which epitomizes under our eyes the history of the race, each day sometimes representing perhaps the race-development of centuries."[8] Dewey, a former student of Hall, constructed his own philosophy of psychological and social growth in reaction to these emerging theories of the 1890s. While Dewey offered an innovative approach to these issues, his philosophy must also be understood in the context of certain evolutionary assumptions that most social scientists shared, despite the fact that many of these ideas were largely discarded in the decades that followed. There were four main assumptions: that the nature of a thing lies in its linear development and history; that the psychological growth of the individual somehow corresponds with or recapitulates the development of the human race; that inherited instincts affect and/or direct the intellectual, physical, and ethical growth of the individual and race; and that the dualism inherent in classic economics, formal logic, and traditional pedagogy needed to be updated in light of the findings of the new psychology.

Dewey's first book on education was *The Psychology of Number and Its Applications to Methods of Teaching Arithmetic*, which was co-authored with James McLellan, principal of the Ontario School of Pedagogy in Toronto. The study was the 33rd volume in the International Education series edited by William T. Harris, who was the U.S. Commissioner of Education. In a letter to Harris addressing the book, Dewey revealed, "It may interest you to know—what I shouldn't like to give away to the public—that I started first by trying to turn Hegel's logic over into psychology and then that into pedagogy."[9] While this letter implied that Dewey had moved beyond his Hegelianism by 1894, Harris did not seem to pick up on this. In fact, in the editor's preface, Harris immediately made a connection between the contents of McLellan and Dewey's book and the education approach of Hegel, because, according to Harris, the German philosophy first recognized the "multiplicity" and "unity" present in the psychology of number explored by the authors. By this Harris meant that each quantity was both a whole in itself (i.e., dime) and part of something else (i.e., a tenth of a dollar). The formal arithmetic of traditional schooling failed to address this relationship properly. Harris shared with Dewey and McLellan an antagonism toward the excessive emphasis on arithmetic in the elementary school as a way of allegedly developing the faculty of pure reason. He also agreed with McLellan and Dewey that "the science of number is indispensable for the conquest of Nature in time and space."[10] Thus Harris insisted that number had a qualitative element revealed through the development of the race that quantitative arithmetic had failed to address; this qualitative element was the psychological value of number. This was the major argument of McLellan and Dewey's book.

Regarding *Psychology of Number*, Dewey flippantly remarked in a letter to his wife in summer 1894, "I furnish the psychology, Dr. McLellan the methods, the teacher drops his nickel in the slot—and the pupil does the rest, as usual."[11] This comment reflected Dewey's cynicism toward straightforward methods textbooks as an effective means of reforming the school; perhaps this is why he did not write a practical textbook on specific teaching methods until *How We Think* in 1910. Dewey contributed the first three chapters of *Psychology of Number*, which made a case for why the new psychology should serve as the foundation for education reform in the elementary classroom. McLellan wrote the thirteen practical chapters that followed addressing the specifics on how to apply the new psychological approach to arithmetic, addition, subtraction, multiplication, division, measures, multiples, fractions, decimals, and percentages.

Dewey's opening chapters briefly introduced several themes that he would explore during his years at the University of Chicago, such as how divisions of traditional subject matter betrayed the organic unity of reality, how the form and content of the curriculum had been unnaturally severed from one another, how the stages of child development were part of the underlying unity of mind as opposed to distinct mental faculties, and how teachers needed to be reflective, informed practitioners. However, the major argument of *Psychology of Number* was that "number is to be traced back to measurement, and measurement back to adjustment of activity." Thus a number was not an ideological abstraction floating in metaphysical space, but rather was an outgrowth of the history of the race and needed to be taught as the reliving of this evolutionary process. As Dewey argued, "Number is the tool whereby modern society in its vast and intricate processes of exchange introduces system, balance, and economy into those relationships upon which our daily life depends." The Hegelian movement toward unity was revealed in the assertion: "All numerical concepts and processes in the process of fitting together a number of minor acts in such a way as to constitute a complete and more comprehensive act." Education was the process of realizing this unity, or as Dewey put it, "the work of supplying the conditions which will enable the psychical functions, as they successively arrive, and pass into higher functions in the freest and fullest manner." Such an educative process, Dewey insisted, could only take place "by a knowledge of psychology."[12]

McLellan and Dewey's approach to number was challenged almost immediately by H. B. Fine and D. E. Philips. Fine argued: "This book makes a false analysis of the number concept, but advocates methods in teaching arithmetic which are in the main good." He argued that counting did not originate with measurement, but instead he insisted that "men must have counted long before they knew how to measure in any proper sense."[13] Philips also questioned the evolutionary origins of number as outlined by Dewey, but not the idea that the child and primitive man were analogous. Drawing upon the experiments of G. Stanley Hall, Philips argued that students came to school with a series-idea that anticipated measurement. "Long before there is any conscious idea of number," Philips explained, "children delight in reproducing or following a series of any kind." Throughout the review essay Philips drew upon both child study and ethnographies of primitive cultures to draw comparisons between "the savage and the mathematical prodigy."[14] Maintaining the savage/child analogy, Dewey responded to Philips: "It is absurd," he insisted, ". . . to suppose that the savage or the child has a perfectly clear definite and ready-made concept of number before he ever counts up any quantity, and then proceeds to measure the quantity or find out how much there is."[15] Dewey insisted that knowledge was gained not through rational reflection, but through activity. Therefore, measurement was the first meaningful activity in which the child and savage engaged and thus must be the true root of the number concept.

William James directly influenced Dewey's approach to the psychology of number presented in the book. As Dewey later reflected, James's "substitution of the 'stream of consciousness' for discreet elementary states" and his "biological conception of the *psyche* . . . worked its way more and more into all my ideas and acted as a ferment to transform old beliefs."[16] One of Dewey's first references to James was in an 1894 essay on the theory of emotion. A decade earlier James had argued that emotion was a consequence of willful behavior, not a mere mechanical reaction of the brain: Humans perceived certain objects or events, their bodies instinctively reacted, and then the mind and body *felt* the emotion. Therefore, the mind did not directly cause emotions, as Darwinians suggested, but rather the mind mediated the response to emerging instincts as the body discharged these motor and organic responses into consciousness. Dewey called this innovation the James-Lange discharge theory because Danish psychologist Carl Lange simultaneously discovered the idea. In his 1894 essay on emotion Dewey expressed his appreciation for the James-Lange theory, although, he explained in a footnote, "a crude anticipation of James's theory is found in Hegel's *Philosophie des Geist*."[17] Like James, Dewey explained that emotion is not a passive response to a stimulus, but instead "is a mode of behavior which is purposive, or has an intellectual content, and which also reflects itself into feeling or Affects."[18] Emotion for Dewey was the "felt process of the realization of ideas," or the unity of body and mind in reaction to a felt need or problem. Thus just as the number concept represented the unity of the mind and external world through activity, so too did emotion represent the unity of a felt problem and the appropriate response through activity. As Dewey concluded—anticipating his famous critique of the reflex arc (see below)—"*the idea and the emotional excitement are constituted at one and the same time . . . they represent the tension of stimulus and response within the coordination which makes up the mode of behavior* [italics in the original]." [19] That is, the mind was not a passive recipient of stimuli but rather approached a stimulus (or object) with a purpose and focus that affected what course the response would take. Likewise, the response organically contained coterminous emotional and cognitive elements. In all cases, through action the mind mediated the relationship between the spontaneously arising instincts and the emerging problem in the environment.

In a review of H.M. Stanley's book *Studies in the Evolutionary Psychology of Feeling*, Dewey again referenced the James-Lange discharge theory to critique the dualism inherent in Stanley's Darwinian approach that "it is pleasure-pain which forces all action." Instead, Dewey rebutted, "When pain is stimulating to action, it is so, I think, not immediately, but through the medium of thought or some sensory *quale.*" Dewey suggested that Stanley's account of the evolutionary origins of emotion fell short because it failed "to recognize that the James-Lange theory, taken together with Darwin's theory, afford a complete account" for the genesis of emotion.[20] Dewey defined his James-inspired theory of mind in the following way:

> This theory, it may be recalled, accounts for the evolution of feelings by reference to habits of use in maintaining life, whether getting food, attack and defense in relation to enemies, or reproduction; and holds that the emotional stress of feeling emerges, when formed habits conflict with the line of action demanded by a changed situation, when, accordingly, it is necessary to readjust the habit.[21]

Dewey insisted repeatedly in his discussions of the origins of thought and emotion that the Darwinian natural selection model of spontaneously emerging thoughts, actions, and reactions inadequately assigned purpose (or teleology) to an activity after the fact, thereby locating the meaning of the activity outside of the act itself. However, Dewey's James-influenced view located the teleological process of growth within the mind and body of the savage and child. This rescued the individuality and volition of the savage/child, making him an active contributor to his learning and growth—an important factor in Dewey's view of social evolution.

The Psychology of Number revealed several concepts that Dewey would continue to explore for the next few years. First, he conceptualized psychology and pedagogy in linear historicist terms. The best way to approach any problem or to learn any content was to relearn it in the manner that the race originally discovered it. Whether it was math, reading, or science, content was best taught through the act of repeating how savages and their descendents originally created this knowledge through necessity, innovation, and reflection. In this way knowledge would be organically linked with action. Next, the book revealed Dewey's appreciation for the psychology of William James. Particularly, Dewey emulated James's idea of the unity of mind and body as co-conspirators in a situated action. The mind was not merely a passive recipient of outside stimuli and satisfactions, but instead acted upon the environment in a process that transformed the individual as well as physical and social context surrounding it. Finally, the book demonstrated remnants of Dewey's Hegelian idealism. Besides praising Hegel outright, Dewey and McClellan also presented a pedagogical approach that William Torrey Harris mistook as a straightforward application of Hegel's ideas. Indeed, Dewey's innovative approach to pedagogy was subtle, perhaps even too subtle for most reviewers to perceive. In fact, the idea of using the race history as the foundation for the curriculum (i.e., recapitulation) was shared by many other scholars of the period. Dewey distinguished his approach from these others only by directly attacking their philosophical assumptions, which he did the following year.

THE HERBARTIANS

Although there was general agreement among leading social scientists about the correspondence between the growth of the individual and race, there were still major issues to be worked out about the mechanism of development, which had immediate implications for the new pedagogy. The debate pitted William T. Harris against the Herbartians, who represented the two leading approaches to curriculum in 1895. The issue thrust Dewey onto the national educational scene, and outlined his organic, functional approach to the educative process. Drawing in the ideas he had developed in *The Psychology of Number*, Dewey outlined the theoretical ideas he would work out the next year at his laboratory school. First, he would need to rationalize to himself and others why he would not simply be implementing the popular idea of German philosopher Johann Frederich Herbart. In fact, before Dewey arrived at the University of Chicago to become the head professor of Philosophy and Pedagogy, he explained in an 1894 letter to his wife, he had received a request "from 9 schoolmaams in some West side ward asking me to please form a class and then teach them Herbartian pedagogy." The request by these teachers demonstrated how popular Herbartian theory had become among progressive-minded teachers. "But," Dewey explained to his wife, "I shan't indulge in that cruelty."[22] As Dewey later explained, he dismissed the Herbartian system because the theory did not adequately account for biological impulse and instinct, it overemphasized the dualistic and formal presentation of content and objects independent of the contexts that engendered them, and it failed to create an organic "unity among ideas."[23] Dewey's own views on pedagogy were sharpened and clarified during the debate that erupted over the Herbartian idea of interest. In fact, in 1895 Dewey presented his first sole-authored major work on education, *Interest in Relation to Training of the Will*, in the context of this debate.

Herbartianism was the first educational fad to engage the American imagination. The theory generated a great deal of excitement among many educators in the 1890s, yet by the early 1900s the theory disappeared as quickly as it had arrived, due in large part to the popularity of Dewey's ideas. Nevertheless, Herbartianism reinforced the movement toward historicist and genetic approaches to the curriculum. Johann Frederick Herbart was a German philosopher who tutored three Swiss boys in the late eighteenth century. Based on this experience he constructed an innovative educational scheme, which was further developed by his German disciples Karl Volkmar Stoy, Tuiskon Ziller, and Wilhelm Rein. Ziller compiled the specific Herbartian steps of learning: (1) the analysis and/or explanation of facts; (2) the synthesis, or assimilation of these facts; (3) the identification of the most important facts; and (4) the applications of the learned principles. Through this process the content was not only learned, but "apperceived." The term *apperception*—the idea of making one's experience clear in one's consciousness—was coined by German psychologist Wilhelm Wundt.[24] By apperception the Herbartians meant that the facts had been incorporated into a psychic command center of the mind, which controlled the organization of all subsequently acquired knowledge. These "apperceptive masses" were coterminous with the soul. They guided the tastes and aided in the cultivation of the mind. Learning had not truly taken place until the content was associated with previously apperceived content and directed toward more complicated, difficult material. According to Herbartians, to make the apperception of material occur more naturally, teachers were to relate the contents of the curriculum to one another through "correlation" or "concentration." Teachers were encouraged to explore the connections among the different disciplines and bodies of knowledge and present them in a correlated manner. Like Dewey, the Herbartians agreed that history was considered the great synthetic subject and all other subjects could be incorporated within it.[25]

As we have seen, Herbartian curricular ideas entered the discourse in the 1890s in the context of historicist theories of mental development and the emerging American functionalism of William James. The Herbartian concepts of correlation, apperception, culture-epoch, and interest shared a number of assumptions with the mental faculty approach it hoped to replace, but it also included a number of innovative assumptions. The Germans had incorporated many Herbartian ideas into their own schools, and many German-trained scholars had brought these concepts back to the United States. In fact, G. Stanley Hall and William Torrey Harris praised the Herbartians for their concept of correlation, and they generally bought into the idea of apperception. Like Hall, the Herbartians also subscribed to the theory of recapitulation, which they referred to specifically as the culture epoch theory. In this manner, the Herbartian scheme served as a transition from the German curricular approaches to the pragmatic and functional ones that followed.

In the 1880s a number of influential American pedagogues, including Charles DeGarmo, Charles and Frank McMurry, and C. C. Van Liew, had studied the pedagogical and philosophical theories of Herbart in Germany. When they returned to the Unites States, they began disseminating Herbart's ideas, including the culture epoch theory (also known as the theory of correspondence or just recapitulation), in educational journals, lectures, and textbooks such as Charles De Garmo's *Essentials of Methods,* published in 1889.[26] As Van Liew explained, "There are certain very distinct and striking parallel lines in the development of the child and the race, both from the formal and material points of view. These parallel lines are traceable in the intellectual, emotional, and volitional development of both."[27] Hall believed that his laboratory research had confirmed the validity of this theory, and many other American social scientists, such as James Mark Baldwin and Charles Judd, subscribed to similar developmental schemes. As Baldwin confirmed, inquiries into psychological development of the individual "in the earlier stages of his growth" should shed light upon "his social nature, and also upon the social organization in which he bears a part."[28] However, the most controversial Herbartian theory—and the one in which the Herbartians diverged most from the ideas of Baldwin, Hall, Harris, and the proponents of mental discipline—was the concept of interest.

At the time it was generally believed that children and adolescents spent their leisure time pursuing their childish and trivial (and savage) interests; school was deliberately designed to combat these tendencies, to inculcate them with the culture and knowledge they needed for the future through the exercise and strengthening of the will. "Only concentrated and prolonged efforts in one direction," Hall insisted in 1892, "really train the mind, because only they train the will beneath it."[29] Likewise, influential German pedagogue Wilhelm Diesterweg insisted that pedagogical ideas are "only fruitful if I arrived at them by exertion. . . . Possession without toil means nothing; exertion everything."[30] The process of learning was supposed to be difficult in order to develop the mental faculties and will. Of course, there were precedents for the use of interest in education, including the pedagogical ideas of Rousseau, Pestalozzi, and Froebel, but these romanticists directed their schemes mainly at very young children. But the Herbartians used interest as the foundation for the entire age range of their educational scheme and combined the idea with the anthropological notion of cultural-epochs.

Interest accorded with the Herbartian cultural epoch theory, because it brought structure and sequence to the curriculum in a way that recognized the evolution of social systems. The interests of children were perfectly coordinated with the historical interests of the race. This interest was not necessarily based in biological impulse and inherited instinct in the way that Hall and Baldwin had outlined. In fact, the Herbartians remained ambiguous regarding from exactly where "interest" originated. At first they relied more on logic and metaphysics than any kind of biological research, but later they attempted to incorporate evolutionary notions of "inherited energies."[31] However, in his 1895 outline of the culture epoch theory, Van Liew presented an impressive list of scholars past and present—including Hegel, Froebel, Pestalozzi, Darwin, Spencer, Comte, and Baldwin—who all subscribed to the recapitulation theory in one form or another. The idea had deep roots in the intellectual traditions of Western philosophy and social science.

For many educators in the 1890s, Herbartianism seemed like the ultimate synthesis of the Germanic ideas of the national soul, the student-centered ideas of the romanticists, the mental faculty psychology of college professors such as Harvard president Charles Eliot, and the evolutionary notions of functional development. It brought unity to the contradictory array of theories being used to justify history in the curriculum. The "successive typical thought masses must be so arranged as not only to conform to the requirements of interest in accordance with the cultural epochs," Van Liew argued, "but also to reveal a clear picture of the growth and nature of our social, industrial, and national institutions, ideals, and needs, and to create a love for them and a lively regard for their welfare."[32] The theory suggested that, with a slight alteration, the mental faculty approach could be reconciled with the emerging theories of genetic psychology and could also instill a love of country. Therefore, its appeal was far-reaching and timely.

On a superficial level the Herbartian scheme looked a lot like Dewey's instrumental approach. In fact, Dewey admired that the Herbartians did "not separate intellectual and moral training," aimed their theory "at unification (organization) both in method and in curriculum," and had "developed a definite, coherent system, not merely truistic generalities" like Harris and Hall had done.[33] However, his praise for the educators ended there. Drawing upon his theories in psychological, biological, and sociological evolution, Dewey constructed an innovative (if somewhat inchoate at this point) approach to learning. He wasted no time in using his pedagogical ideas to challenge the biggest names of the new education.

INTEREST VERSUS THE WILL

Like Dewey, other scholars including Hall and Harris immediately viewed the Herbartian doctrine of interest with suspicion. Although Hall's evolutionary psychology was more empirical than both the mental faculty approach and the Hegelian idealism supported by Harris, Hall was still a strong advocate of training the will, which he asserted was a direct product of the psychical inheritance of the race. Both "history and character," Hall explained, "are written in the habits of muscles, which constitute about one half of the human body and are preeminently the organs of the will." For Hall, the soul represented the harmony between the inherited physical attributes and impulses of the body and the divine force present in the individual. The will was the main instrument for bringing about this alignment. "This power of totalizing, rather than any transcendent relation of elements, constitutes at least the practical unity of the soul" he explained, "and this unimpeded association of its elements is true or inner freedom of will." The will was the crucial element in the process of uniting the laws of nature with development of the individual. The process of learning, he argued, should be driven by exertion but assured by the continual revelation of nature's plan. The effort needed to be both physical and mental, because the will was both the product of the body and the divine guidance of the mind.[34]

In contrast, Harris had little use for the physical attributes of the body, or its inherited instincts and impulses. His Hegelian educational scheme was entirely rationalistic. As a result, the will was even more central to his theory, because the will of the individual represented the objective alignment with the universal will of God. Without the universal will present in the individual, all was subjective. In an 1895 essay Harris directly attacked the Herbartian idea of interest, which he asserted was being used in place of will as the guiding purpose of education. The Herbartians "had no place in their psychology for the will as the free self-determination of the soul" and made it "devoid of self-activity and of all multiplicity of attributes." If self-activity was directed by interest instead of the soul-as-will, Harris explained, morality would have nothing to appertain to, resulting in subjectivity and selfishness. The soul, Harris insisted, should always be treated as something transcendental that could never be linked to individual interests. The argument was more philosophical than psychological, but Harris nevertheless reinforced the centrality of self-discipline and exertion to the educative process, an idea he shared with Hall and mental disciplinarians.[35]

American Herbartian Charles DeGarmo responded to this attack. He agreed with Hall that the child only gained moral insight by mastering the elements of civilization, but insisted that "Herbart says that it is our duty to interest the child in these very studies that produce this moral insight." DeGarmo assured Harris (and his own followers) that "it is the development of will and character that Herbart emphasizes, and this is the important thing."[36] Harris replied that he did not object to interest being brought into education, but to place education entirely upon it "falls into the doctrine of pleasure, or that modern Utilitarian doctrine of Bentham and his disciples."[37] Harris revealed his underlying fear that any indulgence in student interest could be a slippery slope toward narrowly conceived utilitarianism, wherein students studied only those topics that had immediate relevance to their occupations. Education, he insisted, was about discovering the transcendent truths of man, which could never be achieved solely through interest.

Harris was arguing against a caricature of Herbartianism; it was never really based solely on interest. But he did point out the inconsistencies in the theory, especially its awkward amalgam of transcendentalism and biological evolutionism, which were mutually exclusive theories of mind and matter. Dewey weighed in on the debate in media res. In a rhetorical move Dewey would use numerous times over the next 50 years, he asserted that will and interest should not be viewed as opposites, but rather, if refashioned into "self-expression," they should be viewed as the same thing. Dewey denied the idea that any cultural object or product was inherently more interesting to the child than another. This erroneous idea, supported by both Harris and the Herbartians, Dewey explained, was the "German schoolmaster's psychology, not the psychology of the child"; it was used to emphasize authority and the formation of individual character toward a predetermined path. Instead, education should be based upon "securing in the school the conditions of direct experience and the gradual evolution of ideas in and through the constructive activities." The interest of a child should emerge and be linked to particular historical problems. Interest for Dewey, employing a definition that confused many, is "primarily a form of self-expressive activity—that is, growth through acting upon nascent tendencies." Interest was expressed through action, not prior to it, and it was expressed through an external product in relation to this action, not drawn to particular products on an a priori basis.[38]

In his response Dewey attempted to forge a theory of mind and society that combined the generative and creative elements of the rational mind with the inherited biological impulses of the race. According to Dewey, Harris and the Herbartians had ignored the latter, while Hall had not adequately accounted for the former. Interest did not merely emerge from biological impulses toward particular bodies of knowledge from the history of the race, but rather interest was a product of the biological impulse toward any object that met the immediate demands of an emerging problem. For Dewey, *interest* was the "annihilation of the distance between the person and the materials and results of his action; it is the instrument which effects their organic union."[39] What others had called "will through exertion," Dewey refashioned as need directed toward satisfaction. The natural human impulse of the child desired exertion (or will) toward resolution of an immediate felt need or problem.

Responses to Dewey's ideas were mixed. At an 1896 meeting in Jacksonville, Florida, several educational scholars remarked that Dewey's use of the concept "interest as self-expression" was ambiguous and inconsistent (in a later edition of the essay Dewey replaced "self-expression" with "growth"). Dewey responded, "Of course, the term interest, taken without explanation or discussion is ambiguous. If it had a meaning which was fully elaborated and universally recognized, no scientific interest would attach further study." Dewey explained that his essay merely tried to bring the latest psychological theory to bear on an issue that had been mainly framed as a philosophical debate. He humbly, if not disingenuously, insisted that more discussion was needed. At the meeting, after expressing his confusion with Dewey's essay, Harris insisted that interest was guided by pleasure, but pleasure did not necessarily educate in the way that divinely directed will did. "Will wills will," Harris proclaimed confidently. Charles McMurry, in a response aimed at Harris, remarked, "Those who advocate interest as a vital element in teaching are charged with ambiguity, ... The opponents of interest, however . . . deny interest *in toto*." McMurry insisted, "They are at least as much at fault as the supporters of the theory of interest."[40] The Hegelian idealism posited by Harris did not adequately account for interest at all, an element that common sense suggested obviously somehow played into the learning process. Inconsistencies in the use of interest, McMurry argued, should not be used to dismiss the idea altogether.

In an essay published in February 1896, Frank McMurry continued to defend the Herbartian doctrine of interest and its relationship to the culture epoch theory. Making interest the aim of education, he explained, did not mean entertaining or amusing the child; it meant that the instructor chose subject matter with careful reference to the learners, and that content would fit "as closely as possible to their past experience, in order that [students] may feel genuine appreciation of it." Again, Herbartians believed that the contents of the past experience of the child recapitulated the contents of the past experience of the race. Just as the race had developed an abstract sense of duty as a product of the civilized mind, so would the child. "The study of the great men in history," McMurry argued, "is continually furnishing practice for the feeling of approval or condemnation and the accompanying one of obligation to imitate or shun the same kind of action." Interest, not the will, guided children toward the higher ideals of the civilized mind as they were confronted with the lessons of the past.[41]

In May 1896 Harris again weighed in on the interest-will debate. A year had passed since Harris first expressed confusion over Dewey's position on the issue. Upon further reflection and in accordance with his introduction to *The Psychology of Number*, Harris decided that Dewey's essay, in fact, supported his own Hegelian scheme. According to Harris, Dewey's insightful essay had saved the doctrine of interest from narrow utilitarianism and hedonism by linking the concept to "a higher and defining principle"—self-expression.[42] If interest was conceived of as part of the process of revealing the divine will in the individual and world, then it was an acceptable way of looking at things. Thus Harris interpreted self-expression as the third and highest stage in his own evolutionary scheme that involved movement from the "atomistic" stage to the "pantheistic" stage to the "self-activity" stage, which employed the higher faculties of reason.[43] Using Dewey's view of interest as self-expression, Harris offered up a truce with the Herbartians:

> [Interest] is a very great question for pedagogy, and the Herbartians claim to have preempted the field. All other schools of pedagogy will ask permission to assist in this great enterprise. Hitherto it has not been possible to secure a good understanding between them and the followers of the established order. But I believe that a new study of interest in the light of Professor Dewey's discussion will lead to a mutual understanding and hearty cooperation. Interest must be acknowledge as subordinate to the higher question of the choice of a course of study that will correlate the child with the civilization into which he is born.[44]

Harris suggested a compromise, which he kindly attributed to Dewey, that interest could have a significant part of the new pedagogy as long as it aimed to cultivate the child with the greatest achievements of the race. As long as the interests were directed toward the divine will, it did not directly contradict his Hegelian theory. Harris requested that Herbartians lead pedagogues in their effort to catalogue the interests of children through their entire evolution. These interests could then be coordinated with the appropriate "higher"' cultural content and products.

This interest-will compromise was immediately recognized and endorsed by some educators. For example, W. E. Wilson, a Herbartian professor at the State Normal School in Providence, Rhode Island, explained: "Interest is not at all the sensation of gliding downhill on ice. It is rather the sensation of exertion, of rising to a higher position against gravitation." Thus interest reinforced the cultivation of the mind toward the higher achievements of civilization by directing and enforcing the will (i.e., exertion). Interest, Wilson explained, "is not merely the best motive for learning, but it is itself among the primary ends of education."[45] Appealing to common sense, Wilson explained how the knowledge students learned would not only be acquired more efficiently, but it would also be retained longer if students were interested in it.

Likewise, Henry Tucker, an instructor at a high school in St. Louis, agreed that interest and exertion needed to be considered in conjunction with one another. Citing Dewey as an influence, Tucker explained that "effort must be exercised and interest must be maintained in reasonable proportion; the relative ratio of the two will depend upon the subject, the topic, and the ability of the teacher." He suggested that historical instruction needed to be connected immediately to the present social world and to current events. "As history teachers," Tucker explained, "we need to arouse the interest of the pupil in order to get the fullest expression of his mind." But these historical connections to the present would enhance instruction in history, "so long as such consideration serves only as a sidelight and does not overshadow the lesson in hand."[46]

Like these teachers, Harris and the Herbartians praised Dewey, and they considered him in general agreement with their own respective approaches to curriculum. For example, in his 1903 revised textbook, *The Elements of General Method*, Charles McMurry incorporated the innovations of Dewey into his pedagogical scheme. The sources of interest for the child in the curriculum, he explained, "as conceived by Herbart, by recent child study, and by Dr. Dewey," demonstrated how to link "the strong and growing tendency to place instinctive, spontaneous interests of childhood" with the "the best culture materials which the history, literature, and science of the world furnish, and also the whole range of typical modern industries and social life."[47] Thus McMurry used Dewey to link his Herbartian pedagogy to social theory, because Herbart had not directly addressed the sociological aspects of schooling. Concerned mostly with psychological process of learning, which in the 1890s was referred to as "child-study," McMurry employed Dewey's philosophy to fill in the holes of his Herbartian theory in regard to how schools should cultivate the mind in specific reference to an evolving democratic society. Since Herbart constructed his theories for an imperialist German monarchy, not a democracy, McMurry essentially used Dewey to Americanize his Herbartian educational scheme.

However, Dewey did not fully agree with either Harris or the Herbartians. As I will show in the next chapter, in 1896 Dewey published a pointed critique of the Herbartian culture epoch theory, and in 1898 he published a respectful, but negative, review of Harris's text, *Psychologic Foundations of Education*. Dewey wrote that he considered Harris's approach "a fair statement of existing practice" and lamented that "Dr. Harris should throw his deservedly great authority in the direction of what seems unduly conservative and reactionary."[48] Despite Harris's attempt to incorporate the findings and theories of the new psychology, he still relied too heavily on an outdated metaphysics that had largely been dismissed in light of the Darwinian approaches to mind and behavior. Harris never took biological instinct and inherited impulse seriously enough, and he always directed his educational scheme toward the "high ground of the spirit of civilization"—a content-rich curriculum representing the five windows of the soul (mathematics, geography, literature, grammar, and history).[49] Thus, according to Dewey, both the Harris and Herbartian curricula were geared excessively toward the acquisition of content, not at underlying processes that lay beneath them, and both failed to incorporate the latest findings of psychology and sociology.

By addressing and critiquing the biggest names in American pedagogy in 1895–1896, Dewey completed his movement away from Hegelian idealism and fully embraced the pragmatic views of James. By reading Dewey solely through his critiques of these scholars, however, we may overlook how he borrowed a little bit from each one on the road to developing his own views. From Harris and Hegel, Dewey retained the idea of an active mind moving toward organic wholeness, but stripped the theory of its metaphysical aspects and replaced that with a more nuanced form of social mediation. Like the Herbartians, Dewey agreed that these sociocultural mediations could be organized hierarchically as the phases of cultural development and agreed that each stage could be coordinated with the relevant phases of child development. However, Dewey argued that each stage should be focused on the appropriate activities (or social occupations), not the abstract products or content from each epoch. From James, he borrowed the idea that the volition and creativity of man were outgrowths of evolution itself that could be subordinated to the individual and social mind. Thus Dewey agreed with James that man was a participant in social evolution, not a passive observer. As Dewey later reflected, his growing interest in education, which matured precisely at the point in which he was constructing his instrumental views, "fused with and brought together what might have otherwise have been separate interests—that in psychology and that in social institutions and social life."[50] He reconciled these disciplinary approaches through his pedagogy. In addition, Dewey's estimation of "the savage mind" as culturally, but not biologically, deficient played a central role in his reconciliation of sociology, psychology, and pedagogy. For this reason, Dewey would continue to make repeated references to "the savage" in his works in the 1890s and beyond.

In accordance with the general argument of this book it should also be pointed out what Dewey, Harris, Hall, and the Herbartians all had in common—a general acceptance of the genetic and linear historicist view of the mind and society. It was never a matter of whether human development corresponded with the development of the race, but rather a matter of how the two fit together and how to explain the exact mechanism for growth, innovation, and progress. Dewey never questioned the basic idea of correspondence between the stages of sociological and psychological development. In fact, the curriculum he designed at the University of Chicago laboratory school was based on this very idea.

TURNING THEORY INTO PRACTICE

When Dewey opened his experimental elementary school in 1896, he had no elementary school teaching experience, and so he had to rely heavily on the experienced female teachers he hired to implement his ambitious vision. In particular, his wife, Alice, and Ella Flagg Young were significant additions to the laboratory school faculty. They both had a critical role in turning Dewey's ambitious vision into reality. Dewey later commented that Young was the "wisest person in school matters with whom he has ever come in contact in any way."[51] However, Young and Alice Dewey both joined the school after it had already been established. It was Clara Mitchell—a forgotten name in educational history—who was first charged with the nearly impossible task of translating Dewey's theory into practice. In fact, the advertisement for the University of Chicago "primary school" issued in January 1896 declared that "Miss Clara Mitchell will be in immediate charge."[52] In Dewey's letters to Mitchell in the fall of 1895 he demonstrated both the precision of his theoretical ideas and the vagueness of their applications. In the rambling and at times incoherent letters to Mitchell, Dewey listed idea after idea in what must have been an overwhelming barrage of drawings, theories, and concepts with few concrete applications for the classroom. Drawing in the ideas he had outlined in *The Psychology of Number* and *Interest in Relation to the Training of the Will*, Dewey put forth an innovative vision of schooling that would combine theory with practice, intellect with action, and academics with industrial content. Dewey's vision was held together by his views on the sociocultural evolution of the human race and how the savage had solved the historical problems of the past.

The issue to be explored at the laboratory school, Dewey explained to Mitchell, was "to hit upon a genuine spontaneous activity and interest . . .

to so utilize it, that it becomes an effective habit instead of a more or less temporary impulse." To do so, the activity would have to have an "end or object" that must be "social, because only a social end can focus and direct the impulse." All the subjects could be integrated within the circuit of activity, Dewey insisted, because "its analysis gives us material on the physical side, its synthesis on the social side." Dewey's first concrete pedagogical idea to demonstrate what he meant by this was using combustion connected to cooking as a means of teaching science. Each activity not only had to lead to scientific knowledge, but it had to demonstrate social utility as well. "Combustion as the scientific fact of combustion would have little interest," he proposed, "while combustion as involved in his own keeping warm or in the relation of sun to growth of a seed would have great interest." The activity of cooking, Dewey explained, would not only link the curriculum to the child's prior knowledge of the home, but it would also organically contain elements of chemistry, physics, and history. Arithmetic, Dewey suggested, should be focused on "the materials in cooking and carpentry"; literature should be focused on "how people lived and what they did"; and geography should be taught as "the environment as entering into the life of man and the life of man as modifying the environment." Each subject would be related to the present and to historical social occupations that would have immediate meaning for the students. In response to Dewey, Mitchell expressed some general confusion about how these ideas cohered. "The only principle I see in any of these points," Dewey replied, "is that all 'facts' should be 'correlated' with some process and not with one another." These carefully selected processes arranged historically would bring unity to the disparate facts of the world in such a way that students could apply their spontaneously emerging instincts and interests toward constructive social activities, thus leading them down the path to scientific knowledge.[53]

History was the correlating subject for the curriculum. As Dewey first explained to Mitchell, "if we take history as a record of past social activities, it doesn't belong here at all, and won't fit into the scheme. But if taken as sociology expanded, the opening made into the present social activities so as to see into them more deeply, it comes in at once." Therefore, during the planning stages of the school, Dewey suggested to Mitchell that the curriculum be based upon the "selection of typical activities, within present social organism reduced now to tendencies or to parts, & expansion of them into a whole of society."[54] Likewise, in his general principles for his laboratory school, Dewey insisted that the curriculum be "taken up historically" because history "permits and requires greater definiteness, corresponding to the gain of mental concentration," and "requires attention to the sequence and order of progress in its larger more obvious features."[55] Accordingly, as Dewey outlined in his privately published plan for the school, the curriculum began with the immediate world of the students through the processes (or social occupations) of constructing shelter, manufacturing clothing, and growing and preparing food. From here, the teacher led the children into "larger relations upon which they depend—i.e., the consideration of wood, stone, and food takes in a large sphere of existing social activities, and takes one back to previous states of society out of which the present has grown."[56] From this early concentration on household occupations, the curriculum expanded through the phases of human development eventually evolving into a fairly straightforward chronological presentation of historical content. The sequence of units at the Dewey School was based on "progress through invention and discovery," "progress through exploration and discovery," "local history," "colonial history," "colonial history and revolution," and "European background of the colonists."[57] As Dewey explained, while the early years should be directed toward the child's immediate world, historical knowledge must ultimately arrive at "a more thorough and accurate knowledge of both the principles and facts of social life [providing] . . . preparation for later more specialized historical studies."[58] The disciplines (and the facts they produced) were themselves products of human evolution and, according to Dewey, did not exist prior to being formulated and discovered. Students would only appreciate the products of the disciplines if they understood the context from which they emerged and the functions they served.

Dewey's ambitious project would take a couple of years to work out, and, apparently, Mitchell was not up the task; her name was not mentioned in the Mayhew and Edwards's account of the laboratory school, *The Dewey School*, published in 1936. After the first year, Dewey desperately searched for new, more qualified teachers to meet the growing demand of local parents (when it opened, the Dewey School enrolled only 16 children; the next year it had 32, and by 1902 it had 140 students and 23 teachers).[59] Dewey was optimistic, but unsatisfied with what his school had accomplished in its first year. "The instruction is relatively scrappy and clear below the children's real capacity," he explained to a colleague. "The history wants to be worked out along the lines of the relation to the environment, control of food supply, same with the geography."[60] Dewey, with the help of his teachers, did eventually work out the historical portion of his curriculum, and he drew upon his successes to establish himself as one of the leading intellectuals in the country. While his pedagogy reinforced his philosophical views, it was his ideas on society and evolution that allowed him to reach a wider audience by allowing others to see the social utility of his theory.

As demonstrated above, from the beginning Dewey's philosophical approach to education was based upon linear historicism and genetic psychology, ideas he shared with most forward-thinking intellectuals. In light of sociocultural evolutionism and the emerging anthropological ethnologies of primitive societies, scholars were reconceptualizing the mind as a biological organ that adapted to the environmental and social factors it encountered, rather than as a purely rationalistic and metaphysical entity. Two of the most influential social scientists that subscribed to these views were at the University of Chicago when Dewey arrived in 1895: Albion Small and Thorstein Veblen. Both had identified education as a key component of their respective theories, which directly challenged the laissez-faire social Darwinism of Herbert Spencer. Dewey's curriculum was as much a criticism of nineteenth-century sociological theory as it was a reform agenda for American schools.

DEWEY IN CHICAGO

Albion Small, like his intellectual mentor Lester F. Ward, believed in the power of man to redirect and renew society through rational interventions such as education. Small chaired the first sociology department in the United States at the University of Chicago, which had quickly established itself as the center of post-laissez-faire thought. In 1896 Small authored an essay titled "Demands of Sociology upon Pedagogy," in which he directly attacked the mental faculty approach and the suggested curriculum of the Committee of Ten, published a few years earlier. In 1893 the National Educational Association (NEA) had summoned the Committee of Ten to establish uniformity between high school programs and college entrance requirements. Headed by Charles Eliot, president of Harvard, the Committee suggested a complete reformulation of the curriculum, including a system of electives and the inclusion of modern subjects like history and foreign language. Like most scholars, Eliot and the members of the Committee of Ten subscribed to the faculty psychology—that the distinct faculties of the mind, like imagination, memory, and judgment, could be strengthened like muscles. In response, Small argued that the Committee's "judgment" rationale for history instruction was based upon a "medieval psychology" that pieced together "educational courses out of subjects which are supposed to exercise, first the perceptive faculty, then the memory, then the language faculty, then the logical, etc, etc." In contrast, Small suggested a unified theory of mind, wherein students organically experienced the whole of reality. "The prime problem of education," Small insisted, "is how to promote adaptation of the individual to the conditions natural and artificial within which individuals live and move and have their being." History should not be approached as a record of the past, but rather as how the current anatomy, physiology, and psychology of social relations came to be. The study of history, he specifically outlined, should focus on the sociological aspects of interdependence, order, and progress and continuity. Students should appreciate that "beginning with the family, and extending to the compass of the race, society is a network of interdependence." The biographical aspects of the history, which emphasized individual achievement, should be deemphasized in light of the evolution of social forces. Relations between cause and effect should be considered in light of the present.[61]

A similar historicist view was endorsed in Veblen's classic 1899 text *The Theory of the Leisure Class*. Drawing upon his view of the individual as the "organic complex of habits of thought which make up the substance of an individual's conscious life," Veblen directly attacked the formalist models of classic economics by introducing the idea that over time a distinction had evolved between "industrial" and "pecuniary" economic functions.[62] The former included the work of laborers and technicians, and the latter represented the work of business owners, middlemen, and money handlers. Veblen argued that in recent years science and modernization had exacerbated the divide between the two groups, and as a result, the leisure-class lifestyle of the pecuniary group was being threatened by "new women," functionalism, and working-class radicalism. In the final chapter of the book, Veblen related his theory specifically to changing educational conditions. He argued that the kindergarten and new education movements were the result of leisure-class women's revolt against the traditionalism of higher education that had excluded them. Accordingly, Veblen saw the evolution of the secondary and college curriculum from classical to modern studies as further evidence of the revolt against the leisure class. In a passage demonstrating Veblen's functionalism, historicism, and radical iconoclasm toward the classical curriculum (ideas he shared with Dewey), he explained, "For the purpose at hand, canons of taste are race habits, acquired through more or less protracted habituation."[63] Thus there was no value to certain studies and classic texts other than the fact that they had been used habitually in the past; Veblen argued that these classic texts had no inherent worth in and of themselves beyond the value that had been placed upon them historically and socioculturally.

Furthermore, Veblen considered the "useless" and "wasteful" learning of classical languages as a form of "conspicuous consumption" that was deliberately designed to "derange the learner's workmanlike aptitudes." The leisure class deliberately acquired useless knowledge in order to distance themselves from the utilitarian learning of the workers. As Veblen concluded, "the tenacious retention of the classics by the higher schools, and the high degree of reputability which still attaches to them, are no doubt due to their conforming so closely to the requirements of archaism and waste." [64] He considered democratic education a rejection of this leisure-class knowledge, and he proposed the adoption of more scientific and useful studies. Veblen agreed with Dewey that democratization of knowledge required the unity of intellectual and utilitarian learning. As Dewey later commented, he "always found Veblen's own articles very stimulating, and some of his distinctions—like that between the technological side of industry and its 'business' aspect—have been quite fundamental in my feeling ever since I became acquainted with him."[65] Dewey agreed with Veblen that the industrial era had exacerbated a division between productive and business classes, which had manifested itself as waste in education. Veblen's theory provided additional support for Dewey's vision of a more functional, organic curriculum. "When you think of the thousands and thousands of young 'uns who are practically being ruined negatively if not positively in the Chicago schools every year," Dewey lamented in a 1894 letter to his wife, "it is enough to make you go out and howl on the street corner like the Salvation Army."[66] Along with Veblen, Dewey sensed a growing estrangement from nature that traditional schools had helped to foster. "The defect of the present school," Dewey explained in an 1895 letter to Clara Mitchell, "is that it isolates . . . and devotes itself to techniques or symbols (discipline) without reference either to the necessity either of an end or concrete tools. . . . It thus defeats itself, giving a mechanical habit which cannot be applied to new materials or new purposes."[67] In order for learning to be relevant to a rapidly modernizing society, education would need to be reformulated. Education would need to equip students with the skills to adapt to changing industrial and social conditions.

Dewey's concern for the problems of industrialism was underscored by the Pullman railroad strike, which was under way when Dewey first arrived in Chicago in 1894. The newspapers of the time sided with railroad entrepreneur George Pullman and depicted his counterpart, Eugene Debs, as an agitator. Dewey had spoken with a strike organizer on a train one day and was converted by the experience. Although Dewey believed that the strikers would lose in the short term, he nevertheless considered the movement "a great thing & the beginning of greater."[68] However, he found himself at odds with many of his progressive colleagues, who were disturbed by the disruptive tactics of the strikers. To Dewey, the Pullman strike reinforced his ideas about the organic, interconnectedness of modern society, and the wastefulness and inadequacy of the laissez-faire economic approach. More significantly, the strike created a context for an important exchange with his new friend Jane Addams, in which Dewey reexamined his Hegelian beliefs about the necessary and productive elements of conflict.

Addams was a sociologist and founder of Hull House, a settlement house that offered educational opportunities to the urban poor. Hull House was in essence a sociological laboratory that fostered assimilation and uplift. She emphasized the importance of assuaging, not embracing conflict. As Dewey explained to Addams in reference to her response to the strike, "I can see that I have always been interpreting the dialectic wrong end up—the unity as the reconciliation of opposites, instead of the opposites as the unity in its growth, and thus translated the physical tension into a moral thing."[69] Moral conflict, Dewey concluded, was not a necessary generator of unity, but rather was a barrier to genuine unity, preventing both sides from realizing the futility of conflict. "Not only is actual antagonizing bad," he continued, "but the assumption that there is or may be antagonism is bad. . . . I'm glad I found this out before I began to talk on social psychology."[70] Addams's important lesson—that the social world worked best when multiple players worked together to realize their organic, collective ends—played a central role in Dewey's emerging social, psychological, biological, and educational views outlined above.

Drawing on the ideas he had outlined in *The Psychology of Number* and *Interest in Relation to the Training of the Will,* his exposure to the ideas of Small, Veblen, and Addams, as well as the brief but informative experiences he had in 1896 with his laboratory school, Dewey outlined a comprehensive vision for democratic education in the new century. Originally published in *School Journal* in 1897 and then reprinted the same year with Small's essay on the demands of sociology on education (discussed above), Dewey's "My Pedagogic Creed" became one of his most enduring and succinct writings on education. The famous essay linked content to pedagogy to social reform in a seamless and logical continuum. Dewey's sprawling vision, however, was held together by two overarching ideas: linear historicism and genetic psychology. "The child has his own instincts and tendencies, but we do not know what these are until we translate them into their social equivalents," Dewey explained. "We must be able to carry them back into a social past and see them as the inheritance of previous race activities." That is, the past demonstrated how knowledge had originally been formed, and so history pointed to the most effective path of knowledge construction. If the curriculum was approached as a reenactment of the race experience, then it would not only be more socially appropriate for the twentieth century, but it would also be intrinsically interesting to students. In two of his most cited passages, Dewey declared that education "is a process of living and not a preparation for future living," and therefore "the school, as an institution, should simplify existing social life; should redirect, as it were, to an embryonic form."[71] The line between school and society should not only be blurred, Dewey asserted, it should be abolished.

Dewey explained how starting with home life and then reliving the social experience of the race was "the only way of securing continuity in the child's growth, the only way of giving a background of past experience to the new ideas in school." A study of the social occupations of the home such as cooking and sewing served as a perfect bridge to the broader knowledge of the history of the race. The curriculum, he explained, should "mark a gradual differentiation out of primitive unconscious unity of social life," and should "work along the same general constructive lines as those which have brought civilization into being." The child was like the primitive in his instinctual reactions to the emerging problems of the past. The child's interests were also "the signs and symptoms of growing power" that "prophesy the stage upon which he is about to enter." That is, each stage of growth built upon the prior stage, fulfilled the needs of the present, and anticipated the subsequent stage in a linear process of progressive growth. Perhaps the most ambitious and radical statement in "My Pedagogic Creed" was that "education is the fundamental method of social progress and reform," and as a result, every teacher was a "social servant set apart for the maintenance of proper social order and the securing of the right social growth."[72] By leading students through the psychological and sociological stages of the race history, teachers were ushering in a more humane and progressive world. Dewey placed an almost religious faith in education as a means of preparing and transforming citizens for the scientific, democratic world they were about to enter.

In summary, the contemporary events and influential figures of Chicago in the mid-1890s reinforced Dewey's emerging pragmatic beliefs, leading him toward a more social and historicist view of education. Taken together, the unified theories of mind that emerged during these years from modernist sociologists, psychologists, and historians directly challenged the laissez-faire individualistic, mental discipline approach suggested by most scholars of the previous generation. Compared to the previous generation, the view of mind by Dewey and like-minded colleagues was less rationalistic and more holistic and functional; less individualistic and more social; less competitive and more cooperative; less grounded in content and more in process; and less interested in justifying the present than in securing the future. These post-laissez-faire theorists pointed to the significance of social and cultural inheritance—that is, history—as the most significant explanatory force affecting the present and directing the future.

Chapter 2

Repeating the Race Experience

In 1896 Hegelian educator Susan Blow sent a letter to her mentor William Torrey Harris describing her visit to Dewey's laboratory school at the University of Chicago, which had recently opened in the winter. She was not impressed. "The whole principle they were working on seemed wrong," she explained to a presumably sympathetic Harris. "In general the way they work on the imagination will I think nauseate the children." In particular, she was disturbed by Dewey's attempt to turn the young children into savages. "Their purpose for why we should inflame the minds of our little civilized Aryans with the ideal of a savage Indian life I can't see." In the end, Blow was glad to "see their method defeated."[1] In a 1900 essay titled "A Day with the New Education" that was published in the progressive periodical *The Chautauquan,* Laura Runyon related a far more enthusiastic portrayal of what Dewey had accomplished at his school: "Dr. Dewey had discovered a way to abbreviate the amount of knowledge a child must have to be respectable, so that it could be learned in elementary grades." That is, Dewey had managed to remove the waste that he and Veblen had identified in traditional education. Of course, the Dewey School students were not lower-income or minority children. On the contrary, they were mostly the children of University of Chicago professors (not quite members of the leisure class, but far from poor). Nevertheless, Runyon was impressed with what she saw. She reported that "in all classes the children talked—sometimes two at once—but with a freedom of expression and an ability to stick to the point which surprised me."[2] At first, Runyon was concerned about the apparent lack of book learning. She inquired about this further by asking several of the teachers and was assured that books were occasionally used to supplement class discussions and for research, but most of the days were filled with activity. She described one such lesson in full:

> [A teacher] directed me to a class in primitive life where children had spent some weeks in working out, with the aid of the teacher, what the earliest people must have done when they had no clothing, or food, or shelter, or means of defense. She told me how they had thought of a spear by fastening a stick between the split

ends of a club; how they had made bowls out of clay, and discussed
caves as the first homes, and skins as the first clothing. How they
had moulded [sic] in clay their ideas of man and animals in those
days, and had become so interested that they had begged to write
a report on their work for the school paper.[3]

Through the children's "rediscovery" of the spear, the Dewey School students successfully subordinated the environment through socially cooperative means. They had used reflective thinking to solve a problem of the past as a problem of the present. In the rhetorical climax to Runyon's article, she asked a teacher, "but all of this has been found out by past generations; why not give the children the results? Why require them to repeat the process?" The teacher replied, "*Because the process is the valuable part* [italics in the original]."[4] Runyon agreed and was so impressed with what she observed that she joined the Dewey School as a teacher.

In accordance with Dewey's historicist view of knowledge, the complex knowledge of the modern world could not be fully understood without an appreciation of its historic development from earlier forms. In practice, this meant that children at the Dewey School had to relive the carefully selected social aspects of the history of human civilization. An effective education, he argued, required the child to relearn the lessons of the race in a manner that corresponded with how this development originally took place. "In the history of the race, science is the outgrowth of race activities, and not the result of investigation undertaken for its own sake," he insisted. "Thus the child is repeating the race experience when his activities lead him into the path of knowledge."[5] The symbols of civilization such as letters and numbers (i.e., the three Rs) were not introduced until the race had invented them; likewise, students did not learn about the usefulness and products of scientific inquiry until the human race had done so. In this manner, history, organized as an indirect sociology, served as the foundation for the entire curriculum.

HISTORY AT THE DEWEY SCHOOL

In 1906 Runyon wrote her master's thesis for the University of Chicago on the history curriculum at the Dewey School. Her paper represents the fullest available account of how history was approached at the school and demonstrates that Runyon fully understood and subscribed to Dewey's linear historicism and genetic psychology. Rather than basing the elementary curriculum upon the biographies of famous people, as many schools were doing at the time, Runyon insisted that the curriculum was based upon "new problems . . . the student is living out, in the sense of through race development." The early years, she continued, were devoted to "the discovery of one thing after another which makes life comfortable and which the child dimly realizes he is the inheritor of." In this manner students did not take the intellectual and physical inventions of present for granted.[6]

Learning took place, she insisted, when students relived the race experience, "for [the student] is primitive man, striving to find out by tracing how he may control nature, and in this experimentation discover nature's laws."[7] In this manner, the curriculum was not only set up as an indirect sociology, but, by discovering the laws of nature, students were themselves scientists and sociologists. Through the process of trial and error guided by the teacher, students would appreciate that the discoveries were not only useful for the individual but also for the entire race and society. Thus scientific discovery was inherently generic and social.

According to Runyon, after students had established an appreciation for the complexity of life through the study of shelter, food, inventions, discoveries, ideas of government, and clothing, they were ready to comprehend "the discoveries and inventions which usher in the stage of progress we call 'civilization.'" Runyon concluded that the life of the Phoenicians provided the most effective link between primitive and civilized man. At this time, Dewey School students were introduced to symbolic systems of writing, reading, and arithmetic, not as distinct abstractions of the adult world, but rather "from the child's point of view, [as] an attempt to solve the problem of how he, a merchant trader from the Phoenician tribe, could tell the value of his merchandise as compared with that of other merchants, and how he could record promises to give him or receive from him merchandise." Through this pedagogical approach, Runyon again asserted, students "were studying the progress of people toward the conveniences which we now have."[8] The students of the Dewey School were guided through the discoveries and inventions of primitive or "savage" man so that they would fully appreciate the intrinsic value of civilized man. Students "have been taken through the history of the development of the race," Runyon explained, "not because a child necessarily lives through these stages in his development, but because in passing through typical stages of this development he can most easily gain the acquired inheritance of the race." By the age of 9, however, according to Dewey and Runyon, the reliving of the race experience was no longer necessary. The child no longer needed to reenact and relive the experiences of the past but, having gained an intrinsic appreciation for it, could now accumulate, recall, and use historical facts. "History now becomes less empirical," Runyon explained, "and more a matter of authentic record, so that the question of a definite recall of what has been studied comes into the scheme."[9] With a strong foundation, students were then able to appreciate the products of the discipline (i.e., facts).

After children reached age 9 the innovative elements of the Dewey curriculum began to drop out and the historical content of the school began to look more like a traditional one. A reader of Runyon's account of the curriculum for the intermediate years (as well as Mayhew and Edwards's 1936 account of the school) would likely be struck by how much specific historical content is listed. In fact, Runyon admitted that beyond the third grade, "topics studied do not differ greatly from the usual selection of topics in United States history." For example, in the study of the settlement of Virginia, students discussed "the main events in Virginia's history, such as the first years of struggle, the Indian troubles, the loss of the charter, Bacon's Rebellion, the charges which came with the Cromwellian supremacy in England, the trouble with navigation laws, the French and Indian wars."[10] Although content was not delivered through traditional methods of textbook recitation, historical facts were nonetheless transmitted directly from the teacher and textbook to students. Therefore, those critics who accuse Dewey of being antagonistic to books also overlook the actual content of Dewey's curriculum at his experimental school.[11] "To discover [the facts of history] the child must be referred to books where he can find the facts," Runyon explained, "and in thus following out a line of thought he is getting a methods of historical investigation as well as the power of drawing conclusions from facts."[12] Furthermore, in a letter to Clara Mitchell, Dewey explained succinctly, "See no objection to books as books. Question is to the principle in using them."[13]

Despite its traditional reliance on the transmission of facts and the use of books, Dewey's intermediate history curriculum was innovative in two ways. The first was its emphasis on social history instead of merely political and military history, which most schools were focusing on at the time (although these were also covered in the Dewey School). Through social history the facts of the past build naturally upon the social occupations, explorers, and early civilizations. Runyon sought to "give the study of American history the same balance and completeness" as the "Phoenicians and early word explorers. . . . In each of these years the effort was made to gather together the knowledge of the two preceding years and grasp its significance as a whole in larger relations."[14] Second, instead of mere memorization and recitation, students were engaged in the process of inquiry. The "method of attacking history," Runyon explained, outlining a sequence that foreshadowed Dewey's *How We Think*, "is similar to that of science. There is first the recognition of new conditions, an attempt to relate the situation to any previously studied; then a hypothesis as the effect; and then the generalizations of realities." The inquiry approach to history, however, did not involve individual students engaging with primary source documents, but instead was done through discussions guided by the teacher. In this manner, the facts were presented through questions relating to social life, but the teacher was always at the center of this process, and the evolutionary elements of the content were emphasized. For example, in one sample activity—revealing the linear historicist concepts underlying the entire curriculum—students were instructed to "compare the American rivers with those of Africa, the Indians with the Negroes, and the degree of civilization of tribes in America with that of other peoples he has studied."[15] Through such comparisons, the Dewey School students were to arrive at the conclusion that modern civilized society had surpassed the primitive Indian and Negro ones. The past was presented as a simplified version of the present, and past cultures were presented as simplified versions of present ones.

Overall, history served two major functions at the Dewey School. First, it provided a theoretical basis for Dewey's interpretation of how humans interacted with the world. An assertion had no value beyond the experience that produced and sustained it. Accordingly, students could not comprehend a fact or idea fully without understanding the context from which it emerged and how it had increased its social usefulness over time. Second, history united all the disciplines of the curriculum because all knowledge, Dewey insisted, emerged from the problems of the past. From this perspective, history had two meanings for Dewey—a functional and disciplinary aspect. The functional aspect involved how history was present in every idea and object of use to the individual and race; it represented the accumulated efficiency of mankind as enacted through the experiences of its social occupations. On the other hand, the disciplinary aspect was simply the accumulated facts produced by historians, scientists, and anthropologists (i.e., academic scholarship). For Dewey, the disciplinary aspect was circuitously related to the functional one. Just as scientists produced facts about the natural world and writers produced literature, historians produced facts about the past that could be transmitted to students. All of these expressions were united in the history of the race because they all emerged as civilization went about the business of making its living.

DEWEY ON THE SAVAGE MIND

Using his work at the laboratory school, in 1902 Dewey wrote a lesser-known essay on anthropologists' view of the "savage mind." Drawing upon his historicist view of knowledge and the work of a colleague, University of Chicago anthropologist William I. Thomas, Dewey argued that the savage mind had been unfairly dismissed as lacking, inchoate, and incapable, when in fact the savage had much to teach social scientists about the "present mind." The short essay was one of the few times Dewey, the consummate interdisciplinarian, directly addressed evolutionary anthropological theory. In the savage mind essay, Dewey demonstrated that his earlier evolutionist ideas about racial development were reinforced by his pedagogical work at the laboratory school. The traits of the savage, Dewey insisted, reiterating his argument about how children learned, "are outgrowths which have entered decisively into further evolution, and as such form an integral part of the framework of present mental organization."[16] Thus the innovations of the past were holistically and inherently present in the occupations of contemporary civilization.

In the article Dewey specifically outlined the shortcomings of the "comparative method" and its relationship to primitive man. Dewey offered three critiques that, once again, grew directly out of his historicist view of knowledge. First, Dewey insisted that current anthropological theory ripped the "static" facts of individual societies from their cultural and environmental contexts. However, Dewey insisted, these contexts were critical to understanding the specific environmental problems to which the primitive civilizations were responding. Social context, not merely the biological habits, determined the outcome of environmental interaction. Next, Dewey complained that most sociologists and anthropologists describe the primitive mind negatively in terms of a lack, absence, or incapacity, instead of viewing it as a necessary progression inherent in the civilized mind. Once again, because social context and inheritance dictated the capabilities of the primitive mind, it was not fair to judge it against the social context afforded the modern mind, to which the primitive mind had no exposure.

Finally, Dewey insisted that anthropologists do not "have a coherent scheme of mind"; instead they rely on the outdated faculty psychology of "loose aggregates of unrelated traits."[17] Dewey was not the only one to attack this scheme. As we saw in the last chapter, the various theories of the child study movement (i.e., G. Stanley Hall, James Mark Baldwin, American Herbartians) were unified in their opposition to the faculty psychology, which had been used to justify the place of Latin and Greek in the curriculum because these subjects were believed to strengthen the mental faculties. Neo-Lamarckian evolutionism was also based in part upon this theory, because it was believed that the traits acquired through the exercise of the mental faculties were passed on biologically to the subsequent members of the race. By attacking the faculty psychology, Dewey was also indirectly attacking the psychological implications of neo-Lamarckianism and also the passivity of the mind as described by Darwin.

Dewey argued that current anthropological theory inadequately conceptualized habit and impulse as decontextualized and atomistic. All impulse, he insisted, was an impulse from something toward something and could not be understood independent of its entire circuit. To demonstrate his theory, Dewey presented an example of how the hunting psychosis had evolved over time in relation to changing social conditions. Dewey argued that the inherited impulse to hunt was the same for the savage and civilized man, but the manner in which the mind acted upon itself evolved as it was mediated by its social context. The civilized mind, Dewey explained, has "not so much destroyed or left behind the hunting structural arrangement of mind, [as it has] set free its constitutive psycho-psychic factors as to make them available and interesting in all kinds of objective and idealized pursuits—the hunt for truth, beauty, virtue, wealth, social well-being, and even heaven and of God."[18] The civilized mind, Dewey insisted, reinterpreted the instinct to hunt both reflectively by reconditioning it as play and projectively by redirecting it toward new forms of hunting. In this process, what was once a survival instinct (hunting as necessity) had become entertainment (hunting as sport). In the process the civilized mind had reconstructed itself by incorporating the interpretation of the old activity into the new and directing it toward new satisfactions of the impulse in the environment.

Dewey attributed his ideas about the refashioning of the hunting instinct to his colleague William I. Thomas. Dewey cited Thomas's 1901 essay "The Gaming Instinct," and commented in a footnote that his reliance on Thomas's theory was such that "this article is virtually a joint contribution."[19] Thomas's "Gaming Instinct" essay traced the various ways in which the instinct of gaming had manifested itself in both positive and negative ways in modern society. In the spirit of Lester F. Ward, Thomas asserted the importance of social environment to racial and individual development. "Psychologically the individual is inseparable from his surroundings," Thomas explained, "and his attitude toward the world is determined by the nature of suggestions from the outside." The inherited instinct of the race and individual was still significant, but like Dewey, Thomas asserted that instinct could be directed toward a number of different ends by the social environment. Thomas argued, "The instincts of man are congenital; the arts and industries are acquired by the race and must be learned by the individuals after birth."[20] Dewey broadened Thomas's theory by relating it to the process of problem solving in general, through which the inherited instincts were reconciled with the social inheritance of the race.

The unity of the special functions of the primitive and civilized mind could only be appreciated, Dewey concluded, through an understanding of social occupations—the very idea that he had used to bring unity to the laboratory school curriculum. In the savage mind essay, Dewey again asserted that "occupations determine the fundamental modes of activity, and hence control the formation and use of habits."[21] The process of social occupations both initiated the inquiry and directed its outcome. The idea of social occupations represented the heart of both Dewey's anthropological and pedagogical outlooks because it was through occupations that man acquired a more socialized intelligence.

By 1903 Dewey had successfully merged evolutionary anthropology with developmental psychology, reformulated the culture epoch theory into an innovative pedagogy of social occupations that he implemented at his laboratory school, and drawn upon his historicist view of knowledge to offer nuanced critiques in the related disciplines. However, I have not answered the fundamental question of why. Why did Dewey conceptualize knowledge in linear historicist terms, and why did his pedagogical approach require students to relive the race experience? Surely there were easier, more efficient ways to generate and transmit knowledge (as Runyon had pointed out in her initial visit to the Dewey School).

Like his contemporaries (i.e., Veblen, Small), Dewey worried that the modern world was evolving so fast that students and adults would lose their sense of connectedness with the organic unity of experience. Although the emerging forces of industrialization, specialization, immigration, and scientific innovation held great promise for the improvement of society, they also held the potential to estrange and disenfranchise modern Americans from each other and their world. Dewey explained:

> The newcomers into civilization find themselves face to face with technical, mechanical, and intellectual devices and resources in the development of which they have no share or lot; and which are so far beyond them that they have no instinctive or natural means of understanding them. The problem of education—the problem of establishing vital connections between the immature child and the cultural and technical achievements of the adult life—thus continually increases in difficulty. It is coming to be recognized that the historical method, more than any one thing is the key which unlocks difficulties.[22]

Dewey put his faith in history as the force that unified all useful knowledge and experience, especially when conceptualized in terms of social occupations. If knowledge was delivered in a decontextualized manner, ripped from the environment and mentality that engendered it, then it would be superficial and shallow. But if knowledge was understood and developed organically through context, experience, and inquiry, then it would be intrinsically appreciated and fully connected to the objective, generic world students inherited. This would allow them to adapt further to subsequent change.

Dewey's linear historicist ideas on the development of cultures were in sync with the major currents of European and American social science. Although Dewey offered a less ethnocentric form of social evolutionism than Herbert Spencer or Lester F. Ward, his theory still relegated aboriginal, African, and American Indian civilizations to inferior status. Dewey's curriculum identified Northern European industrial society as the most fully realized (and most socially efficient) culture and thereby placed Euro-American society at the top of a hierarchy of civilizations. Other, more primitive cultures were not necessarily viewed as inherently inferior, but they were certainly not to be taken on their own terms as alternatives. Instead, they were to be studied as prior steps toward the "structure of the present mind."[23] The primitive cultures of the past were geniuses in their own context, but for Dewey they had nothing to offer present civilization because it had progressed beyond them. Culture at the Dewey School was not purely qualitative, it had a quantitative element as well—a matter of "how much" or "to what degree." Progress, for Dewey, was based upon an appreciation of the most advanced, most socially efficient means of social occupation, which inevitably led students to conclude that American society represented the pinnacle of civilization. In fact, as demonstrated by Runyon, in some cases students were specifically led to reach this conclusion (these ideas will be explored further in subsequent chapters).

Despite these limitations, Dewey drew upon his historicist view of knowledge and genetic psychological view of growth to construct an innovative curriculum at the University of Chicago laboratory school.[24] He sought to capitalize on the inherited instincts of the child, such as hunting and gaming, by redirecting these instincts toward more civilized educational endeavors. Dewey organized all the content of the curriculum around a narrative of social and intellectual progress. Dewey's selection criteria for what content to include in the curriculum was self-consciously presentist. He selected only those facts from the past that continued to inform the thoughts and actions of the present. However, all content for Dewey was a circuit, because the knowledge that was so crucial to his "repeating the race experience" curriculum was the product of scientists, historians, and anthropologists, who were themselves the products of the latest stage of the race experience.[25] So knowledge had two components, what Dewey called "content" and "form" values.

As Dewey explained in *Ethical Principles Underlying Education*, published in 1897, the study of content should "introduce the child to a consciousness of the makeup or structure of social life," as well as give him "command over the instrumentalities through which the society carries itself along. . . . The former is the content value and the latter is the form value." The content of subject matter determined its form, but the form produced its content. That is, through the study of the historical growth of a subject, students learned how and why its method (form) had come about, but the content of the subject about which these students learned was itself the product of that same method. The paradox was inescapable, and so the whole form/content circuit needed to be taught simultaneously. Dewey explained, "Studies cannot be classified into form studies and content studies. Everything has both sides."[26] To overcome this inherent paradox, Dewey worked out two solutions at the Dewey School: First, teach the content of the race experience not as static, predetermined facts, but as a set of simplified, unraveling processes involving concrete problems and tools corresponding with the development of the race; second, coordinate the progress of the race with the psychological stages of the child. Thus the history of the race dictated the selection of what "content" to teach and the psychological stage of the child dictated the appropriate "form" the content took.

Regarding the selection of content, Dewey explained that the "type phases of historical development may be selected which will exhibit as through a telescope, the essential constituents of the existing order."[27] To organize the content of the curriculum (and to capitalize on the inherited instincts of the students), Dewey insisted that "a study of still simpler forms of hunting, nomadic, and agricultural life in the beginnings of civilization; a study of the effects of the introduction of iron, iron tools, and so forth, serves to reduce the existing complexity to its simple forms."[28] The idea was that the historical content presented to students would not be historical as such, but rather would be presented as immediate problems, which also happened to have historical and scientific significance. After students had mastered the corresponding form and content for each stage, they would eventually arrive at the modernist stage, which included the introduction of the techniques of the professional and/or expert. However, students would only appreciate the techniques of the expert if they were viewed as a natural progression from prior social forms. "With increasing mental maturity, and corresponding specialization which naturally accompanies it," Dewey explained, "these various instrumentalities may become ends in themselves."[29] Therefore, knowledge construction at the Dewey School was not open-ended; it was always directed toward the previously discovered generic, more socialized knowledge of the past and present. Both the prescriptive and descriptive elements of Dewey's curriculum could be found in specific linear stages he outlined repeatedly during the early and middle years of his career. However, Dewey forged a subtle, but original, position on the theory of recapitulation, which he used to critique many of the evolutionary theories of the day.

ONTOGENY RECAPITULATES PHYLOGENY

As explained in Chapter 1, the biogenetic theory that ontogeny recapitulates phylogeny appeared in many different manifestations throughout the psychological, anthropological, and educational research of the nineteenth century. The theory's most prominent proponents were Ernst Haeckel, Herbert Spencer, and G. Stanley Hall, and its most ardent educational practitioners were the Herbartians. As Spencer explained, "The education of the child must accord both in mode and arrangement with the education of mankind conceived historically."[30] And Hall reiterated as late as 1904, "The child relives the history of the race in his acts just as the scores of rudimentary organs in his body tell the story of its evolution from lower forms of animal."[31] Likewise, as leading Herbartian Charles McMurry explained, in order to learn, children needed to "reproduce in themselves the experiences of suitable epochs in history."[32] According to the proponents of the cultural epoch theory, the contents of the elementary curriculum needed to be coordinated with the historical stages of race.

There were at least three pedagogical interpretations of the cultural epoch theory as demonstrated by elementary curricula of the period. The first suggested that the facts from each particular stage of civilization be transmitted to students, not necessarily in chronological order, but in the order of anthropological development. One such curriculum began with the early Aryans, then covered life in Ancient Egypt, nomadic life among the Hebrews and Phoenicians, primitive life in Japan and Africa, primitive life among Native Americans, and then life among the American colonists. The objective was to demonstrate the evolving social modes of living, which were believed to coordinate with the biological impulses of the child. Another interpretation of the theory focused on the evolving forms of the historical discipline itself that developed from myths, fables, and legends to historical sagas, to "scientific history." Thus students explored the evolution of the race through the various forms "history" took, which once again were believed to correspond with the natural impulses of the child. Finally, a third form suggested that certain literary selections from each epoch (such as *Robinson Crusoe*), regardless of whether or not it was actually produced during the period it represented, best capitalized on the natural interests of the child. Despite these variations, each interpretation stressed the importance of relating the social developments of man through carefully selected products of each epoch in a sequence that coordinated with the evolution of the child's developing mind.[33]

In 1896 Dewey published an essay that directly addressed the Herbartian strand of the *cultural epoch theory*, which Dewey defined as the idea that "the cultural products of each epoch will contain that which appeals most sympathetically and closely to the child at that epoch." Specifically, he objected to the presiding interpretation of the cultural epoch theory on three grounds. First, he opposed the idea that cultural epochs represented a rationale for a purely biological basis of the curriculum, wherein content should be selected solely on the emerging instinct stages of the child. Many or most of the phases of recapitulation, Dewey explained, "are of no educational significance at all, however interesting they may be to the anthropologist." Second, Dewey objected to the idea that cultural epochs somehow determined a particular body of content, or what he called "cultural products" to be presented to the child. "The interpretation of the fact of correspondence, as meaning necessarily or even primarily, study of cultural products in history and literature," Dewey explained, "seems to me to rest upon confusion theoretically." He objected to the idea that a particular choice of content (such as *Robinson Crusoe*), would be more meaningful to the child simply because it referred to a specific historical epoch without any consideration for the process of learning.[34]

For Dewey, the content of the curriculum should neither be presented as the "products" of the past, nor should it be presented only in relation to the child's natural impulse. Instead, he argued, content should be presented as an interest, "*which demands primarily its own expression* [italics in the original], and not simply an acquaintance, second-handed with what that interest affected at some remote period."[35] Dewey argued that the content of the curriculum should be immediately relevant and intrinsically interesting to children as they themselves discovered the inheritance of the race. The curriculum should reflect the point where the inherited impulse of the child and mature content of the disciplines overlapped and/or met.

Despite these significant criticisms of the presiding interpretation of the culture epoch theory, in the article Dewey admitted that he did "not question the fact of correspondence in a general way," but he argued that too much emphasis had been placed on selecting the proper content and/or on exploiting the child's biological impulses, without examining how these two factors came together.[36] The reconciliation required accounting for both psychical development and sociocultural evolution. The history of the race was not relevant on its own terms, but rather was relevant in how it informed the decisions and actions of the present, which required a focus on evolutionary process. Accordingly, Dewey concluded that the focus should be on recapitulating the experiences, not the products, of human development. In this manner, students' impulses and the content of the curriculum would be united through the child's engagement with historical problems.

While Dewey was working out his curriculum at the laboratory school and espousing his ideas in numerous journal articles, he was also teaching in the newly formed teacher education program. Dewey's course syllabi demonstrate that he struggled with finding the right terminology to describe the nexus where biological impulse joined with the historical bodies of knowledge to subordinate the environment. At first he used the metaphor of the "circuit." While constructing the curriculum for the laboratory school, Dewey insisted to Clara Mitchell that "there is a circuit in any material" and explained: "This, of course, is the principle of correlation everywhere—Life, the circuit of nature through vegetable, animal and human (including industrial) formed back into itself."[37] The circuit, he explained, represented how natural objects became subordinated to human expression, which is also where the circuit began. Dewey referred to the point where impulse met subordination as the child's "interest." In his syllabus for his educational ethics course he explained how there was "No Succession of Studies [i.e., epochs], but only the Same Material Lived Through, with Different Types of Interest." As a suggested exercise he asked his university students to "observe workings of spontaneous recollection in the child with reference to the principle that it is not 'faculty' which grows but interest."[38] Here, through an observation exercise, Dewey had his students affirm his own pragmatic theory, as well as dismiss the old "faculty psychology." Faculty psychology, he explained, makes learning "a mere formal training of certain distinct powers called perception, memory, judgment, which are assumed to exist and operate by themselves, without organic reference to subject matter."[39] It was "interest" through the holistic employment of the mind, Dewey insisted, not the separate faculties that grew when a young child interacted with the environment.

A year later, in his syllabus for a course in educational psychology, Dewey again insisted that there was "no serial growth of faculties, but development of types of interest and complexity of activity . . . no serial order of subjects, but one world lived through with increase of comprehension and change of interest."[40] Critiquing both the psychology of mental faculties, as well as the Herbartian cultural epoch theory that a particular "order of subjects" would spark learning, Dewey argued that "interest" more accurately represented how the mind worked. In *Interest in Relation to the Will* Dewey reiterated how "Interest marks the annihilation of the distance between the person and the materials and results of his action; it is the instrument which affects their organic union."[41] Thus interest united the physical and psychical worlds in a circuit of experience. However, Dewey later replaced the term *interest,* which he now used to designate solely the first stage of psychological development, with the more generic term *growth.* In the syllabus for his philosophy of education course, Dewey concluded that education was "growth as organic process" and "growth as reconstruction."[42] Although not exactly synonyms, the terms *circuit, interest,* and *growth* all served the purpose of designating the point through which inherited impulse interacted with a perceived problem emerging from the environment, the solution to which in some way aligned with the mature thought of the discipline and race. Once again, for Dewey, learning was the subordination of environment (or the reconstruction of experience) that added to the efficiency of the individual and race to solve an emerging problem.

Overall, Dewey agreed with the idea of correspondence between the growth of child and race in a general sense. But instead of merely presenting the child with the corresponding products of a cultural epoch like Hall and the Herbartians prescribed, Dewey argued that the student needed to engage directly in the experience of constructing knowledge corresponding with the evolutionary innovations of the epoch. This subtle refashioning of evolutionary anthropology did not escape the eye of a contemporary educator, who wrote to the *Public-School Journal* with the following comment:

> I wish to say here that Dr. Dewey had never attacked the doctrine of the Culture Epochs, rightly understood, . . . but only certain misconceptions of the theory. . . . He is not an opponent,

but a friend of the doctrine in question, viewed in the light of
his philosophy. . . . It is somewhat amusing to find one who
is attacking the idea of the Culture Epochs, at the close of his
argument utilizing the conceptions of the doctrine of evolution.
The Culture Epoch theory is merely an application of the doctrine
of evolution to the development of the child after birth.[43]

Indeed, the commenter was correct that, despite his significant variations,
Dewey retained the basic idea of linear historicism and genetic psychology—
that the innovations of the past themselves revealed certain knowledge of the
present that could only be arrived at by passing through a particular sequence
of lived (or relived) stages and experiences. The products of past discovery
and knowledge should not be presented as such, but rather as a process of
knowledge construction.

THE SAVAGE AND SOCIETY

As I have shown, Darwinian theories of mind and behavior had a clear impact on the "new psychology" of learning in the 1890s, but they also had
an equally profound impact on theories of social development. Evolutionary,
genetic, and historicist notions of racial development not only dominated the
intellectual currents of anthropology and sociology during the latter half of
the nineteenth century, but also permeated the thoughts of the other social
sciences including economics, political science, and psychology. Influential
nineteenth-century social scientists such as Adam Smith, Auguste Comte,
John Stuart Mill, Karl Marx, and Herbert Spencer all attempted to demonstrate that modern Western history was propelled along a progressive course
of industrial development by natural and/or historical laws. For anthropologists and sociologists, these laws were designed to explain why certain civilizations had arrived at the top of a hierarchy of races and nations while others
had been left behind in what appeared to be earlier stages of development.
For historians, these laws were designed to explain why the institutions of
Western Europe had evolved logically along rational lines. For many social
scientists, these civilizations were largely viewed as having unique characteristics and/or "souls" that had been developed (or not developed) over centuries through a combination of biological, environmental, and cultural means.
Within the broad parameters of biological and social evolutionism, there was
a wide range of interpretations and models of how and why these disparities
and varieties came to be. But social scientists agreed that all of human history
could be subsumed within a single linear evolutionary scheme that included
the stages of savagery, barbarism, and civilization.[44]

Social science in the late nineteenth century was directed toward the discovery of the positivistic and pragmatic laws that drove social and civil development. There were two major camps. There were those, like Comte and Spencer, who believed that, just as in science, there were fixed, transcendent laws of society. For example, Spencer's theory of laissez-faire social Darwinism proposed that society had always been and will always be driven by movement from the state of homogeneity toward greater heterogeneity. On the other hand, there were those, like Lester F. Ward and Dewey's colleague, Albion Small, who believed that social change itself was governed by laws. They posited that all societies passed through specific developmental stages, with Western European civilization at the top of this hierarchy of races.[45] Both approaches sought to impose order on a rapidly changing society that many believed, if not fully understood, threatened to derail human progress. "If it cannot be shown that society is a domain of true natural forces," Ward argued, "the claim to the possibility of a social science must be abandoned." Consequently, Ward insisted, "social phenomena can be controlled as physical phenomena are controlled by knowledge of the laws according to which they occur."[46] For Ward and his followers, the discovery of the laws of change would allow progress to occur in a more orderly and democratic manner.

In accordance with his contemporaries, the nature of historical development (particularly the unity of the rational mind and natural world through experience) played a critical role in Dewey's genetic and historicist approach to knowledge. However, unlike the positivists and Hegelian idealists, Dewey did not subscribe to transcendent laws of social change, which, he believed, did not adequately account for individual and social innovation. Dewey asserted, "The transformation and evolution of successive social states depend upon the introduction of new factors and forces into industrial production and exchange."[47] For Dewey, progress was dependent upon human invention, innovation, and creativity, an idea he shared with contemporaries Ward and Small. Society was not driven or restrained by transcendent laws that existed independent of human use; rather, man created laws to subordinate the world he inhabited. That is, the development of positivistic (i.e., Marx, Comte) and/or idealistic (i.e., Hegel) social laws was not part of a process of alignment with some a priori or transcendent laws or ends, but rather the social laws were an outgrowth of social evolution itself. Therefore, the aim of humanity, according to Dewey, "is to subordinate the materials and forces of the natural environment so that they shall be rendered tributary to life functions."[48] That is, knowledge was constructed as the mind subordinated the psychical and social world through the experience of the individual as he increased his social efficiency by either contributing to or drawing upon the cumulative historical experience of the race. For Dewey, human evolution was gradual, incorporative, and context-bound. Therefore, Dewey concluded, pragmatism "may be compared to the theory of 'economic interpretation of history,'" because it reflected how the history of a civilization undertook "the primary business of making its living."[49] By "making its living," Dewey did not mean narrowly conceived vocational or utilitarian action. Instead, he meant going about the activities of life in a manner through which the environment was subordinated to the needs of present growth of the individual and race.

THE REFLEX ARC

From a philosophical and social standpoint, the turning point in Dewey's philosophy and educational theory is generally believed to be his essay "The Reflex Arc Concept in Psychology," published in July 1896.[50] In this influential article, Dewey attacked the dualistic concept of stimulus-response, which was the foundation of several emerging sociological theories. Having been influenced by the James-Lange notion of an active mind that organically controlled and focused it on particular problems, Dewey questioned whether a stimulus and response could really be viewed as separate and distinct entities. He explained how the reflex arc model "breaks continuity and leaves us nothing but a series of jerks, the origins of each jerk to be sought outside the process of experience itself."[51] Instead, Dewey suggested, actions should be viewed more holistically as a "circuit," because the response of a prior stimulus was itself the stimulus of the next action and because neither stimulus nor response could be exclusively sensory or motor. Thus human learning should not be divided up into mechanistic bits of information, but rather should be viewed organically as growth and united through experience. As I demonstrated above, the circuit metaphor made its way into Dewey's pedagogical writings and syllabi.

Dewey's instrumental view of knowledge united the social and psychological aspects of human and racial development by arguing that if viewed as the reconstruction of experience in relation to specific felt needs and problems, then they were the same thing. As a result, Dewey critiqued dualistic psychological theories that did not adequately account for the sociological aspects of growth, and, inversely, he critiqued sociological theories that did not adequately account for the psychological aspects of growth. This can be seen in Dewey's critical review of two prominent nineteenth-century thinkers who attempted to construct coherent theories of human development, Lester F. Ward and psychologist James Mark Baldwin. In both cases, Dewey posited that these influential thinkers did not base their theories on an adequate theory of mind and society. Through examples he employed in these reviews, we can get a clearer idea of how Dewey conceptualized individual and social growth as coterminous.

In *The Psychic Factors of Civilization,* as in his earlier works, Ward aimed his sociological theory directly at Herbert Spencer's laissez-faire social Darwinism, which rebuked human intervention in natural processes such as poor laws, social welfare, and public education. In contrast, Ward argued that man was not merely subject to, but also the master of, natural processes. Through innovation and the psychic forces of mind, man could overcome the natural restraints of biological evolution. The ability to do so is what distinguished man from the other organisms on the earth. Ward's ambitious study sought to accomplish two goals: to demonstrate how mind constituted the groundwork for social forces and "to point out in what manner the social forces can be brought under control of the intellect."[52] Ward outlined the characteristics of the subjective and objective mind—categories he borrowed from Kant—and argued that progress was contingent upon the ability of the objective mind to direct the subjective mind, which was the "dynamic element of society . . . properly called the soul of man."[53]

Dewey reviewed Ward's text from the perspective of a "new psychologist." Accordingly, in his review Dewey suggested that "Mr. Ward gives back considerably more to the psychologist than he succeeds in borrowing from him." Dewey praised Ward's theory as superior to Spencer's because it accounted for human initiative and control of the environment. However, Dewey objected to Ward's dualistic concept that sensation and notion are separate entities—an empiricist epistemological view that Dewey felt had been disproved in light of new evolutionary psychology. "Mr. Ward is so under the spell of the old psychology," he quipped, "that he fails to recognize the radical psychical fact, although just the fact needed to give firm support to his main contentions—I mean *impulse,* the primary fact, back of which, psychically we cannot go [italics in the original]." For Dewey and James, impulse was biological but it became psychological when it entered consciousness and was mediated by interest, at which point the two could not be separated.[54]

The evolution of intelligence, Dewey insisted, was not about the direct action in response to stimulus, but rather involved "checking the natural, direct action, and taking a circuitous course." Impulse both initiated the action and guided the response to it in a holistic manner, not as a series of mechanistic stimuli and responses of pleasure and pain, which Ward's theory implied. What Ward had done, Dewey asserted, was merely substitute a psychological theory for Spencer's biological one, instead of treating the two as "psychological equivalents—a theory of consciously organic activity."[55] To support his point about the shortcomings of the dualistic view of social development—particularly to critique Ward's individualistic view that actions are developed purely to satisfy the self—Dewey again provided an example of the development of savage life, thus linking his circuitous theory of learning to social development.

Dewey explained that when a savage competed with other organisms, he was indeed being egotistical and individualistic, but when he interacted with inanimate objects, his mind became detached, scientific, and social. "When the savage makes a bow and arrow, his ultimate aim, indeed, is still gratification of appetite," Dewey argued, "but for the time being his attention must be taken up with a purely objective adjustment—with general utility, not of simple personal profit." Therefore, Dewey concluded, "scientific discovery and speculative genius are simply farther steps on this same road."[56] In other words, when the savage created an object that had social utility, even if he did so for personal profit, he still added to the social efficiency of the race, and therefore his action was inherently social and scientific in nature. His impulse took on social meaning when it produced a useful result. Therefore, the savage's invention not only affected his own life, but also the lives of other savages, even those with whom he never came into contact, because the invention and use of the bow and arrow impacted the entire social and physical environment in which the other savages were embedded. In this manner the savage impulse was simultaneously biological and social.

A similar example appeared in Dewey's review of Baldwin's 1897 book *Social and Ethical Interpretations in Mental Development: A Study in Social Psychology*. In the review, Dewey essentially offered the same critique he aimed at Ward. He accused Baldwin of placing too much emphasis on the socially constructed contents of the mind (compiled through imitation) at the expense of its biological impulses. As a result, the individuality of human cognition was not adequately accounted for. The process of imitation did not adequately explain how innovation and growth occurred. To develop his critique, Dewey once again presented an example of how the innovations of the individual affected the development of the entire race:

> The real social work done by the inventor of the telegraph is not the number of people who imitate either his act or his thought; it is the readjustment of actions, and of exercise of interests that he makes necessary. It is the new stimulus he gives, the new mode of control he introduces. The invention changes the price of daily bread, makes the daily newspaper, compels new methods of doing business—all of which affect me profoundly as a social being, even though I use the telegraph but once a year. And in making itself valid in this interplay of forces there is plenty of room for struggle, for existence, and for selection. The psychological is no longer set over against the biological.[57]

Taken together with the example of the savage creating the bow and arrow, we can see how Dewey viewed innovation in light of his genetic evolutionary scheme. Humans were driven by biological impulse and instinct, but this impulse was not deterministic; it was both initiated by particular social needs and directed toward particular social ends. Even if the individual is not consciously aware of it, the individual's interests and actions are mediated by the social inheritance of the race. Therefore, the savage mind and the civilized mind were psychically the same. They differed only in the mental contents of their social inheritance, not in their biological and psychic capabilities. The enhanced inheritance of the race was not carried biologically from one generation to the next, but rather it was transmitted through different, cumulative reactions to its genetically derived impulses. The origins of the impulse were both initiated and shaped by the evolving reactions to the environment. Thus Dewey's philosophy attempted to overcome the theories of both environmental and genetic determinism.

Dewey believed that his genetic and historicist pedagogy aligned perfectly with his pragmatic view of knowledge. As he later explained in an essay about the effects of pragmatism on education, knowledge is not a "copy" of the facts of the universe, but rather "the expression of man's past most successful achievements in effecting adjustments and adaptations, put in a form so best to help sustain and promote the future still greater control of the environment."[58] Knowledge for the race and for the child was warranted so long as it is useful for solving present and future problems. What united both of these points was the importance of history as a means of revealing a more socialized, holistic version of knowledge—one that he optimistically believed would eventually overcome philosophical and social antagonisms. "And history," Dewey argued, "shows that the advance of science represents the gradual victory of the more generic or social point of view over purely individual points of view, opinions, and merely class points of view."[59] Retaining the organic and historicist elements of his Hegelian idealism, Dewey posited that humanity—just like the savage he referred to in his review of Ward's book —would progress and evolve as it discovered more scientific, generic forms of knowledge, such as the bow and arrow.

For this reason, the history of the social occupations of the human race, organized through social occupations, served as the foundation for the entire curriculum at the Dewey School. "The education of the human race," Dewey insisted, "has been gained through the occupations which it has pursued and developed . . . . If occupations were made fundamental in education, school work would conform to the natural principles of social and mental development."[60] The social occupations of man organized historically not only united the disparate subjects of the curriculum and indicated "what is important and what is trivial in the mass of facts that has come down from the past," but they also accorded with the development of the mind and race.[61] Dewey wanted schoolchildren to engage in the same social activities through which their ancestors had struggled. With guidance from the teacher, stu-

dents would arrive at the same innovative solutions their ancestors had discovered, only do so in less time and with greater efficiency. In this manner,
Dewey hypothesized, students would appreciate the intrinsic value of the
physical and intellectual discoveries of the present and be better equipped to
take on the physical and intellectual challenges of the future.

THE CHILD, THE SAVAGE, AND SOCIETY

If we step back for a moment we can appreciate the originality and significance of Dewey's savage example presented in his review of Ward's *Psychic
Factors of Civilization* and how it related to his overall philosophical and
pedagogical approach. Let's say there were two hunter-gatherers, Savage A
and Savage B. Through reflective action based upon spontaneously emerging
but context-bound instincts, Savage A successfully subordinated the environment to invent the bow and arrow. This innovation gave Savage A the ability
to hunt his prey more effectively. The ability to form the bow and arrow allowed Savage A to live on, while Savage B starved and died off; thus Savage
A's intellectual trait was naturally selected and passed on to his offspring. To
a Darwinian the invention of the bow and arrow was the result of natural
variation and natural selection, but to the neo-Lamarckian the innovation
was the result of Savage A's creativity and volition, an acquired characteristic
that would become part of the biological makeup of the man. James Mark
Baldwin introduced a compromise via a social element, by suggesting that
Savage B could have imitated Savage A and thus also have lived on, but the
ability to create the bow and arrow would have been passed on socially, not
biologically (although over time the biological potential could also eventually
be passed on).

What Dewey did was add another significant level of social complexity by
pointing out that Savage A could have affected Savage B without ever coming into direct contact with him. Had Savage B approached a valley where
prey had previously been plentiful, but now was empty because of the invention of Savage A's bow and arrow, Savage B would have been profoundly
affected. For Dewey, innovation was not as simple as individual invention or
even direct imitation; rather, innovation subordinated and transformed the
entire environment. Thus something almost metaphysical had occurred between savages that mediated the individuals and environment, even though
the two never came into direct contact. During his Hegelian days Dewey
would have referred to this a priori mediation as divine will or unity, but
under the influence of the new psychology Dewey simply attributed it to the
creation of a new order of consciousness, which he unfortunately referred to
as "objective" and/or "generic" knowledge for a short time, but eventually
referred to as associated form of living, or "democracy" (see Chapter 4).

For Dewey, inherited instincts were the starting point of all educational growth, but the social environment in which these instincts emerged profoundly mediated how they developed. Thus we can better appreciate Dewey's definition of *education*, which he first introduced in *The Psychology of Number*, as "the work of supplying the conditions which will enable the psychical functions, as they successively arrive, and pass into higher functions in the freest and fullest manner."[62] The objective of the teacher was to create a context and environment that would draw out the naturally occurring instincts and then provide the bow and arrow (or its equivalent, like arithmetic) precisely at the point in which it was needed. Then, and only then, would students intrinsically and organically appreciate the innovation in light of the situation as they used the new tool to subordinate the environment (or solve the presented problem). These ideas reverberated throughout *The Child and the Curriculum* and *The School and Society*, two of Dewey's most popular works on education. Dewey's conception of the savage played a central role in both.

The publication of Dewey's *School and Society* in 1900 and *The Child and the Curriculum* in 1902 marked an important turning point in the proselytizing of Dewey's educational ideas. These books, based on popular lectures and published together by the University of Chicago Press, would go through more than 25 reprintings by 1950; the third edition alone sold over 260,000 copies.[63] Often assigned to prospective teachers in normal schools, the books outlined the specifics of what Dewey had accomplished at the University of Chicago laboratory school, but framed his findings in terms of broader philosophical issues. In *School and Society* Dewey explained the pedagogical significance of his repeating the race experience approach. "We can trace and follow the progress of mankind in history, getting an insight also into the materials used and the mechanical principles involved," he reasoned. "In connection with these occupations the historic development of man is recapitulated." Through reenactment of the social occupations of the past, "children shall be led out into a realization of the historic development of man." Dewey argued that his historicist approach aligned with the latest psychological and anthropological research on primitive societies. Like the developing savage, Dewey related how the laboratory school students "go on through imagination through the hunting to the semi-agricultural stage, through the nomadic to the settled agricultural stage." In this manner, the bodies of subject matter were "seen in their relationship to human activity, so that they are not simply external fact, but are fused and welded with the social conceptions regarding the life and progress of humanity"[64]

In *The Child and the Curriculum*, Dewey reiterated how the linear historicist and genetic psychological approaches to knowledge allowed curriculum theorists to overcome the unnecessary schism between the organized bodies of disciplinary content and the naturally occurring interests and instincts of children. Just as he had done in *Interest in Relation to Training of the Will,* Dewey proposed a middle path between child study advocates who argued for naturalistic approaches to curriculum and traditionalists like William Torrey Harris who insisted that instruction be immersed solely in organized subject matter. If content was approached in terms of social occupations that repeated the race experience, Dewey argued, then this divide could be overcome. Experience, Dewey insisted, "is historic; it notes the steps actually taken, the uncertain and tortuous, as well as the efficient and successful." Therefore, the curriculum needed "to be restored to the experience from which it has been abstracted." It needed to be "translated into the immediate and individual experiencing within which it has its origin and significance."[65] That is, the content of the curriculum needed to be taught in a manner that both capitalized on the emerging, inherited instincts of children, but also directed them toward the organized bodies on knowledge in the same linear sequence and manner in which the race had originally discovered them.

In summary, Dewey forged a curricular and social vision of democratic schooling that used the race experience as its unifying feature. And like his contemporaries, Dewey's innovative approach to the savage mind played a central role in his estimation of the abilities and worth of primitive societies and young children. Both groups were geniuses in their own limited contexts in their abilities to solve emerging problems for themselves. Both groups have much to teach us. Instead of viewing children and savages as inchoate and lacking, they should be approached on their own terms, as prior, necessary steps toward the civilized mind. Dewey used his anthropological view of the savage and child to critique the psychology of other scholars and bring coherence to his laboratory school curriculum. Such an approach reflected Dewey's historicist view of society as moving along a single, linear path. This sociological approach was mirrored and supplemented by his genetic approach to psychological and social development, which is the subject of the next chapter.

Chapter 3

THE MIND AT EVERY STAGE
HAS ITS OWN LOGIC

A s I OUTLINED in the introduction, Dewey viewed knowledge construction in historicist and genetic epistemological terms. By this I mean
that he considered the modern disciplines of history, psychology, sociology, and anthropology as products of the historical development of the
race itself, which he believed corresponded with the development of child and
adult. In other words, the theories and schemes of social scientists (including
Dewey's own theories) were not universal truths waiting to be determined,
but rather they were tools to further subordinate the environment. As a historicist, Dewey related all facts to prior facts, and as a genetic epistemologist,
he considered any historical fact as having incorporative contextual meanings
organized hierarchically. "The mind at every stage of growth has its own
logic," Dewey insisted in *How We Think*. "The only way in which a person
can reach the ability to make accurate definitions, penetrating classifications,
and comprehensive generalizations is by thinking alertly and carefully at his
own *present* level [italics in the original]."[1] As I discussed in Chapter 2, for
example, the hunting instinct did not have a single static meaning. Instead,
its meaning evolved from survival instinct to recreational activity as the race
progressed, and, accordingly, its meaning also evolved as an individual recapitulated the history of the race. For Dewey, to understand any fact and its
relationship to an individual or society, one had to understand its history.

Throughout Dewey's early and middle years he made reference to specific stages of child and social development. Stage theories were common for
sociologists and psychologists during this period, but Dewey put his own
stamp on the correspondence idea by identifying the organic nature of these
stages and how each subsequent stage necessarily incorporated the previous
one. This is not to suggest that these stages had any a priori existence in
the structures of the mind; Dewey rejected such Kantian dualism outright.
Consequently, because Dewey's pragmatism prevented him from referring
to any essential or a priori knowledge, he could only draw on the past as a
foundation for any individual or social knowledge. As philosopher Richard

Rorty explains, historicists like Dewey "must emphasize narrative form" because "historicism will not permit him to think of his work as establishing a relation to real essence; he can only establish a relation to the past, . . . to a larger past, the past of the species, the race, the culture."[2] For this reason, the specific stages of Dewey's scheme were a central part of his work at the University of Chicago because they guided the instruction of his teachers regarding how to best capitalize upon the emerging interests of the students. These stages of growth would not spontaneously emerge from the child as if actualizing some latent potential waiting to be released. Rather, the stages provided a road map, based upon the narrative of the race itself, to best satisfy the emerging potentials of the child by subordinating the environment.

STAGES OF PSYCHOLOGICAL GROWTH

For Dewey, the stages that a child progressed through were products of racial inheritance. As Dewey explained, "all conduct springs ultimately and radically out of native instincts and impulses," such as curiosity, interest, imitation, hunting, and gaming. Therefore, teachers needed to "know what these instincts and impulses were in order to know what to appeal to and what to build upon." All subject matter was "empty . . . until it is made over into terms of the individual's own activities, habits, and desires."[3] Throughout the early and middle years of his career, Dewey referred to these specific developmental stages in course syllabi, lecture notes, articles, and two of his major books, *School and Society* and *How We Think*. Although Dewey continually revised his language, the basic characteristics of each level remained the same.

Dewey first applied developmental levels to pedagogy in *The Psychology of Number*. He identified the first stage, which lasted until age 12–15 months, as the stage of bodily control. The second stage begins when the instinct of imitation "ripens and takes the lead." The third level is the "stage of conscious recognition of meaning."[4] In a later essay in which he defends his psychology of number against critics, Dewey linked each stage to the development of specific mathematic concepts. In the first stage the child and the savage learn to count and thus develop a vague sense of number: "The point is simply that the savage and the child begin with vague concepts of plurality, corresponding to the series, and with an equally vague sense of the totality or unity (quantity) which is split up into this plurality." The ideas of unity and plurality are developed simultaneously in relation to an emerging problem. During the second stage of the instinct of imitation, counting emerges "as spontaneous play." And during the third stage of conscious recognition "the relation between counting and magnitude is so obvious that nothing further need be said." At the third stage the counting process is used as a means and not merely as a playful end; counting is applied to magnitudes to measure or define them, a process that, according to Dewey, implied ratio.[5]

He addressed the "epochs of child psychology" again in a syllabus for his Educational Psychology course in 1896. The first epoch of early infancy was that of physical coordinations, in which sensory and motion instincts were gradually acquired. The second epoch of later infancy was that of "Free Use of Formed Coordinations." This stage included the "dawn of imagination" and "social aspects of play." The next epoch was the "Symbolic Period," which included interest in symbols and tools (i.e., numbers and letters). The last epoch of adolescence was that of "Reflective Interest, The Coordination of One's Activity as a Whole with That of Others in Society."[6] By 1898 Dewey had slightly altered his stages, most notably by substituting the term *consciousness* for *interest*. In a later class syllabus, he identified four stages: first, "direct experience"; second, "consciousness of means and ends as distinct"; third, "consciousness of organization itself"; and fourth, "consciousness of calling or function." These stages corresponded respectively with the early elementary, later elementary, secondary, and higher educational levels.[7]

For most readers, *School and Society* presented the fullest description of Dewey's psychological stages and how he had coordinated race activities to each one. He identified the first stage (ages 4 to 8) as "characterized by directness of social and personal interests, and by promptness of relationship between impressions, ideas, and action."[8] The subject matter for this stage included those objects and activities in his immediate social surroundings that could be translated into play, stories, and art. Historical occupations such as cooking and weaving best fit these criteria. The second stage (ages 8 to 12) included a "growing sense of the possibility of more permanent and objective results and of the necessity for the control of agencies for the skill necessary to reach these results." Dewey found that social processes of early American history best matched with the characteristics of this stage. In this stage students acquired the use of letters and numbers as "the tools which society has evolved in the past" and "the keys which will unlock to the child the wealth of social capital which lies beyond the possible range of his limited individual experience."[9] Thus we can see how the carefully selected and sequenced subject matter expressed both the "content" and "form" of knowledge to students.

Based on the amount of space (eight pages) Dewey devoted in *School and Society* to the second stage and its possible hurdles and shortcomings, it is clear that he considered it the most significant one. This was the stage that most schools had gotten wrong. Without an intrinsic appreciation of the form and content of symbolic systems (i.e., numbers for mathematics, letters for literacy, maps for geography) and their historical and present use, all subsequent abstract study would be disconnected and dull. Therefore, the ultimate goal of the second stage was to convince the child that he did not need to be a passive recipient of others' knowledge, that he had "the power or skill which he can now go ahead and use independently."[10] The third stage was characterized by mastery of "the methods, the tools of thought, inquiry, and activity, appropriate to various phases of experience, to be able to special- ize upon distinctive studies." At this level students would engage in the sci- entific acts of deduction and induction for each subject. Regarding the fourth stage, Dewey related that when *School and Society* was first published in 1899 his school had not "been in existence long enough so that any typical infer- ences can be safely drawn."[11] By the next year, however, Dewey was confident enough to outline the characteristics of this stage, which he addressed in an essay simply titled "Mental Development."

The "Mental Development" essay differed from previous ones because Dewey incorporated and synthesized the work of many of his colleagues who were working on child study. The essay began with a lengthy bibliography of research on physical development, periods of mental development, play and games in children, children's art, language of children, and adolescence, and included the major works of James Mark Baldwin. For the most part, Dewey largely drew upon the research of others to provide further evidence for the stages he had outlined earlier. Beyond this, the most original contribution of the "Mental Development" essay was the outline of the fourth stage of development—adolescence or youth—which extended to age 24. This last stage, Dewey explained, marked "the epoch of securing the final adjustment on the part of the individual of himself to the fundamental features of life." Students at this stage fully appreciate the social inheritance of the race and sought to contribute to it in some way. "In history," Dewey explained, ". . . the tendency at this time is to see larger wholes, to try to gather together facts otherwise scattered and to mass them as parts in the comprehensive whole."[12] Thus students seek to bring order to the overwhelming mass of facts the world presents. This was the social constructivist stage. Students and adults at this level learned how to construct new knowledge for the sake of learning and growth.

Dewey briefly revisited his developmental stages again in *How We Think*. In this 1910 text he made few direct references to the "repeating the race experience" curriculum he enacted at the Dewey School. Instead, his stages were abstracted into three incorporative levels of curiosity: the physical, the social, and the intellectual. The first stage (physical) was represented by "an expression of an abundant organic energy"—a tendency that young children shared with animals. They were impulsive, energetic, and constantly "getting into things," yet there was no central coordination of these unrelated acts. The second stage (social) included "the influence of social stimuli," in which children asked questions of others. Children recognized parents, other children, and adults, but did so only in relation to what these figures could do to further their own desires and impulses. Play took place during this stage as a form of imitation, but (reiterating his critique of Baldwin) Dewey insisted that this action was not intended to please others, but merely to act out impulses for its own sake. In the third stage (intellectual), "curiosity rises above the organic and the social planes and becomes intellectual in the degree in which it is transformed into interest in problems provoked by observation of things."[13] Students now wanted to have their actions achieve some end. Throughout the progression through these stages, the goal of the teacher, Dewey insisted, was "to protect the spirit of inquiry, to keep alive the scared spark of wonder and to fan the flame that already glows."[14]

As a genetic psychologist, Dewey subscribed to the beliefs that humans progressed through linear, observable, sequential stages of consciousness; that these stages emerged as a biologically inherited impulse—mediated by the mind—and interacted with a socially informed external stimuli; that these stages included evolving manifestations of the same inherited instinct (i.e., hunting, gaming, interest, curiosity); that each stage incorporated the prior one; and that they corresponded with the social development of the race. "For in the truly genetic method," Dewey explained, "the idea of genesis looks both ways; this fact is itself generated out of certain conditions, and in turn tends to generate something else."[15] That is, each stage both emerged from the form and content of the prior stage and then led to the form and content of the subsequent stage. The new attainments of each stage, "in turn, become the instruments of others."[16]

In conclusion, according to Dewey, the entire psychological history of the child could be summarized in the following way: First, children engaged in impulsive curiosity (Stage 1), then they analyzed and incorporated these impulsive curiosities into a centrally coordinated playful curiosity (Stage 2), then they analyzed and incorporated these playful curiosities into a purposeful intellectual curiosity of means-toward-an-end (Stage 3), then they analyzed and incorporated these purposeful intellectual curiosities into a calling or function (Stage 4). The calling or function stage was what disciplinary experts did; they produced knowledge and/or products (i.e., theories) for consumption by others. Stage 4 logic not only involved the act of constructing new knowledge, but also the ability to analyze the knowledge of other experts, which involved analyzing the act of knowledge construction itself. Stage 4 was the social constructivist stage, the level in which disciplinary experts use the discourse of their disciplines to produce original knowledge. As I show below, these stages of mental development corresponded with the intellectual growth of the entire race.

STAGES OF SOCIOLOGICAL GROWTH

At the turn of the century virtually all social scientists agreed that human history could be organized hierarchically within a single evolutionary scheme that included the stages of savagery (primitive), barbarism, and civilization.[17] As demonstrated above, Dewey referred to these stages of social development throughout the early and middle years of his career. "Many anthropologists have told us there are certain identities in the child's interests with those of primitive life," Dewey explained in *School and Society*. "There is a sort of natural recurrence of the child mind to the typical activities of primitive peoples."[18] Thus Dewey, along with most psychologists of the time, established the recapitulational link between development of the individual and race. In *School and Society* Dewey related how, through the coordination of social occupations to the past, "the historic development of man is recapitulated."[19] Using his scheme, Dewey coordinated specific content with each stage of human development. As Dewey insisted, the content and form of past cultures "absolutely must be transmitted to the succeeding and immature generation if social life itself is not to relapse into barbarism and then into savagery."[20]

Dewey was careful to explain that the stages of history would not spontaneously emerge from the impulses of the child, as the Herbartians were suggesting. "Points of similarity in the interests of the child with those of various periods in the race," he explained, "are indicated not on the ground that the child is predestined to recapitulate the cultural development of the race, but because, having the same career to achieve, there is a present organic necessity for the genesis and growth of similar attitudes."[21] That is, the historical reliving of the innovations of the race was the most effective way to organize the content and form of the curriculum, not because it necessarily made learning inherently easier, but because the growth of the race and the growth of the individual occurred through the same stages of consciousness when faced with similar environmental and social problems. Thus, for both the historicist and genetic psychological elements of Dewey's thought, history was the key to appreciating the nature of any issue or content. As Dewey explained, "History sets forth the temporal background, the evolution of the gradual control of the activities by which mankind had enriched and perfected its experience."[22]

The historical stages of the race were most clearly outlined in Dewey's 1900 essay "Some Stages of Logical Thought," in which he traced the "modes of thinking easily recognizable in the progress of both the race and individual."[23] In the first stage of racial development "beliefs are treated as something static." Words are reflective of things that are believed to be unchanging and fixed. Any doubts that arise are either squashed and/or subsumed within the preexisting beliefs. These fixed customs and attitudes are habits of understanding that inhibit growth and progress. As Dewey explained, "We find an apt illustration of fixed ideas in the rules prevalent in primitive communities, rules which minutely determine all acts in which the community as a whole is felt to have an interest." The second historical stage, characterized by the Greeks and Hebrews, includes the questioning of static beliefs through the introduction of prophecy, argumentation, and discussion. The shift from the first "primitive" stage to the more advanced second stage occurs as the "scheduled stock of fixed ideas grows larger," and "their application to specific questions becomes more difficult, prolonged, and roundabout." The weight of the conflicting evidence challenging the fixed belief system becomes so great "that it cannot sustain itself without a readjustment of the center of gravity." As a result of this social dissonance, a new society emerges that entertains discussion and argumentation. As Dewey argued, "Where all was fixity, now all is instability; where all was certitude, nothing now exists save opinion based on prejudice, interest, or arbitrary choice." [24]

The third stage of social growth includes transition from the Greek mode of "mere thinking" to the "elaborate system of checks and balances found in the technique of modern experimentation." During the third stage the ideas that had logically been outlined and intellectually demonstrated now have to be proven empirically in the physical world. "The transition from the second to the third stage," Dewey explained, was best characterized as "the transformation of discussion into reasoning, of subjective reflection into proof." The fourth stage moves from positivistic proof to inference, to "pushing out the frontiers of knowledge, not at marking those already attained with signposts." It involves discovering better, more nuanced ways of explaining the world, with an acceptance of the process of self-correction inherent in such an approach. Theories are contingent and variable. Social and scientific laws are no longer seen as unchanging restraints on the world, but instead are considered agreements and compacts with the facts themselves, as statements of their order. As Dewey explained, in the fourth stage "the observable world is a democracy." The specializations of the disciplines emerged organically during the fourth, social constructivist stage.[25]

Just as with his psychological stages, Dewey emphasized that the sociological stages could not be skipped. Each had to be adequately lived through because each level of consciousness incorporated the previous one. The modern disciplines emerged organically out of the previous stages. Regarding the fourth stage, Dewey wrote:

> Instrumentalities of extending and rectifying research are, therefore, themselves organs of thinking. The specialization of the sciences, the almost daily birth of a new science, is a logical necessity—not a mere historical episode. Every phase of experience must be investigated, and each characteristic aspect presents its own peculiar problems which demand, therefore, their own technique of investigation.[26]

That is, the discrepant facts that emerged from the world were no longer best subsumed within a single system of form and content such as the scientific method, but, rather, these "apparent exceptions, negative instances, extreme cases [and] anomalies" were best investigated by new disciplinary points of view.[27]

In conclusion, according to Dewey, the entire sociological history of the race could be summarized in the following way: First societies established fixed beliefs, customs and laws (Stage 1); then they analyzed and incorporated these beliefs through discussions, dialogues, and judgments (Stage 2); then they analyzed and incorporated these discussions into a positivistic science of induction and deduction (Stage 3); then they analyzed and incorporated positivistic science into differentiated sciences based on contingency and inference (Stage 4). The final contingency stage produced the modern disciplines and the subdisciplines within them, each of which had its own socially constructed symbolic forms of knowledge and communication. The modernist stage was not only the level of "democracy," but also the level of the modern specialist. The Dewey School did not address this final stage because it went beyond the psychological and sociological scope of its curriculum. Instead, the Dewey School teachers focused on developing thinking at Stages 1 through 3.

COORDINATING PSYCHOLOGICAL AND SOCIOLOGICAL GROWTH

The central problem explored by Dewey and his teachers at the University of Chicago laboratory school was how to coordinate the psychological stages outlined by the child study movement with the sociological stages Dewey outlined in "Some Stages of Logical Thought." As Dewey explained, "The ultimate problem of all education is to coordinate the psychological and social factors"; that is, to coordinate the emerging instinct stages of the child with the historical modes of occupation that best represented them.[28] For the most part, the curriculum that the Dewey School teachers constructed, especially for the primary years, was a success. The fullest account of the curriculum appeared in 1936 in Katherine Camp Mayhew and Alice Camp Edwards's *The Dewey School: The Laboratory School of the University of Chicago, 1896–1903*. In this exhaustive description of the theory and practice of the school the authors related that "the study of primitive forms of spinning and weaving is given in connection with the primitive history to illustrate further the life of people whose mode of living is simple and in direct contact with nature." Young students at the Dewey School proved that their instinctive responses to historical problems matched the stages of consciousness of the historical epochs. As Mayhew and Edwards explained, "The child himself often made the process of transition from the present to the past an easy one." They continued, "With something of the intuition of the true scientist he frequently chose an ancient method of historical approach and solved the problem of how to begin his study with 'Let's pretend.'"[29] That is, the student responded to the problem in the same "ancient" way his racial ancestors had done. The subject matter and form of the curriculum was organized historically and hierarchically to correspond with the development of how the race had evolved in relation to emerging social and environmental problems. As I have pointed out, even reading, writing, and arithmetic were not introduced until students learned about how and why their historical counterparts (the Phoenicians) had invented them.

Dewey's genetic approach to curriculum was not only implemented at his famous school, but also influenced other progressive reformers. One of Dewey's first disciples was Katherine Elizabeth Dopp, a former normal school teacher and instructor at the University of Chicago. In the 1910s Dopp developed and published a series of textbooks based on Dewey's "repeating the race experience" curriculum, including the *Place of Industries in Elementary Education, The Tree-Dwellers, The Early Cavemen, The Later Cavemen,* and *The Early Sea People.* As Dopp explained, "Since the experience of the race in industrial and social processes embodies better than any other experiences of mankind those things which at the same time appeal to the whole nature of the child and furnish him the means of interpreting the complex processes about him, this experience had been made the groundwork of the present series." In the preface to her books, Dopp thanked Dewey "for the suggestions he has given me with reference to this series," and she also thanked William I. Thomas (see Chapters 2 and 6), "for suggestions upon anthropological phases of many of the subjects presented."[30] Accordingly, Dewey provided an enthusiastic review of Dopp's curriculum in *The Elementary School Teacher,* in which he reiterated how "the historical method is invading the business of education and is likely to be one of the most fundamental forces in directing its immediate future." Regarding Dopp's implementation of the genetic pedagogical method, Dewey concluded, "Dr. Dopp's book is the most helpful thing that has yet been published."[31] Like Dewey had done at his laboratory school, Dopp had coordinated the instincts of the child with the hunting, fishing, pastoral, agricultural, feudal, handicraft, and industrial stages of historical development.

Dewey addressed the broader impact of evolutionism on social science in his commonly cited 1909 essay, "The Influence of Darwinism on Evolution." He explained how, prior to Darwin, philosophers were engaged in determining the eternal and essential nature of things. Even when recognizing the growth and evolution of an entity, the objective was to discover its "fixed form and final cause," thus ascribing a latent potential to what was actually always in a state of constant flux. "The influence of Darwin upon philosophy," Dewey insisted, "resides in his having conquered the phenomenon of life for the principle of transition."[32] As we shall see below, Dewey also applied the genetic psychological and historicist approach to educational ethics by demonstrating how all ethical systems, including the modern form, were transitional and based upon the transient needs of their users.

EVOLUTIONARY ETHICS

Dewey first specifically addressed ethics in the classroom in the short essay "Teaching Ethics in the High School," written in 1893, in which he suggested that social ethics should be incorporated into the teaching of history, which "will constantly introduce new material, new problems, new methods of the ethical imagination that is occupied with making real for the individual the world of action in which he lives."[33] In 1896 Dewey again argued that social ethics should be added to the high school curriculum, so students could appreciate how the individual added to the social inheritance of the race. History, he explained, afforded "opportunity for discussions of questions of habit and character, purpose and motive."[34] However, Dewey most directly addressed educational ethics in one of his first essays on education, "Ethical Principles Underlying Education," first published in 1897.

The stages of Dewey's genetic approach to morality were not conspicuously referenced in this work, but his linear historicism was fully on display. "Ethical Principles Underlying Education" was published in the 1897 Herbart Society Yearbook and was later reprinted with slight revisions as *Moral Principles Underlying Education*. The general argument of the essay is that morality should not be taught explicitly as a list of prescriptions, rules, and desirable traits, but rather it should emerge organically through content-based instruction and through the social interactions of the embryonic community of the school. "The child ought to have exactly the same motives for right doing," Dewey argued, "and be judged by exactly the same standard in the school as the adult in the wider social life to which he belongs."[35] In essence, Dewey argued that ethics is best taught by ignoring it as a set of stand-alone lessons. Thus, if the teacher approached the curriculum in the proper manner, then moral development would essentially take care of itself. Accordingly, much of the essay is about how to approach instruction properly in a way that connect theory and practice, form and content, and the social and psychological aspects of the curriculum. Like the savage, students would feel the moral dissonance referenced above and appreciate how their instinctual moral habits and intellectual responses were no longer appropriate, and they would organically grow to meet the needs of the emerging social problem. This is not to suggest that morality was something that simply emerged biologically. Rather, the emerging impulses would only find satisfaction if the social and moral environment presented by the school was reflective of the larger community (past and present). The students' present stage of moral growth was not indulged. Instead, it was recognized and challenged by a more complex ethical environment.

Specifically, in "Ethical Principles Underlying Education" Dewey again identified history as the most significant subject for teaching morality: "The ethical value of history teaching will be measured by the extent to which it is treated as a matter of analysis of existing social relations—that is to say as affording insight into what makes up the structure and working of society." Outlining his genetic approach to the curriculum—one that reduced "the existing complexity to its simple elements"—Dewey explained how the Greeks represented "what art and the growing power of individual expression stand for" and how the Romans demonstrated "the political elements and determining forces of political life on a tremendous scale." Both would be used in coordination with the third psychological/ sociological stage outlined above. The contributions of these civilizations needed to be presented to students so that they could appreciate how the remnants of the past were organically contained in the present social world. Everything depended, Dewey explained, upon history as "a method of social progress" and "upon history being treated from a social standpoint, as manifesting the agencies which have influenced social development, and theoretical institutions in which social life has expressed itself." In summary, Dewey insisted that "when history is taught as a mode of understanding social life it has positive ethical import" because the ethical lessons of right and wrong action were organically and inherently contained in the content of the past.[36]

A year after Dewey published "Ethical Principles Underlying Education," Dewey wrote the essay "Evolution and Ethics" (1898) responding to the 1893 Romanes Lecture by the recently deceased Thomas Huxley titled "Ethics and Evolution." During the nineteenth century Huxley had been one of the strongest proponents of the straight Darwinian view of psychic evolution—that the mind was merely the biological outcome of natural selection of inherited traits that had best "fit" the environment. However, at this famous Oxford lecture Huxley seemingly reversed his position by arguing for the significance of human intervention in the evolutionary process by drawing a distinction between "cosmic" and "ethical" evolution. The former referenced the selfish, individual biological inheritance, but the latter involved the acquired cooperative and selfless aspects of modern life. Dewey, of course, agreed with Huxley's revision, because he considered human innovation to be a significant factor in the evolution of the race, but Dewey disagreed with Huxley's mechanism for the moral growth. Similar to the savage example he used in his review of Lester F. Ward's book (see Chapter 2), Dewey explained how ethical evolution should not be based upon a dualistic view of mind and environment, wherein the former simply passively responded to (or "fit") a purely materialist version of the latter. Instead, Dewey insisted that the ethical growth was the act of the mind subordinating the social and physical environment:

> That which was fit among the animals is not fit among human beings, not merely because the animals were non-moral and man is moral; but because the conditions of life have changed and because there is no way to define the term "fit" excepting through these conditions. The environment is now a distinctly social one, and the content of the term "fit" has to be made with reference to social adaptation. Moreover, the environment in which we live is a changing and progressive one.[37]

Dewey argued that the physical word was not merely such, but was subordinated to and permeated with the innovations of the social world. The human of the present was not merely the result of the accumulation of naturally selected or acquired characteristics, but rather was the expression of the relevant traits as mediated by the present social environment. "The past environment," he explained, "is related to the present as part of the whole." Therefore, any attempt to separate the moral from the physical word was misguided, because they were both organically united. Dewey concluded, in accordance with the curricular ideas he introduced in "Ethical Principles Underlying Education," that "whatever is necessary to life we may fairly assume to have some relevancy to moral living."[38] Dewey developed these ideas further in his popular textbook, *Ethics*.

The first edition of Dewey's textbook on *Ethics* was copublished with James H. Tufts in 1908. Tufts was Dewey's colleague at the University of Michigan for 2 years and was his colleague at the University of Chicago for 10. Tufts was a specialist in ethics and so he wrote the first section of the book tracing the "beginning and growth of morality," and Dewey wrote the chapters addressing the theoretical aspects of the topic. However, they cowrote the preface and introduction in which they profess the pedagogical potential of the historical approach to the topic. "To follow the moral life through typical epochs of its development enables students to realize what is involved in their own habitual standpoints," the authors explained. "It also presents a concrete body of subject matter which serves as material of analysis and discussion." They explained four specific benefits to studying the early stages of moral development. First, by using "genetic study," the complexity of modern morality was broken down into a simpler form. Dewey had obviously employed this idea at his laboratory school, and Dewey and Tufts used a similar method with their college-age students. Second, genetic study allowed students to realize that rudiments of the earlier forms of ethics have survived into the present. In accordance with Dewey's essay on the savage mind, the authors were giving credit to these racial ancestors for making the necessary adjustments, many of which had organically remained within the moral systems of the present day. Thus anthropologists should view savages and primitives as necessary steps toward the present—as geniuses of their own age—not as morally deficient. Third, Dewey and Tufts argued, the distant past provided material that could be studied more objectively than the present. "Our moral life is so intimate," they explained, ". . . that it is hard to observe impartially." Finally, genetic study emphasizes the "dynamic, progressive character of morality."[39] By studying how morality was shaped and guided by the social contexts from which it emerged (and how morality was contingent upon its context for its effectiveness), students would view their own inherited moral system with a greater degree of intrinsic appreciation.

The introduction to *Ethics*, once again, outlined the specific stages of moral development of the child and race. Progress through the individual and social stages occurred because "the habits formed at one age of the individual's life, or at one stage of race development, proved inadequate for more complex situations." When the "child leaves home" or "the savage changes to agricultural life," the new social and physical environment in which he found himself created a dissonance that could only be assuaged by constructing new habits to better meet the emerging needs of the situation. Specifically, the three stages of moral development were the "instinctive" stage, the "transition from impulse to will" stage, and the "well-organized character" stage.[40] Growth through these stages allowed man to become more rational, social, and moral. All three stages were incorporated in modern civilized life, but "only the first two are found in savage life."[41] Drawing upon an impressive number of ethnographic works by modern anthropologists, Tufts outlined the social, moral, and religious characteristics of each of these stages over the course of 180 pages—much more than the average student needed, but the book was not intended merely for students but also for scholars. As a result, it received excellent reviews from scholarly critics, who appreciated the book's historical background, its scientific approach to the topic, and how the authors brought morality out of metaphysics and into the real world.

To give the specifics of the moral views Dewey outlined in *Ethics* would take us beyond the scope of this book. Instead, I merely wanted to demonstrate that Dewey's genetic psychological and historicist approach united all of his areas of interest, extended into his philosophical writings on ethics, and was shared by his intellectual peers. *Ethics* fleshed out the linear historicist ideas he had presented a decade earlier about how morality was an outcome of overall social growth. *Ethics* also demonstrated that Dewey approached his elementary and college students from a similar pedagogical perspective, by tracing the history of the object of study from its origins to the present. Therefore, it is fitting that "Ethical Principles Underlying Education" (1897) and *Ethics* (1908) more or less bookend the time Dewey spent at the University of Chicago laboratory school during which he worked out how to coordinate the historical phases of social and moral life with the emerging stages of child interests, and do so in a way that demonstrated how the knowledge of the past was organically contained in the present. Dewey was mostly successful with his ambitious task although, as his shifting vocabulary demonstrated, he was never fully satisfied with how to describe the psychological and sociological stages of growth. As explained below, the stages of individual and social growth were referenced in Dewey's most influential educational work, *How We Think*.

HOW WE THINK

How We Think was a culmination of Dewey's work at the University of Chicago laboratory school. Accordingly, in the introduction he thanked his wife and Ella Flagg Young for their encouragement and help in bringing his ideas "concreteness as comes from embodiment and testing in practice."[42] The text can be seen as a sequel to *School and Society* because the earlier work focused almost exclusively on education during the primary grades (Stages 1, 2, and 3), yet *How We Think* addressed the "scientific thinking" of Stages 3 and 4. The generic elements of reflective thinking that made such a long-lasting impact on curriculum designers were identified as "(a) a state of perplexity, hesitation, doubt and (b) an act of search or investigation directed toward bringing to light further facts which serve to corroborate or to nullify the suggested belief." He fleshed out these steps more specifically as "five logically distinct steps: (i) a felt difficulty; (ii) its location and definition; (iii) suggestion of possible solution; (iv) development by reasoning of the bearings of the suggestion; (v) further observation and experiment leading to its acceptance or rejection; that is, the conclusion of belief or disbelief."[43] These steps were organically contained in each stage of development, although they took on qualitatively different forms.

In *How We Think* Dewey outlined the stages of psychological growth into the physical, the social, and the intellectual stages. Dewey specifically cited L. T. Hobhouse's *Mind in Evolution* as evidence for existence of these psychological states. "Evolution is a single continuous process," Hobhouse explained in his 1901 text, "the different phases of which are only truly seen in their significance when treated as parts of the whole to which they belong"—a notion with which Dewey clearly concurred.[44] Like Dewey, Hobhouse considered his brand of evolutionary views contrary to the positivism of Comte, Mill, and Spencer and more aligned with the views of Lester F. Ward. Specifically, Hobhouse believed that at a certain point in the evolutionary history of the race, the mind was no longer a passive recipient of environmental forces, but instead became an active contributor to its own evolutionary process. This transition was intimately related to the development of reflective and/or logical thinking.

In accordance with the views of Hobhouse, Dewey demonstrated his allegiance to historicism and genetic psychology throughout *How We Think*, although in this work he made clearer distinctions among the types of thinking present at each stage and their relationship to the larger process of growth. As Dewey explained (in words echoing Hobhouse's account above), "the *psychological* and the *logical*, . . . are connected *as the earlier and the later stages in one continuous process of growth* [italics in the original]."⁴⁵ Thus we can see the tension developing between the progressive movement of the organic process of social growth and the contextual nature of each stage— or, to put it another way, the tension between the latent potential in each stage waiting to be actualized and the open-ended interactionist nature of his overall pragmatic approach. An activity was not educative on its own terms, but was educative in qualitatively different ways depending upon the level or stage of consciousness. Yet the entire process was driven by a movement toward unity and growth in the direction of the expert. In *How We Think* Dewey asserted that "in natural growth each successive stage of activity prepares unconsciously but thoroughly, the conditions for the manifestation of the next stage," and "what is abstract at one period of growth is concrete at another."⁴⁶ An appreciation for the future role of each stage of reflective thinking could only be recognized by a teacher who was cognizant of the next level and thereby extracted the latent potential of the student. Since metaphysics could not be appealed to in order to determine and utilize what this next level should be, Dewey could only appeal to the history of the race, that is, to levels of thinking that had already been discovered and utilized by Western civilization. Therefore, in accordance with Dewey's linear historicism, the past demonstrated what reflective thinking at each level of growth looked like. To underscore this point, Dewey once again addressed the levels of sociological growth he outlined in "Stages of Logical Thought":

> In the history of the progress of the human knowledge, out and out myths accompany the first stage of empiricism, while hidden essences and occult forces mark its second stage. . . . Scientific method [as the third stage] replaces the repeated conjunction or coincidence of separate facts by discovery of a single comprehensive fact, effecting this replacement by breaking up the course of gross facts of observation into a number of minuter [sic] processes not directly accessible to perception.⁴⁷

Therefore, like the development of modern ethics, logical thinking was an organic outgrowth of experience as necessitated by the continual complexity of the natural and social world. Furthermore, like his study of ethics, Dewey brought logical thinking out of the a priori realm and into the real world.

One of Dewey's major weaknesses as a writer was his failure to explicate his abstract ideas through concrete real-world models. Examples such as the savage discovering the bow and arrow that he employed in his review of Lester F. Ward's book are few and far between in Dewey's writings. However, the centerpiece of *How We Think* is the three real-world instances of reflective thinking he presents in Chapter 6 of the book. The instances not only provide specific examples of the concepts he presents throughout the rest of the study, but also demonstrate how Dewey extracted the generic aspects of thought from its stage-specific modes. The first example describes a person who had 40 minutes to make it to a meeting uptown and was pondering whether the subway or a "surface car" would be more efficient. Based on his knowledge of where the subway car let out, he chose to take the subway instead of the surface car to his destination. The second example depicts a person staring at a ferryboat on the horizon trying to identify a flagpole-like object on its bow. After exploring several possibilities of what the object could be (e.g., wireless telegraph, ornament, pointer), the person hypothesized that the pole was probably there to show the pilot what direction the boat was headed. The third example describes a person who discovered bubbles moving from the outside to the inside of tumblers when washing them in soapy water and placing them on a plate. He hypothesizes that the air inside the tumbler expanded upon removal. Upon several experiments with different tumblers (some were shaken, some were prevented from collecting air), he confirmed his hypothesis that air from outside the tumbler expanded within it, causing the bubbles to move across the glass. These three examples, Dewey explains, "form a series from the more rudimentary to more complicated cases of reflection."[48] If we compare these stages with the sociological and psychological stages outlined above we can see that the first, subway example corresponded roughly with the Stage 2 discussion/dialogue phase. The second, ferryboat example corresponded roughly with the Stage 3 positivistic science of induction/deduction phase. Finally, the third, tumbler example corresponded roughly with the Stage 4 inference/contingency phase. Each one incorporated the prior one as part of the organic process of growth. Dewey essentially confirmed this interpretation later in the book:

> The three instances cited in Chapter Six represented an ascending cycle from the practical to the theoretical. Taking thought to keep a personal engagement is obviously of the concrete kind. Endeavoring to work out the meaning of a certain part of the

boat is an instance of an intermediate kind . . . the problem was theoretical, more or less speculative. . . . The third case, that of the appearance and movement of the bubbles, illustrates a strictly theoretical or abstract case.[49]

The mind contingently developed through these stages of logical growth as it engaged emerging problems of the social world.

LATENT AND CONTINGENT POTENTIALS

Despite his successes, Dewey's genetic psychological and historicist approach to knowledge and pedagogy contained an inherent contradiction that became more obvious over time. How could his historical approach to content and morals be both interactional and yet contain linear, universal stages of growth? How could the present contain both historical contingencies and realized universal principles and stages? For example, in "Ethical Principles Underlying Education" Dewey insisted—in language that made him sound like a sociological positivist—that it must be recognized that "social forces in themselves are always the same—that the same kind of influences were at work 100 and 1000 years ago that are now."[50] In *The Child and the Curriculum* Dewey remarked that "development is a definitive process, having its own law which can be fulfilled only when adequate and normal conditions are provided."[51] Thus knowledge (on both the psychological and sociological level) for Dewey resulted from a linear sequence that was moving toward a convergent "unity" through ahistorical "forces" and "laws," yet was inherently dynamic, interactional, and bound to its social context. Knowledge, for Dewey while he was at the University of Chicago, was fluid and open-ended, yet at the same time moving linearly toward a more generic and socialized consciousness that necessarily constituted progress. As we shall see in Chapter 5, Dewey still needed to develop his ideas on the necessity of interaction with a pluralistic universe for actualizing potentials, which he did not do until 1915–1917. At this point, Dewey's focus on the internal factors of growth at the expense of satisfying external factors left his scheme ambiguous and somewhat incomplete.

Similarly, although Dewey conceived of knowledge growth in stages, each stage also contained a constant element—reflective thinking. Dewey never phrased it in these terms, but the reflecting thinking process was biologically based potential; it was a manifestation of the inherited instincts that began with bodily energy but were conditioned numerous times to subordinate the evolving, complex world around it. Thus reflective thinking was a universal human faculty, even though, at any one time, it existed in the world simultaneously in various psychological/sociological forms corresponding with various stages of human development. However, once again, the universality of reflective thinking represented somewhat of a contradiction for Dewey because the idea of historicism emphasized the dynamic evolution of all things, including (presumably) the linear developmental sequence he outlined and implemented at the Dewey School. Richard Rorty recognized this very contradiction in *How We Think,* writing: "Dewey wants to praise certain ways of thinking which he thinks have become more common since the seventeenth century, but he cannot specify these ways too narrowly, for fear of erecting an abstract formalism as constrictive as any of his more 'rationalistic' predecessors."[52] That is, Dewey wanted to demonstrate that although the forms and contents of reflective thinking were transient, the stages of reflective thinking themselves were universal, despite the fact that his historicism and genetic approach denied the universality of anything.

Dewey addressed this issue directly in 1902 in a series of essays on the historical approach to ethics. Dewey began by critiquing the two most common forms of genetic approaches to content: the materialist and idealist. The materialist approach assumed that "early forms of a historical series are superior to later forms," and, inversely, the idealist approach assumed that "various members of the series . . . [possess] different degrees of reality, the more primitive being nearest zero." Thus Dewey denied the idea that either earlier or later forms were more real than the rest of the series; instead, the reality was the entire series itself. Unlike most other historicist schemes of the time, Dewey's historicism (in theory) denied that earlier forms of reality contained a latent potential of later forms. As Dewey later explained in *Democracy and Education,* "Instead of latent intellectual powers, requiring only exercise for their perfecting, they [native impulses] are tendencies to respond in certain ways to changes in the environment so as to bring about other changes."[53] A particular social context was needed to draw out the potential, which was not necessarily latent, but instead was activated by the same social context as previous iterations of the form.

In practice, however, the Dewey School teachers necessarily led students from one stage of thinking to the next in a predetermined sequence, implying that each stage did, in fact, contain a latent potential for the next. Dewey insisted that emphasis should not be on any one form, but rather "the process operative in reference to all forms."[54] The generic stages of thought outlined in *How We Think* represented this "operative process." According to Dewey, the object of study should not only be to discover the "operative process" in all things, but also to study the diversity of ways the process had manifested itself (i.e., its history). Nevertheless, Dewey's pedagogical approach reduced all content and forms to those factors that contribute to progress, while ignoring those that did not, leading to the impression that (at least at a pedagogical level) society contained a teleological force leading to the present. As Dewey later explained, "All thinking is original in a projection of considerations which have not been previously apprehended." Thus a child who discovers something "is really a discoverer, even though everybody else in the world knows it."[55] The challenge of teaching, he argued, "is to keep the experience of the student moving in the direction of what the expert already knows." Therefore, Dewey was not really arguing on behalf of open-ended inquiry in education; he was arguing on behalf of directed inquiry toward the preexisting knowledge of the expert. For the teacher, the knowledge of and from the past may have been contingent, but the teaching of this knowledge was predetermined.

This contradiction runs throughout *How We Think*; it is the work that links his research at the laboratory school with his later broader interests in education and democracy. To say that *How We Think* is transitional is to say very little because all of Dewey's works were transitional; Dewey was constantly reconstructing his views in light of new ideas and issues. But *How We Think* most conspicuously outlined both the historical and ahistorical nature of his linear historicism. In this work Dewey outlined the specific generic steps of inquiry contained in all reflective thought. In terms of direct influence on the curriculum, these steps were the most cited and influential ideas he ever came up with.[56] However, curriculum theorists past and present have failed to recognize that *How We Think* was as much about genetic psychology as it was about the universal steps of reflective thinking—about how to satisfy the potential (latent or otherwise) of thought.

At the same time, the generic steps of reflective thinking presented in *How We Think* democratized the curriculum by making it more about process than content. In other words, any student regardless of his cultural and biological background could potentially engage in reflective thinking about any emerging "real-world" issue. Dewey deliberately chose examples in Chapter 6 that were not part of the "conspicuous consumption" curriculum of Veblen's "leisure class," such as determining the correct Latin verb to use or which mathematical law applied to a theoretical problem. Instead, logical thinking emerged from the experience of everyday interaction such as determining how to travel uptown most effectively. Even his example of experimental "scientific thinking" emerged from the daily activity of washing dishes. On the other hand, Dewey's allegiance to historicism and genetic psychology reinforced the ethnocentric approach to curriculum that he helped implement at the Dewey School, wherein the thoughts and ideas of Western culture were identified as the most advanced, most efficient, and most socialized end point of progress. As we have seen, this Eurocentric "repeating the race experience" scheme solved a lot of problems for Dewey, but as U.S. schools became more populated with members of the alleged "barbarian" and "savage" races of the present, the innovative curriculum he had worked out became less relevant.

This issue relates to the closing words of Dewey's essay on Darwin's influence: "Intellectual progress usually occurs through sheer abandonment of questions . . . an abandonment that results from their decreasing vitality and a change of urgent interest. We do not solve them; we get over them."[57] Dewey never solved the dilemma of how to reconcile the ethnocentrism of the University of Chicago laboratory school curriculum with his emerging interactionism, nor did he ever solve the dilemma of how to establish a curriculum based upon the emerging potentials of universal stages and, paradoxically, the contingency of interactional satisfactions. He and his peers simply "got over" even worrying about these problems. In particular, Dewey's interests broadened from the psychological and biological interests of the child to the institutional structures of the American high school. This led him to engage two issues that had moved to center stage during the twentieth century: the democratic value of vocational education and cultural value of non-European groups. These are the subjects of the next three chapters. Addressing these two issues moved Dewey away from his linear ethnocentrism toward a more interactionist and pluralist approach.

In fact, by the mid-1900s, Dewey had exhausted the influences and ideas of his University of Chicago colleagues. While designing his Dewey School curriculum, he had adopted their post-laissez-faire convictions as well as their historicist and genetic approaches to knowledge. However, these ideas turned out to be intellectual dead ends as the ethnocentric implications of these modernist approaches became apparent. After 1904 Dewey no longer drew upon the ideas of Small and Veblen. Rather, he would be most affected by the ideas of William I. Thomas because his sociological ideas had most accurately anticipated the significance of the pluralizing world. Dewey's reorientation was slow to emerge, but it was aided by his sudden departure from the University of Chicago in 1904.

Angered by a new administrative arrangement for the University of Chicago laboratory school that demoted his wife, Alice, Dewey resigned in protest. The "gist of it is simply that I found I could not work harmoniously under the conditions which the President's methods of conducting affairs created and imposed," Dewey explained to William Torrey Harris. "So it seemed to be due both him and myself that I should transfer my activities elsewhere."[58] Despite President Harper's pleas for reconciliation, Dewey had had enough of his escalating administrative duties and sought a new intellectual environment. Dewey also was frustrated with the intellectual limitations of the teachers with whom he was working. "So many teachers," he complained to Harris, "are simply looking around for something that somebody else has said, and are so willing to swallow it all whole, that I hesitate about putting any additional temptations in their way."[59] With help from his friend James Cattell, he quickly found a home at Columbia University, where his work would reach a much broader audience. As Cornell West commented, "Dewey got his start in Michigan and excelled in Chicago, but in New York he became a star."[60]

Chapter 4

THE OBSERVABLE WORLD
IS A DEMOCRACY

IN 1903 JAMES CATTELL surveyed American psychologists and instructed them to rank their most eminent peers. Dewey was ranked eighth behind William James, Cattell, Hugo Munsterberg, G. Stanley Hall, James Mark Baldwin, Edward B. Tichener, and Josiah Royce. However, he was ranked in front of behaviorist Edward L. Thorndike, who was at Columbia University when Dewey arrived in 1904.[1] Dewey's relatively low ranking in the survey could be attributed to the fact that, to most, Dewey was not a psychologist, he was a philosopher. Despite his term as president of the American Psychological Association, Dewey did not engage in the kind of scientific laboratory research psychologists were expected to do. In fact, after he left the University of Chicago, he never again stepped foot in a laboratory. For these reasons, when he arrived at Columbia University, Dewey was housed in the philosophy department, not the school of education.

Dewey had accomplished a great deal at the University of Chicago. His laboratory school was nationally known, and according to William James, Dewey and his peers had established an entirely new school of thought. In fact, James commented that Harvard had thought but no school, and Yale had a school but no thought; only Chicago had both.[2] Despite these successes, Dewey did not become one of the nation's and the world's leading public intellectuals until he began asserting his authority and expertise on the ideals of democracy. As intellectual historian Henry Steele Commager famously remarked in *The American Mind*, "It is scarcely an exaggeration to say that for a generation no major issue was clarified until Dewey had spoken."[3] It was during Dewey's years at Columbia University that he spoke often and authoritatively on the broader concerns of education in a democracy.

For Dewey, democracy was not just a form of government, nor was it simply an associated form of living; it was the final stage of social and individual development. At the fourth stage of consciousness, Dewey explained, "the observable world is a democracy," in which science was ushering in an age of expanded insight, interactive living, contingent knowledge, and continual growth. The new democratic age required a complete reconstruction of the U.S. public schools. "If there is especial need of educational reconstruction at present time," Dewey insisted, "it is because of the thoroughgoing change in social life accompanying the advance of science, the industrial revolution, and the development of democracy"[4] The details of exactly how to incorporate the transformative effects of science, industry, and democracy occupied Dewey in the years between his arrival at Columbia University in 1904 and his travels abroad in the 1920s. These were transitional years for Dewey, during which his interests expanded beyond the specific pedagogy and curriculum of the Dewey School to broader areas of life. Less interested in how to coordinate the biological instincts of children with the stages of social development, Dewey took a greater interest in the educational policies of the day, such as vocational education and progressive pedagogy. However, while Dewey introduced many new insights and applied his educational philosophy to new areas of interest, his ideas were still imbued with the linear historicism and genetic psychology he had worked out in Chicago.

DEMOCRATIC EDUCATION

In a 1903 essay titled "Democracy in Education" Dewey reiterated his view of democracy as a logical outcome of social progress and growth in the modern world. Democracy was a matter of proper, linear, and desirable development. Democracy meant "freeing intelligence for independent effectiveness—the emancipation of mind as an individual organ to do its work." He commented on how the organizational aspects of the American school had lagged behind the social movement toward democratic ideals because it still employed a top-down model of administration. Just as the traditional curriculum venerated the authority of predetermined texts and knowledge, which were then delivered uncritically to students, the traditional structure of schools approached teachers as passive receptors of authority from above. Instead, he argued, teachers should be viewed as autonomous professionals with their own wisdom to impart. "For no matter how wise, expert, or benevolent," Dewey exclaimed, "the head of the school system, the one man principle is autocracy." Dewey asserted that democracy means "the individual is to have a share in determining the conditions and aims of his own work . . . through the free and mutual harmonizing of different individuals."[5] Dewey's vision implied that if the school was to serve an embryonic democratic community, not only would the curriculum and teaching methods need to be updated, but the entire structure of the school would need to be transformed as well. Likewise, if the school was truly to serve as an embryonic community, then it would have to blend more seamlessly with its immediate social context. Accordingly, in an influential essay, "The School as a Social Centre," Dewey outlined what the ideal relationship between the school and community should be.

According to Dewey, the public school would need to become the "centre of full and adequate social service" to achieve its full potential. True to his linear historicism, he began the essay like he did many others, by tracing the history of the school. The function of education, he explained, "since anything which might pass by that name was found among savage tribes, has been social." However, as society evolved during the classical and middle ages, the school was gradually severed from its social origins. Only in modern times did the explicit goal of citizenship education once again link the school to its social element. As a result, "our community life has suddenly awakened." Dewey recognized that unlike savage, classical, and medieval life, modern life included a complex range of economic, scientific, and democratic issues with which schools would have to contend. Significantly, it was in his "Social Centre" essay that Dewey first considered the pluralistic makeup of American society and first dealt directly with issues of racial and religious intolerance. He did so, however, with his ethnocentric linear historicism intact.[6]

"We find our political problems involve race questions, questions of assimilation of diverse types of language and custom," Dewey explained. "The contents of the term citizenship is broadening; it is coming to mean all the relationships of all sorts that are involved in membership in a community." He recognized that citizenship needed to be broadened beyond the traditional view of White Anglo-Saxon Protestants, because the modern world had evolved. However, this democratic process still involved "assimilation."[7] Dewey outlined four specific ways in which the modern school was linked to the evolving broader social context. First, the modernization had made transportation and movement much easier, leading to greater interaction, especially in cities. In fact, Dewey's career had coincided with the rapid urbanization of America. For instance, in 1871 when Dewey was still in high school, there had been only 14 cities in the United States with over 100,000 persons, but by 1910 there were 50 such cities.[8] Dewey recognized that the new urban environment forced different cultures to interact with one another whether they liked it or not. "The centralization of industry had forced members of classes into close association with, and dependence upon, each other," Dewey explained. "Bigotry, intolerance, or even an unswerving faith in the superiority of one's own religious and political creed, are much shaken when individuals are brought face-to-face with each other, or have the ideas of others continuously and forcibly places before them." Cultural isolation caused bigotry, Dewey boldly suggested, not science or reason. Second, Dewey argued, with increased cultural interaction came "a relaxation of the bonds of social control," and so "the community must find methods of supplementing it and carrying it further outside the regular school channel." When traditional cultural values were questioned and assimilated with those from other groups, a natural breakdown of order occurred. Therefore, it was the job of the modern school to reorient these traditional values toward the scientific, democratic values he espoused. Third, Dewey continued, the ideas of knowledge and culture changed from the German model of eternal polish to the more useful sort: "The simple fact is that we are living in the age of applied science."[9] Finally, due to the more complicated nature of the modern, scientific, democratic world, schooling had been prolonged. This not only led to rising enrollments in high schools, colleges, and professional and graduate schools, but it also meant that modern citizens would be expected to be lifelong learners. Modernism required continual, unending change and adaptation. Schools needed to recognize this and prepare its citizens appropriately.

Dewey proposed three functions the modern school could fulfill to meet the needs of a changing world. First, Dewey suggested that schools should encourage "mixing people up with each other . . . by doing away with the barriers of caste, or class, or race, or type of experience that keep people from real communion with each other." Simply put, schools should help students assimilate to American life. Second, the school should house meetings for social purposes to meet the communal needs of local adults. This way students' parents could engage with one another like their children were doing at school. Third, the school should serve the goal "of continuous social selection of a somewhat specialized type." The idea was not that adults would sort the students, but that the students would sort themselves based on their interests and abilities by being exposed to various occupations and equipment. Perhaps Dewey underappreciated the degree to which students would simply select the roles they felt most comfortable in—that is, the role of their parents—thus society would merely be reproduced not reconfigured or advanced. Nevertheless, in Dewey's vision the school could potentially even the playing field of an inequitable society by allowing its students and their parents "the fullest opportunity for development." Egalitarian, if not a little naive, Dewey was disturbed by "the unutilized talent dormant all about us."[10] He wanted the schools to unleash the potential of talented students in all areas of life.

Regarding Dewey's views on race and its relationship to his genetic psychology and linear historicism, it is clear that at this point he was proposing an assimilationist, not a pluralist model of education consistent with these views. "The power of public schools to assimilate different races to our own institutions, through education given to younger generation," Dewey argued, "is doubtless one of the most remarkable exhibitions of vitality that the world has ever seen." In fact, Dewey addressed the issue of immigrant parents who might resent the acculturative function of U.S. schools that denigrated their cultural heritage by denationalizing their children. To solve this problem, Dewey proposed that schools could recognize the cultural elements of students' countries of origin by celebrating the "historic meaning in the industrial habits of the older generations—modes of spinning, weaving, metal working, etc. . . . [that were] disregarded in this country because there was no place for them in our industrial system."[11] When these abandoned occupations were appreciated in their own context as "historic," Dewey proposed, family life would be enriched. Thus we can see how, like the savage mind, Dewey considered the lifestyles of immigrant families as psychically equivalent, but socially deficient. The immigrant cultures were to be appreciated as prior steps toward the more advanced modern, scientific, democratic world of the United States, but not as culturally unique perspectives to be valued, celebrated, and maintained.

Overall, "The School as a Social Centre" was one of Dewey's most original and ambitious essays on education; in 1902, no one else was proposing such a radical reconceptualization of the schools. Nevertheless, Dewey's vision was prescriptive, not descriptive, because the University of Chicago laboratory school had done few of the things he had outlined. The Dewey School did not have a culturally or socioeconomically diverse student population. In fact, his vision owed more to Jane Addams's Hull House (which Dewey cited throughout his essay) than to anything he had accomplished at the Dewey School. Yet the "Social Centre" essay marked an important turning point for Dewey because he started to shift his attention away from less immediate issues of pedagogy toward broader issues of educational policy. That is, Dewey became less of an educational researcher and more of a general authority on all educational matters. Perhaps no book captures his transition from scientist of the "new education" to prophet of "progressive education" more than *Schools of To-Morrow*, a text he cowrote with his daughter Evelyn.

SCHOOLS OF TO-MORROW

Published in 1915, *Schools of To-Morrow* consisted of thematic descriptions of several progressive schools around the country that demonstrated "tendencies toward greater freedom and an identification of the child's school life with his environment and outlook, and even more important, the recognition of the role education must play in a democracy."[12] In the text, the Deweys highlighted several aspects that these innovative schools shared with the University of Chicago laboratory school, although direct influences of the latter upon the former were not established. In particular, aspects of the "repeating the race experience" approach were outlined. For example, the Deweys wrote that at the Elementary School of the University of Missouri, "pupils study the history of shelter from the first beginnings with a cave or a brush thicket, through the tents of the wandering tribes and the Greek and Roman house, to the steel skyscraper of today." That is, they traced the industrial history of the Western world. In Chicago schools, the Deweys speculated, "The children are perhaps studying primitive methods of building houses, and on their sand table they build a brush house, a cave dwelling, a tree house, or an eskimo snow hut." Likewise, in Gary, Indiana, the student "learns to handle materials which lie at the foundations of civilization in much the same way that primitive people used them, because this way is suited to the degree of skill and understanding he has reached." Thus, in accordance with Dewey's educational philosophy, these schools had set up their curriculum to coordinate the psychological stages of child development with the sociological stages of the civilized world. In fact, in the conclusion the Deweys reiterated, "When a child learns by doing he is reliving both physically and mentally some experience which had proved important to the human race; he goes through the same mental processes as those who originally did these things."[13] This was the subtle, common link that ran through all the schools studied.

Two of the schools evaluated and praised in *Schools of To-Morrow* were those of Gary, Indiana, and P.S. No. 26 in Indianapolis, Indiana. Critics and scholars have cited Dewey's praise for these schools as evidence of the alleged gap between his theory and practice, and some have even charged Dewey with outright hypocrisy. Specifically, the "platoon" system of Gary has been identified as the most extreme case of anti-intellectualism inherent in the social efficiency approach to schooling, and P.S. 26 represented Dewey's failure to condemn racially segregated schools. Indeed, both cases somewhat contradict the pluralist views he would profess a few years later, but they were fully in sync with the linear historicist outlook he held at the time.

The description of the Indianapolis school said that it was located in the "poor, crowded colored districts of the city and has only colored pupils." It appears in a chapter on social settlements. The Deweys insisted that P.S. 26 was not an attempt to solve the race question, even though they later proclaimed, "the success of the experiment would mean a real step forward in solving the 'race question' and peculiar problems of any immigrant district as well."[14] The fact that the Deweys grouped immigrants and Blacks together is very suggestive, for it reflected their conviction that racial disparity was a result of social, not biological, deficiency. This grouping also implied that, like recent immigrants, the American Blacks were not yet fully American. Full acculturation required time because, like recent immigrants, African Americans were stuck in an earlier form of cultural development. Although the term *savage* does not appear anywhere in the book, the descriptive chapters cited above, which were written by Evelyn, included the term *primitive* instead. Did the Deweys consider these Black students "primitive," as many scholars of the time did? Although the question cannot be answered definitively, they likely made a distinction between American Blacks and those "primitive" Blacks from Africa and other nondeveloped areas. For Dewey, both groups were socially deficient, but to different degrees.

On the other hand, the mere inclusion of a Black school in *Schools of To-Morrow* proclaimed that African Americans were part of the Deweys' progressive vision for democracy and education. This bold, and even brave, step needs to be recognized. But the Deweys' explicit refusal to identify segregated schools as an inherent violation of this vision was conspicuous in its absence, especially in light of Dewey's repeated attacks on the "segregated" approach to vocational education (see below). The Deweys highlighted how the principal of P.S. 26 had done much to improve the social, intellectual, and physical environment of the students. Nevertheless, the Deweys recognized that "changes in social conditions must take place before" the "colored" inner-city inhabitants of Indianapolis could be "independent and prosperous."[15]

What exactly did the Deweys mean by social conditions? The chapter implied that they merely meant the immediate physical and economic infrastructure, not the broader conditions of segregated schools and racist society. Accordingly, African American students of P.S. 26 were mostly being taught vocational content. This knowledge would potentially allow them to transform their immediate environment and improve their economic condition, but the curriculum did not necessarily equip them to question the broader political and social system that segregated and oppressed them. So was Dewey's praise of the segregated P.S. 26 hypocritical? If viewed in the broader content of his linear historicism and genetic psychology, he was not. For Dewey, education had to take place in a particular linear sequence that allowed students to best subordinate their environment. If their environment was considered deficient, they could only go so far because the students required a more advanced culture to stimulate further development. In other words, the students of P.S. 26 could only "repeat the race experience" up to the present time, but if their present was developmentally deficient—a prior step in social development—and could not be mediated by a more advanced form of culture, they could go no further. As a social center, the school needed to reflect the specific culture of its community with all its deficiencies.

Dewey's praise of Gary, Indiana, would be equally controversial. Gary was home of the "platoon" system of schooling, wherein the physical plant of the school was employed to achieve maximum efficiency by having half the student population in classrooms and the other half using its vocational, physical, and technical equipment such as gymnasiums, playgrounds, shops, auditoriums, and laboratories. The student platoons would then switch, so the entire school was in continual use. As journalist Randolph Bourne would claim the following year in his book, *The Gary Schools*, the platoon experiment was "perhaps the most ingenious attempt yet made to meet the formidable problems of congested urban life and modern vocational demands which are presented to the administrators of the city school."[16] In contrast to Bourne's praise for these practical and administrative feats, the Deweys focused more on the curriculum of the schools and how they managed to fuse vocational and academic content. In the first three grades the Gary students "draw, do painting and clay modeling, sewing and simple carpentry," much like the students at the Dewey School had done. Furthermore, in accordance with the developmentally based curriculum of the Dewey School, in fourth grade the Gary students "are now less interested in playing games, so they spend less time playing and more time making things." Every student in Gary spent a minimum of one hour each day working in the shops, and all students received some form of academic knowledge as it related to these activities. Accordingly, the Deweys enthusiastically depicted Gary's fusing of disciplinary knowledge with real-world problem solving. "The chemistry is the chemistry of food," they gushed; "botany and zoology include care of the school grounds and animals."[17] The Deweys highlighted the holding power of the Gary schools, especially for working-class students and the children of recently arrived immigrants.

Dewey never explicitly stated that the schools described in *Schools of To-Morrow* were direct descendents of his laboratory school, even though several of these reformers had cited Dewey as an influence (e.g., William Wirt of Gary, Indiana; Arthur Dunn of Indianapolis). However, in one review of the text prominent educator William Bagley explained how *Schools of To-Morrow* "describes typical schools in which the theories for which [Dewey] is responsible have been worked out—although he modestly refrains from stating this fact." Bagley declared that "contemporary educational theory in America is dominated by America's foremost philosopher—John Dewey," a development Bagley viewed as unfortunate, because Dewey allegedly wished "to have no commerce" with "recorded knowledge."[18] Indeed, in *Schools of To-Morrow* there was far more description of the vocational activities of these schools than there was of their academic content. Bagley was a vocal critic of the functional approach to curriculum, which he believed was gradually displacing humanistic content in the schools and compromising their intellectual rigor. He considered Dewey's praise of these innovative schools as dangerous and misguided. In a published letter Dewey responded to Bagley's accusation that he was antagonistic to recorded knowledge as "insanity" and denied that the educators described in the book were his disciples. The progressive schools described in the book, Dewey insisted, had "sprung up independently under diverse auspices."[19] As Dewey explained, these schools were manifestations of a broader national effort at democratizing students, schools, and society by appreciating the interrelatedness of all three. Nevertheless, Bagley's reading of the text likely reflected that of most readers—that Dewey was demonstrating the pervasiveness of his ideas.

The Deweys' objective for *Schools of To-Morrow* was not only to provide endorsement and support for the burgeoning progressive education movement, but also to weigh in on one of the most controversial issues of the day: the role of vocational education in the public schools. The issue was not so much whether or not to include vocational education as part of the curriculum, but rather whether vocational education should be under "unit" or "dual" control. That is, at the administrative level, should vocational education be under the same bureaucratic structure as the academic part of the curriculum like in Gary, Indiana, or should it be under two separate structures, like in Massachusetts? Most Western European schools had a dual system. So the question was whether U.S. schools should emulate the European model or keep all its students under one system. As we shall see below, Dewey unequivocally sided with the single, unit approach, which he considered more democratic and fair. In an essay opposing industrial education, Dewey insisted that reformers should "first inform themselves as to what is actually being done in this direction in the more progressive schools."[20] In fact, many of the schools outlined in *Schools of To-Morrow* were selected specifically to demonstrate what a unit system that combined vocational and academic content for all students looked like. Accordingly, in the conclusion to *Schools of To-Morrow*, Dewey insisted on the unit system:

> There must not be one system for the children of parents who have more leisure and another for the children of those who are wage-earners. The physical separation forced by such a scheme, while unfavorable for the development of a proper mutual sympathy, is least of its evils. Worse is the fact that the overbookish education for some and the over "practical" education for others brings about a division of mental and moral habits, ideals and outlook.[21]

By 1915 Dewey had constructed a comprehensive vision for democratic public schools, one that was based not only on his work at the University of Chicago laboratory school, but also on the schools that he had read about or observed all over the country. "The democracy which proclaims equality of opportunity as its ideal," Dewey insisted, "requires an education in which learning and social application, ideas and practice, work and recognition of meaning of what is done, are united from the beginning and from all."[22] Having forged his vision, he was now in a position to defend it.

VOCATIONAL EDUCATION

As Dewey mentioned repeatedly throughout his early and middle works on education, much had changed in U.S. schools, society, and culture. The population of U.S. high schools had experienced unprecedented growth. Within a period of 30 years, high school enrollments increased from a little over 10 percent to more than 50 percent of the school-age population; specifically, high school enrollments increased from about 200,000 in 1889–90 to over 2 million in 1919–20.[23] This rapid increase included the influx of immigrants from the so-called less desirable regions of Southern and Eastern Europe. As one educator explained, the immigrants who had arrived between 1820 and 1880 were "skilled workers" who had "some education," "spoke a language more nearly like English," "went to rural communities," and "brought their families and intended to make America their home." In contrast, the immigrants who arrived between 1880 and 1924 were "unskilled workers," had "come from countries where the mass of the people cannot read or write," saw "little reason for learning English," "settled in cities," and "expect to save their money and return to their homes in Europe."[24] These foreign-born students, it was believed, needed immediate attention and required a more relevant, civic-based kind of schooling.

Perhaps no school subject came under more scrutiny than history because it was most closely associated with the outdated faculty psychology and because it was the subject most directly related to the assimilation of these immigrant groups. This is why history was such a central part of the curricula outlined in *Schools of To-Morrow*. But there was no consensus among educational reformers that the approach outlined by Dewey and his followers was the most efficient, progressive, and democratic course to take. Some, like Massachusetts Commissioner of Education David Snedden, used the expanding school population and the alleged demise of the faculty psychology to attack the place of traditional subject matter such as history in the curriculum altogether. "We have abundant evidence now, based upon psychological experimentation," Snedden insisted, that the training of memory or reasoning achieved through historical study did not transfer to other subjects. To suggest otherwise, he explained "is of course, in light of modern knowledge, an educational fallacy."[25] The evidence to which Snedden was referring was the research of Dewey's new colleague, Edward Thorndike.

Thorndike had received his psychology degree under William James at Harvard; he was one of the first American psychologists not to study in Germany. Having abandoned the nonobservable, imprecise methods of his functionalist mentor, Thorndike focused his inquiry on the more precise, scientific, and observable relationships of S-R (stimulus-response) bonds. His first experiments were on animals, but he soon began conducting experiments on human subjects. In 1901 he published a famous empirical study on the effects of one mental function upon the efficiency of others. Thorndike concluded that "improvement in any single mental function rarely brings about equal improvement in any other function, no matter how similar." In other words, Thorndike's laboratory research suggested that improvement in historical judgment, enhanced by, say, critical thought about the causes of the American Civil War, would not necessarily improve a student's ability to judge the contents of the daily newspaper.[26] (Dewey had attacked the assumptions of the faculty psychology as early as the mid-1890s, but, unlike Thorndike, his approach was philosophical, not empirical.) In place of the faculty psychology, Thorndike argued that all learning could be reduced to two laws: exercise and effect. The first law suggested that the more frequently a response occurred, the greater the tendency for it to repeat. The second law suggested that responses resulting in pleasurable outcomes would be likely to become habit, and inversely those that had negative outcomes would be more likely to be stamped out. Therefore, Snedden's behavioral approach to curriculum reflected a broader shift in the field of psychology from the structuralism of Wundt, to the functionalism of James to the behaviorism of Thorndike. With the idea of educational transfer between subjects empirically discounted, Snedden used Thorndike's research to demand a complete reformulation of the curriculum to meet the demands of immediate interest and utility.

Although fully established as serious academic discipline by the 1910s, psychologists at the beginning of the twentieth century had to work hard to carve out an institutional niche for themselves independent from philosophy and physiology. The psychologists listed at the beginning of this chapter had done much to establish the field as a separate area of study, but jobs were still hard to find. As a result, many young psychologists were drawn to pedagogy to find employment. Historian James O'Donnell estimates that over a third of psychologists in 1910 expressed interest in educational problems because, for many, behaviorism essentially was learning theory. The obvious utility of Thorndike's behavioral psychology not only to education, but also to the business world, made the approach popular in an age when "efficiency" was the social buzzword of the day. For these reasons Thorndike's approach to learning and Snedden's approach to curriculum quickly gained popularity in schools of education. This development was underscored by a movement toward scientific, statistical approaches to social problems. "The creation in 1910 of the experimentally and statistically oriented *Journal of Educational Psychology* as an alternative to [G. Stanley] Hall's *Pedagogical Seminary*," O'Donnell explained, "signaled the transformation of educational psychology into a science of behavior."[27] In its emphasis on experience as opposed to a priori mental structures, the new behaviorism was tangentially related to the work of Dewey. But, as I will show, Dewey quickly distanced himself from the emerging field and aligned himself with the competing subfield of social psychology.

On the surface Thorndike and Snedden's approach to curriculum and learning looked a lot like Dewey's own functional approach. However, they diverged on two important issues. First, Dewey objected to the mechanistic dualism of Thorndike and Snedden's behavioral psychology and its connection with educational research. In an essay addressing the relationship between theory and practice in education, Dewey insisted, "It is, I think, strictly true that no educational procedure nor pedagogical maxim can be derived directly from pure psychological data."[28] That is, educational theory needed to include both psychological and social aspects, so basing a curriculum purely on how the mind worked, as Thorndike suggested, was inadequate. Instead, the curriculum needed both descriptive and prescriptive elements based not only on an understanding of how the mind worked, but also on a vision for what kind of society the mind was to be directed toward. Second, Dewey disagreed with Thorndike and Snedden's broader view of how science should be put to use for curriculum design. For Dewey, science was a general disposition that could be applied to all contexts; it was a way of thinking that allowed for adaptation and reflection. Snedden, however, approached scientific curriculum-making in narrower, positivistic terms. Essentially, he approached the curriculum as Thorndike's behaviorism applied to social problems.

Snedden studied at Stanford University under sociology professor Edward Ross, who was a popular eugenicist and author of the influential book *Social Control*. Ross and Snedden's version of social control was much more defensive than Dewey's. While Dewey saw promise and democratic potential in the new immigrant populations flooding American shores, Snedden and Ross saw a potential threat. Like his mentor, Snedden viewed the schools as an opportunity to sort students into their proper social roles and to ease the transition to the modern world through rational means of control. Specifically, Snedden and his scientific curriculum allies proposed a systematic study of the existing social world and a cataloging of the specific skills each student would need to fulfill the role in which they best fit. Any extraneous learning that did not align explicitly with a real-world occupation, he argued, was considered unnecessary and needed to be removed. All learning was to be immediately relevant and utilitarian. Snedden repeatedly referred to his approach as scientific, and he was a strong proponent of the dual system of vocational education, which aligned perfectly with the curricular vision he outlined for American schools.

Dewey first voiced his opposition to the adoption of the dual system in Illinois in a 1913 essay, "Some Dangers in the Present Movement for Industrial Education," originally entitled "An Undemocratic Proposal." He considered the introduction of industrial education as a means of keeping students in school a "mischievous enterprise" and "a blind alley both industrially and economically." Dewey presented three reasons why the idea was misguided. First, on a practical level, the dual system "divides and duplicates the administrative and educational machinery." In an age of efficiency Dewey considered such duplication a waste of public funds. Second, the dual system would "paralyze one of the most vital movements now operating for the improvement of existing general education." That is, the dual system would undermine the adoption of the ideas Dewey had outlined, which many of his followers were now implementing across the country. Third, Dewey explained, the segregation "will work disastrously for the true interests of the pupils who attend the so-called vocational schools," because they would be ill-equipped to question and improve their social role. Dewey recognized the influence of European education on the issue, particularly the dual schooling system in Germany. However, he insisted that basing the U.S. system on a county with such deep "class distinctions" was harmful to the democratic ideals of the country.[29]

This short essay marked Dewey's growing discontentment not only with the German style of education but also with Germany's philosophical and social ideas, an antagonism that grew as the onset of the First World War approached. "In a word," Dewey concluded, "the problem in this country is primarily an educational one and not a business and technical one as in Germany."[30] Two years later in the *New Republic* Dewey reiterated the class-bias theme in another essay opposing the dual system, "Splitting Up the School System." Dewey insisted that splitting up the high schools into different tracks was "designed to divide the children of the more well-to-do and cultured families of the community from those children who will presumably earn their living by working for wages in manual and commercial employments." For years Europeans had predicted that the United States would divide into fixed classes like they had. Instead, assimilation and social mobility, enabled by the public schools, had prevented this from taking place. According to Dewey, the dual system threatened to undermine this process and, more significantly, it threatened to arrest the social development of the democratic way of life. The unit control needed to be defended if democracy was to flourish. "Under unified control," Dewey argued, "the pupils are kept in constant personal association with youth not going into manual pursuits." The unit system allowed students the best opportunity for meaningful individual development and the best opportunity to learn from one another. With a sense of urgency, Dewey stressed that the new progressive education would take hold in all areas once policy makers appreciated what such schools looked like. "A complete education system," Dewey exclaimed, "is in active development."[31] In another essay, he specified the "efforts already put forth in adopting industry to educational ends . . . in Chicago, Gary, and Cincinnati."[32] Appropriately, the innovative schools in these districts were described in *Schools of To-Morrow.*

Dewey's pointed attacks on the dual approach to industrial education provoked a reply by David Snedden. Under Snedden's leadership, the state of Massachusetts had established a dual control educational system in 1906. Snedden argued that besides "securing the greatest efficiency," the dual system "put in immediate charge of a special form of education a group of persons who are primarily interested in its successful development."[33] Not only was such a policy democratic in Snedden's view, it also accorded with his curricular approach of teaching students only the subject matter that had immediate value to the social role students would fill. Dewey replied that he and Snedden had different definitions of the term *vocational*. Snedden's definition included the knowledge and skills to adapt to the existing industrial system, but Dewey's definition, he claimed, was the knowledge and skills to "first alter the existing industrial system, and ultimately transform it." Dewey insisted that industrial and academic education needed to be conceptualized, not as opposites, but as different ways of approaching the same content. Just as the working-class students had much to learn from what had traditionally been considered "academic" content, the middle-class students had much to learn from what had traditionally been considered "industrial" content. Both aspects could be combined if they were approached as "active, scientific and social."[34] Dewey invited Snedden to examine the innovative work being done in Gary, Indiana, another school system depicted in *Schools of To-morrow*. Dewey explored these themes further the next year in his most enduring and respected book on education, *Democracy and Education*

THE SAVAGE IN *DEMOCRACY AND EDUCATION*

Published in 1916, *Democracy and Education* was Dewey's magnum opus on education. He later reflected that his philosophical outlook "was most fully expounded" in this book, and he wrote to a colleague that the book was "the closest attempt I have made to sum up my entire philosophy."[35] *Democracy and Education* appeared 5 years after he had initially signed a contract with Macmillan Publishing Company. Exhausted by the experience, Dewey remarked to his publisher, "I must say that I am 'fed up' on education at the present and it will be some time before I can write another book on that topic."[36] In fact, most of the material Dewey explored in *Democracy and Education* had been addressed in his previous works. A reader of "Interest in Relation to Training of the Will," "Ethical Principles Underlying Education," *The Child and the Curriculum, School and Society*, and *How We Think* would have found little new in Dewey's classic text. The significant exception was the brilliant Chapter 7, "The Democratic Conception in Education," in which Dewey outlined in detail what the fourth stage of democratic consciousness entailed. This important section will be addressed in Chapters 5 and 6 as it relates to the emergence of Dewey's interactionism and cultural pluralism. Most of *Democracy and Education,* however, further developed the ideas Dewey had explored in the numerous essays and books he wrote at the University of Chicago.

The Deweys' consideration of the innovative schools in *Schools of To-Morrow* and how they assimilated immigrants and educated African Americans apparently did not challenge John's previous ethnocentric views, but rather reinforced them. As in his previous works, in *Democracy and Education* Dewey made repeated references to his stages of psychological and sociological growth and how they coordinated with one another. Dewey specifically outlined the "three fairly typical stages of growth" and how they related to subject matter. At the first stage "knowledge exists as the content of intelligent ability-power to do." At the second stage this knowledge is then "surcharged and deepened through communicated knowledge or information." At the third stage "it is enlarged or worked over into rationally or logically organized material—that of one who relatively speaking is expert in the subject." In reference to the psychological/sociological stages outlined in the last chapter, Dewey was actually referring to the second, third, and fourth stages of growth. The final stage referenced was the "consciousness of calling" stage that corresponded with the form and content of the disciplinary expert. In fact, as Dewey explained, Chapters 15, 16, and 17 of *Democracy and Education* specifically addressed "the successive stages in that evolution of knowledge which we have just been discussing." In accordance with his curriculum at the University of Chicago laboratory school, these chapters addressed "Play and Work in the Curriculum," "The Significance of Geography and History," and "Science in the Course of Study," which corresponded with the linear sequence of the historical development of social occupations. The first stage was the age of working and playing for immediate satisfaction. As Dewey explained, "The play and work stage correspond point for point, with the traits of the initial stage of knowing, which consists . . . in learning how to do things and in acquaintance with things and processes gained in the doing." The second stage was the age of history and geography. It initiated movement out of savagery and barbarism by providing "background and outlook, intellectual perspective, to what might otherwise be narrow personal actions or mere forms of technical skill." The third stage was the age of science. "Both logically and educationally, science is the perfecting of knowing, its last stage."[37]

Dewey referenced the stages one more time in his chapter on "Intellectual and Practical Studies." During the first stage, that of the savage, "experience itself primarily consists of the active relations subsisting between a human being and his natural and social surroundings." At the second stage, that of the "Greeks and people of the Middle Ages," the content of social life tremendously facilitates selection of the sort of activities which will intellectualize the play and work of the school." At the third stage life was characterized by the "progress of experimental science." Dewey reiterated that, educationally speaking, "the movement of activity must be progressive, leading from one stage to another." In other words, appropriate activities and content were not merely those subjects that expanded the consciousness and engendered reflective thinking, but specifically those subjects that accomplished these two objectives and relived the race experience in the linear sequence of progress. As we can see, Dewey shifted his terminology regarding these stages and applied them somewhat inconsistently. Nevertheless, stages of psychological and sociological growth played a central role in his educational philosophy and underscored his overall genetic psychological approach.[38]

As in his previous work, Dewey's conception of the savage played a central role in *Democracy and Education* as well. As early as page 2, the savage was introduced as the antithesis of all things "democratic" and "scientific," terms that Dewey essentially used as synonyms for the civilized world. Accordingly, the savage was used as an example of all that was undemocratic, unscientific, and uncivilized, and as a symbol of the distant, "undeveloped" past of Western ideas and institutions. In other words, savagery represented everything that needed to be overcome. Education was the key to moving the individual and society along the continuum of social progress from savagery to barbarism to civilization. In savage tribes, Dewey argued, the gap between adults and children is minimal, but with "the growth of civilization" this gap widens, increasing the need for formal education, which alone prevents a culture from relapsing into the stages "of barbarism and then into savagery." Thus, for Dewey, savage tribes were not merely different; instead, they represented a less developed form of living. Savages had more in common with children than they did with civilized man. Among other things, like children, the savage lacked the use of socially mediated symbols. The idea of the school as a means of this formal education, Dewey reasoned, would "seem preposterous . . . to savages," because such "undeveloped groups" did not store their knowledge in the form of symbols as civilized cultures did. To demonstrate the significance of agreed-upon social symbols to cultural development, Dewey explained that if "two savages were engaged in a joint hunt for game" and a hand signal meant move right to one but move left to the other, "they obviously could not successfully carry on the hunt together."

Symbols permeated the environment of civilized societies that mediated all action and communication, something that was missing, Dewey explained, "in savage and barbarian communities."[39]

Dewey reiterated that despite the contingent inferiority of primitives, the difference between savage and civilized societies was not a result of their biological inheritance or their psychic potential, but rather an outcome of their deficient social environment. Dewey argued, "The mind of savage peoples is an effect rather than a cause of its backward institutions . . . the savage deals largely with crude stimuli; we have *weighted* stimuli [italics in the original]." In another contrast, Dewey explained that a savage adapts himself to the environment, but a civilized man subordinates the environment; therefore, "a savage is merely habituated; the civilized man has habits which transform the environment." That is, civilized society was a positive outcome of its social inheritance, specifically in how it used its advanced scientific knowledge and advanced culture to subordinate the environment further and more effectively than the savage culture had. The same actions and stimuli for the savage and civilized man had hierarchically different meanings based on the efficiency of its meanings and outcomes. "Yet in *meaning* what has been accomplished," Dewey explained, "measures just the difference of civilization from savagery [italics in the original]."[40] The savage was not inherently inferior, but rather he was contingently inferior, the result of a socially deficient environment over which he had no control.

Specifically, Dewey argued that savage societies were held back by superstition, ancestor worship, animism, and magic. Dewey outlined the differences between the savage and civilized man succinctly in this way: "One who is ignorant of the history of science is ignorant of the struggles by which mankind has passed from routine to caprice, from superstitious subjection to nature, from efforts to use it magically, to intellectual self-possession." Yet, as Dewey had explained in his essay on the savage mind, both the primitive and civilized man were psychically the same, and they had the same potential for scientific thought. "What we call magic was with respect to many things the experimental method of the savage; but for him to try was to try his luck, not his ideas," Dewey explained. "Savages are simply falling back upon habit in a way that exhibits its limitations." The savage did the best he could, but without exposure to the innovations and symbols of the civilized man, he could only go so far.[41]

Overall, Dewey's view of the savage was both humane and dismissive. He awarded the savage with all the potentials of the civilized man and considered his lack of culture as a contingent outcome of his isolation from technology and his exposure to a deficient social environment. Yet these savage communities—which, as we have seen, Dewey believed had survived into the present world—were also "undeveloped," "backward," "ignorant," and "simple." He did not consider the discrepancies among the world's societies as mere cultural differences, but rather as undeveloped when compared against the standard of Western civilization. "With increased culture," Dewey argued, clearly using the term in a linear, quantitative sense, ". . . progress takes place." Dewey equated social progress directly with science and democracy. "Civilization is the mastery of [science's] varied energies," he explained. "Science is experience becoming rational . . . past experiences are purified and rendered into tools for discovery and advance."[42] Science, in Dewey's sense of the word, was not a body of accumulated skills and knowledge, but rather an intellectual disposition necessary for democratic, civilized living.

So what, one might ask, are we to do with a savage who has suddenly been transformed from his deficient social environment to the more advanced, civilized, scientific one of the present? To many, including perhaps Dewey, this was the condition of African Americans in the early twentieth century. Those who subscribed to purely biological laws of development would suggest that the savage did not have the psychic potential to ever achieve the level of civilization necessary for modern life. On the other hand, empiricists who believed that the mind was a blank slate would suggest that social deficiency of the savage could be overcome by exposure to the socially appropriate education. Dewey, however, held a middle view. The biological impulses of children/savages could not be ignored. Rather, they were to be redirected toward socially appropriate activities and occupations. "We must strike while the iron is hot," Dewey insisted. "Especially precious are the first dawnings of power." In other words, like other developmentalists such as G. Stanley Hall and the Herbartians, Dewey suggested that if a savage was not exposed to a proper education early on—while the iron was hot—the consequences were irreversible. The adult savage had essentially missed his chance to partake in the scientific, modern, and democratic world. According to Dewey, "The great advantage of immaturity, educationally speaking, is that it enables us to emancipate the young from the need of swelling in the outgrowth of the past." For Dewey, the adult savage, having missed his opportunity for a civilized education, was forever relegated to the premodern consciousness of savagery; he was hopelessly stuck in an earlier stage of social and individual development.[43] Again, this was the argument used by many to deny African Americans equal rights.

INDUSTRIAL EDUCATION IN DEMOCRACY AND EDUCATION

One of the outcomes Dewey recognized of the modern, civilized world was occupational specialization. In *Democracy and Education* Dewey reiterated many of the arguments he had made previously regarding the separation of industrial and academic education. He identified five reasons for the growing support for vocational education in the modernizing democratic world. First, "labor is extolled; service is a much-lauded moral ideal." As industrial and political leaders began to appreciate the interactional and democratic nature of society, all citizens were expected to contribute to the growth of the over-all economy and nation. Second, the growth of industry itself created more jobs requiring specialized labor. Third, as society became more complex, it demanded specific technical skills. Fourth, as society became more scientific and experimental, less emphasis was placed on pure book learning and more emphasis was placed on the practical application of knowledge. Fifth, the emerging functional psychology that Dewey had helped launch focused more on the "increased importance of industry in life." Taken together, Dewey outlined how the transition from the prescientific to the scientific age required a reconceptualization of the ideas of learning and occupational preparation.[44]

Although Dewey recognized the need for vocational education, he nevertheless rejected outright Snedden's utilitarian rationale for the curriculum. Dewey objected to "the notion of preparation for a remote future and for rendering the work of both teachers and student as slavish." He demanded that "the democratic criterion requires us to develop capacity to the point of competency to choose and make its own career. The principle is violated when the attempt is made to fit individuals in advance for definite industrial callings, selected not on the basis of trained original capacities, but on that of the wealth and status of parents." The goal of progressive education, Dewey boldly declared, was to break down social stratification, not to perpetuate it; to correct "unfair privilege and unfair deprivation," not to reinforce it. Dewey did not consider vocational education as inherently undemocratic; it was only so if students were funneled exclusively into vocational tracks that isolated them from the other students and led them to specific social roles. Furthermore, Dewey did not view industrial and academic education as opposites, and so he saw no reason to dismiss vocational learning completely. Under his version of democratic education, they needed to be viewed the same, as equally significant and coterminous. After all, to Dewey all learning was vocational in its focus on subordinating the environment to better meet the needs of man, and all learning was intellectual in its inherent application of socially mediated ideas.[45]

In addition to separating himself from the narrowly conceived vocationalism of Snedden, in *Democracy and Education* Dewey also distanced himself from the behavioral psychology with which vocational education was associated. Although Dewey did not identify Thorndike's behaviorism outright, he did nevertheless attack dualistic-mechanistic approaches to mind and curriculum throughout his famous text. Dewey distinguished education from mere training in three ways. First, he insisted that by merely securing habits that are useful, the student "is trained like an animal rather than educated like a human being." That is, behavioral psychology did not pay enough attention to the social nature of learning. Although instincts were the starting point of all education, they were not just shaped; they needed to be filtered through the social mediations of the cultural environment of the school. The social nature of learning through reflective inquiry and culture was precisely what separated men from animals. "Making the individual a sharer or partner in the associated activity so that he feels its success as his success, its failures as his failures," Dewey explained, is "the completing task" of education. Second, Dewey again objected to the dualistic, mental passivity of behaviorism's stimulus-response epistemology. "Every stimulus does not simply excite or stir up activity in a passive sense," he insisted, "but rather it directs it toward an object." Therefore, he continued, "a response is not just a reaction, a protest, as it were, against being disturbed; it is, as the word indicates, an answer. It meets the stimulus and corresponds with it." The response represents the mind actively subordinating the environment to meet its own needs, not just fitting itself passively to the environment. Third, Dewey insisted that the stimulus-response psychology did not account for how students could meet emerging problems with reflection and innovation. When habits are fixed from the outside, Dewey explained, "they possess us, rather than we them." But on the other hand, in shared activity, "each person refers what he is doing to what the other is doing and vice versa." Therefore, the mind is active, interactive, and social, not passive.[46]

Dewey's view of mind, curriculum, and society precluded him from accepting the testing, sorting, and training of students due to their alleged static potential as individuals proposed by Thorndike and Snedden. But this does not mean that he was entirely opposed to vocational education. As we have seen, vocational education played a central role in Dewey's educational work at the University of Chicago, particularly in how he organized his Dewey School curriculum around the historically arranged social occupations. In fact, Dewey's approach to the industrial-cultural history of the race aligned with the emerging "new history" of his friend and colleague at Columbia University, James Harvey Robinson. Robinson, along with other "new historians" Charles Beard, Carl Becker, and Frederick Jackson Turner, also demanded the reformulation of history in light of changing social conditions.

Robinson and Dewey expressed mutual admiration for one another throughout their years at Columbia, and they shared a belief that knowledge needed to be democratized so that all citizens could share in it equally. In 1911 Dewey wrote his graduate student Elsie Clapp:

> After an interesting talk with Mr. Robinson the other day it
> occurred to me that there is a subtle tendency to take the idea

of progress as itself progressive, dynamic. The desirability of the
idea makes it comfortable to rest upon; so the dynamic concept
becomes particularly static in its force. The tendency, if it exists,
seems to me illustrative of the intellectual class.

In this letter, Dewey was attacking intellectualism for intellectuals' sake. Like
Robinson, Dewey wanted to put knowledge to work for everyone, not just
for the purely intellectual satisfaction of the scholars. Dewey thought that by
expanding freedom of thought to all, not just intellectuals, the "walls [could
be] broken thru and we can escape," and "culture, scholarship, specialized
research, divine philosophy" could all be approached "as the same thing."[47]
Ideas not only needed to be dynamic, but they needed to be accessible and
linked with experience in the real world; otherwise, progressivism and dy-
namism would just themselves become static intellectual truths, detached
from the action. Democracy, Dewey insisted, required continual change and
movement toward progress through the liberation of all minds. In a letter to
his daughter, Dewey explained that, like him, Robinson "knows that history
is about live people and that live people five hundred years ago are very much
like people today." In the letter Dewey referenced Robinson's new textbook
Introduction to Western Europe, which implemented the techniques of the
"new history" that Robinson had helped pioneer by incorporating social and
economic history into the narrative of the past. Dewey, a proponent of using
social history in the classroom, expressed the hope that his daughter could
take some of Robinson's history classes at Columbia.[48]

Robinson later expressed his admiration for Dewey and for their common modernist belief that "everywhere and always there is movement. . . .
Dewey sees that philosophers should justify their existence by showing us
how to think of things in terms of progressive exploration rather than how
they must be."[49] This view was expressed in Robinson's classic 1913 text
New History, in which he attacked the older generation of historians, whom
he accused of merely chronicling the major battles and exploits of kings.
They overemphasized continuity, success, and eternal truths at the expense of
discontinuity, failure, and intellectual adjustments. Such a history, Robinson
argued, would not provide the tools to think critically about contemporary
society, nor to help solve its emerging problems. "We are," he suggested, "in
constant danger of viewing present problems with obsolete emotions and at-
tempting to settle them by obsolete reasoning." He thought that the role of
the historian should be to point out anachronisms in contemporary thought,
and to investigate the origins of present errors.

Robinson's *New History* included an essay, "History for the Common
Man," about the usefulness of history for students in a vocational school.
Like Dewey, Robinson argued that although a history of kings and govern-

ments would indeed be of little interest to these students, a history of industry would be immediately relevant. Such a history would excite the students' imaginations and give them food for thought while toiling in the factories. Such an industrial history would provide the best, "perhaps the only means of cultivating that breadth of view, moral and intellectual perspective, and enthusiasm for progress, which must always come with perception of the relation of the present to the past."[50] For Robinson, the creation of a more functional social history was nothing less than the democratization of knowledge. The transformation of the subject would allow history to serve as a liberalizing and progressive force in society.

In *Democracy and Education* Dewey concurred with Robinson, writing (somewhat naively) that factory workers would find work more meaningful if they understood the historical and social significance of their efforts. The meaning of man's actions would become transformed, Dewey suggested, when he understood their broader implications. History in particular "gives background and outlook, intellectual perspective, to what otherwise might be narrow personal actions or mere forms of technical skill." By appreciating how the industrial tool or machine being used was an outcome of the cultural history of the race and how it fit into the larger social web of meanings, the workers would feel that they had more at stake in their actions. "In the degree in which men have an active concern in the ends that control their activity," Dewey explained, "their activity becomes free or voluntary and loses its externally enforced and servile quality, even though the physical aspect of behavior remains the same." Robinson and Dewey both suggested that there was nothing inherently exploitive or dull about factory work; rather, it was the attitude and knowledge one brought to the job. It must be noted, however, that neither of these scholars had ever worked in a factory.[51]

Ultimately, Dewey and Robinson's approach to cultural history and how it related to present concerns of industrial workers can be summarized in the following paragraph taken from *Democracy and Education*:

> History deals with the past, but this past is the history of the present. . . . Genetic method was perhaps the chief scientific achievement of the latter half of the nineteenth century. Its principle is that the way to get insight into any complex product is to trace the process of its making—to follow through the successive stages of its growth. To apply this method to history as if it meant only the truism that the present cannot be separated from its past, is one-sided. It means equally that the past events cannot be separated from the living present and retain meaning. The true starting point of history is always some present situation with its problems.[52]

The final line of this paragraph became one of the most-cited statements in the history of the new field called "the social studies," a movement in which Robinson played a major role. However, the lines immediately preceding it about the "genetic method" and tracing the "process of its making" through its "the stages of growth," which clearly reveal Dewey's linear historicism, are rarely (if ever) included. But these lines are critical to understanding what Dewey meant by "present situation with its problems." He meant problems from the past, presented as problems of the present. As he further explained, because teachers could not fully and accurately re-create the past "by deliberate experiment" like they could in science, teachers had "to resort to primitive life" in which "modes of organized action are reduced to their lowest form."[53] If all students, regardless of whether they were going to be a doctor or a factory worker, learned about the cultural inheritance of the world through the genetic method (like the curriculum at the Dewey School), they would be equipped to deal with whatever role they might find themselves in the modern economy, and they would have the disposition to adjust to changing conditions as they arose.

In summary, for Dewey, there was nothing inherently wrong with vocational education in a democratic society, if it was conceived of and introduced in the proper manner. Both the industrial and professional classes needed to approach vocational education as the essential act of subordinating the environment through socially mediated means. When the worker and factory owner viewed their actions as different degrees of the same activity, they would have a greater appreciation of one another's role in the organic wholeness of society. For this reason, there was no need to separate both classes into a dual educational system, because both groups required the same kind of education. Dewey contrasted Snedden's shallow form of social control with what he called "genuine social control," which he defined as the formation of a mental disposition, "a way of understanding objects, events, and acts which enables one to participate effectively in associated activities."[54] Control was enforced through an intrinsic desire to have actions coordinated with others, not through the suppression of nonsociable impulses through training. Democratic social control occurred through an active, associated desire to achieve common ends. However, Dewey never outlined what to do when one group did not want to partake in associated living or did not want to be developed in accordance with Dewey's educational scheme. The tension between voluntary association and the forced assimilation was at the center of Dewey's evaluation of the Polish American community during the First World War. Perhaps, more than any other event or idea, the "Polish Question" experience pointed to the limitations of Dewey's linear historicism and genetic psychology in an increasingly pluralistic age and forced him to reconsider his position.

POLISH AMERICANS IN A DEMOCRACY

In an essay published in 1918 called "Philosophy and Democracy," Dewey insisted that democratic living demanded a new definition of *individualism*. "For individualism traditionally associated with democracy makes equality quantitative, and hence something external and mechanical rather than qualitative and unique," he explained, but the new definition meant, "in short, a world in which existence must be reckoned with on its own account, not as something capable of equation with and transformation into something else . . . [but] as association and interaction without limit . . . in which each by intercourse with others somehow makes the life of each more distinctive."[55] This was a very bold vision, one that had immediate consequences for immigrant groups who were expected by many to adhere to a particular Anglo-Saxon type. According to this vision, the immigrants' culture was not expected to be transformed "into something else," but rather to be valued "on its own accord." Dewey had clearly articulated a plan for immigrant children and how their cultural heritage could be valued as prior steps in the industrial evolution of the human race and, thereby, be recognized as contributive to the modern world. However, he had been largely silent on the parents of these children. If the schools were to serve as social centers, as Dewey wanted, then evening classes and social interaction could contribute to the parents' democratic education as well, enabling them to assimilate to the new nation. But what if these groups did not want to assimilate? What if they did not view their values and customs as deficient, like Dewey did? Dewey's study of the Polish American community of Philadelphia revealed that he felt that resistant immigrants needed to be forcibly assimilated. Development toward democratic thinking and life was in their best interest and in the best interest of the nation.

The Polish study began when Albert Barnes, a wealthy physician, enrolled in Dewey's seminar at Columbia. Barnes suggested that Dewey employ some of his graduate students in the study of Polish Americans in Philadelphia who were failing to Americanize to the extent desired by certain policy makers. The Americanization issue was connected with an upcoming conference on President Wilson's policy concerning the postwar status of Poland. Dewey and Barnes's assimilationist stance toward the Poles was outlined from the beginning of the study. As Barnes wrote Dewey, "The idea would be to work out a practical plan, based upon firsthand knowledge, to eliminate forces alien to democratic internationalism and to promote American ideals."[56] In a position that has since been criticized as hypocritical and undemocratic, Dewey recommended that the conference be postponed and that the Wilson administration directly intervene in the internal politics of the Polish American community to ensure that the factions more sympathetic to democracy be better represented. In short, he suggested "bringing about greater unity among the Poles, reducing and eliminating so far as possible their cutthroat and factional methods . . . to unify and intensify support for the war."[57]

In an article in the *New Republic* drawing upon his findings in the Polish community, Dewey attributed the immigrant problem to one of interaction. Dewey blamed both the reactionary elements within the Polish community and the traditional elements within the American community as having prevented the proper development. Within American society, Dewey identified a "conspiracy of economic, denominational, and political forces with personal ambition and love of prestige to keep the newcomers isolated and out of a real share in American life." In a process he called "obnoxious hyphenatedism," Dewey criticized the superficial recognition of cultural leaders who could deliver votes but made no genuine effort to create "a true recognition of the value brought by immigrant groups." Such activities only served to exacerbate the division among the national groups by severing them from the opportunity to assimilate to true democratic life. Dewey chided both the American leaders who benefited from the cultural isolation of the Polish immigrants and the reactionary Polish leaders who pretended to speak for their entire immigrant constituency. The problem was that internal divisions and hierarchies had been carried over from Poland, and because the Poles had been isolated, they were not able to develop adequately (and naturally) along democratic lines. Dewey insisted that these isolated immigrant groups did not need superficial recognition, they needed "unhindered access . . . to human materials." That is, they needed access to democratic education.[58] Only direct intervention by the federal government would allow this to occur, because only it could remove the artificial barriers that prevented cultural interaction.

In accordance with his linear historicism, Dewey's study traced the divisions within the Polish community to historic divisions brought over from their homeland. Dewey believed that the new American environment of science, growth, and democracy required an abandonment of these divisions, which were remnants from an earlier stage of sociological development. When the Poles arrived, they were not industrialized; instead they were mostly traditional and rural. Accordingly, their social values were unscientific and inadequate for the new context. For Dewey the schools were the engines of reform and the assimilative bridge for Polish children, but their parents did not have access to democratic schooling, and so they were vulnerable to exploration and manipulation by reactionary leaders. In certain contexts and particular situations, Dewey argued, governmental intervention was necessary for growth to occur.

When we consider the Polish study along with Dewey's praise of the segregated schools of Indianapolis, two contradictory themes emerge. First, for Dewey, democratic schooling involved the fusing of vocational and academic content in an environment that fostered growth toward the final stage of "consciousness of calling," in which "the observable world is a democracy." Such an education required that students of all backgrounds, races, and creeds be given open access to the path of development toward scientific, democratic thinking. Premature segregation into vocational and academic tracks, Dewey insisted repeatedly, stunted this process. Likewise, artificial barriers to interaction, such as the exploitive reactionary leadership of the Poles, needed to be removed so that this development could take place. One thing about the Polish inquiry that critics of Dewey have failed to appreciate is that Dewey not only blamed the conservative leadership of the Poles for their cultural segregation, but he also blamed the immediate social context created by their American neighbors as well as the broader ignorance of the situation by Americans at large. Dewey not only asked the Wilson administration to intervene politically, but he also called for an increased effort at educating the broader American public about the Polish situation. He assumed that once U.S. citizens were aware of the situation, they would support Wilson's policies. Therefore, the government's job, in essence, was to remove artificial barriers to growth through formal and informal public education.

The second theme is that once artificial barriers of policy had been removed, it was largely up to local communities to meet their own needs in a context-bound manner. The innovations outlined in *Schools of To-Morrow* demonstrated how local schools met the needs of their own population in a number of creative and responsive ways. Gary, Indiana, set up a platoon system to deal with its urban overcrowding, its local industrial economy, and its White immigrant population. P.S. 26 in Indianapolis set up its own school to equip its African American population with skills needed to improve their immediate economic standing, but not necessarily to question their political and social standing. So, why did Dewey not view schools segregated by race as an inherent barrier to development of the democratic way of life? Why did he repeatedly denounce segregation by class, but not by race? The only logical and consistent answer is to accept that in 1915 Dewey assessed Polish Americans and African Americans against different standards. Like his contemporaries, Dewey believed that both groups could be placed on a unilinear scale of development, with the Poles ahead of the Blacks. Both groups were socially deficient, but the cultural distance between the Polish immigrant and scientific, democratic American was small enough to be overcome. However, the distance for African Americans was, at present, too great. The paradox of Dewey's linear historicism was apparent by 1915. Dewey needed to reconcile the pluralist, interactional view he was outlining in his theoretical essays with the policies he was endorsing in his practical work. The process was slow, but he would eventually reconstruct his views to bring these two worlds into alignment, as he realized that his views on culture and race were inadequate for the postwar world.

Chapter 5

THE AMERICAN NATION IS INTERRACIAL AND INTERNATIONAL IN ITS MAKEUP

WHEN DEWEY ARRIVED at Columbia University there were, generally speaking, three positions to take on racial development and education.[1] The first, most conservative perspective posited that the moral and intellectual characteristics of races were immutable—the result of evolutionary changes that had taken place in the early years of racial development. In the mid-nineteenth century, scientists like Samuel Morton and Louis Agassiz had popularized the biological inferiority of American racial minorities, and the social statistics of Herbert Spencer provided "scientific" support for these views. As Agassiz explained in 1863, "Social equality . . . is a natural impossibility, flowing from the very character of the negro race. . . . They are incapable of living on a footing of social equality with the whites."[2] The differences between the races, they believed, were completely biological, hereditary, deterministic, and fixed. For some, called polygenists, Africans, African Americans, aboriginal Australians, and Native Americans were actually considered subhuman or degenerate races. Hungarians, Irish, Poles, Russians, and Italians, on the other hand, were fully human, but they were still composed of inferior biological stock. The cultures of these groups, it was believed, were a direct consequence of their biological inheritance. Therefore, the ability of these "inferior" racial groups to assimilate fully into modern, civilized culture was doubtful. Educating these groups with the products of higher culture was futile because they did not have the intellectual and/or ethical potential to learn the complex material necessary for full participation in civilized, Western culture. German biologist Ernst Haeckel explained in 1904: "[Reason] is for the most part only the property of the higher races of men; among the lower races it is only imperfectly developed. . . . Natural men (e.g., Indian Vedas or Australian negroes) are closer in respect of psychology to the higher vertebrates (e.g., apes and dogs) than to higher civilized Europeans."[3] While most American social scientists had adopted more moderate views on race by the turn of the century, eugenicist authors such as Madison Grant in *Passing of the Great Race* (1916) and Lothrop Stoddard in *The Rising Tide of Color* (1920) maintained and popularized these ideas among White American Protestants well into the twentieth century. In addition, popular school textbooks at the time reinforced these racialist anxieties and admonished students about racial and cultural mixing.[4]

The second, broader and more moderate view of race suggested that while biology indeed played a role in the divergence of races, the social, cultural, and physical environment exerted an equal if not more powerful influence on racial development. Most American social scientists believed that these races could be educated and integrated, but they disagreed about the pace and method of this process. This moderate view grew out of the emerging anthropological research on primitive cultures and the acculturation of immigrants, but it was also a product of pure necessity. Unlike the homogenous Western European nations that could easily marginalize and exclude their minority populations, with whom they had mostly come into contact through colonization, the United States could not simply ignore its rapidly changing ethnic makeup. Due to the closing of the frontier and the clustering of ethnic groups as a result of urbanization, these groups needed to somehow be absorbed into the makeup of a quickly modernizing society. Black, American Indian, and immigrant populations could no longer be pushed aside and ignored. As Charles DeGarmo explained in 1907, "The growth of cities and the disappearance of the frontier have made non-social individualism detrimental to our further progress."[5] In light of this view, a purely biological explanation for racial disparity no longer served as a useful narrative. Instead the moderate environmental/social perspective allowed immigrants and other native racial groups to be slowly worked into the fabric of American society through isolated and experimental interventions. Intellectual historian Axel Schafer explains, "Leading progressives replaced the racialist belief in fixed biological deficiency, not with transracial pluralism, but with the notion of cultural deficiency."[6] Unlike purely biological deficiency, cultural deficiency could be overcome gradually through education.

The third, multicultural and pluralistic view of race expressed full cultural and biological equality among races. This perspective—expressed most vigilantly by "radical Blacks" like W.E.B. Du Bois and progressive White scholars such as Franz Boas and William I. Thomas—asserted that racial difference was purely the product of historical, socially imposed inequality. There was nothing biologically, inherently, or even culturally inferior about non-White races whatsoever. In 1897 Du Bois defiantly proclaimed: "We believe that the Negro people, as a race, have a contribution to make to civilization and humanity, which no other race can make . . . it is our duty to conserve our physical powers, our intellectual endowments, our spiritual ideals."[7] Similarly, the ethnographic fieldwork of Boas had demonstrated the complexity and rich-ness of so-called primitive cultures, thereby debunking the Spencerian theory that civilized nations represented more complicated versions of savage and barbarian ones.[8] In 1904 Boas suggested that studying foreign and primitive cultures could even "impress us with the relative value of all forms of culture, and thus serve as a check to an exaggerated validation of the standpoint of our own period."[9] Although not quite transcending racialist thinking, Ran-dolph Bourne and Horace Kallen also expressed innovative views about the importance of preserving elements of cultural difference, not just adjusting them to the standard of Anglo-Saxonism.[10] These transracial views posited that cultures of immigrant and native minority populations were equal to that of the majority White Protestant one.

In 1909 Dewey argued that "there is no inferior race, and the members of a race so-called should each have the same opportunities of social environ-ment and personality as those of the more favored race," and by 1916 Dewey proclaimed that "the American Nation . . . is interracial and international in its make-up," which at first glance seems to place him in the third pluralist camp.[11] However, a closer look at his racial views prior to 1916 reveals that his linear historicism prevented him from fully embracing the pluralism of Du Bois and Boas until after the First World War.

DEWEY'S VIEWS ON RACE

Dewey first addressed race directly in a 1909 essay. Prior to this, Dewey was essentially silent on race. Although it is true that he never explicitly addressed the topic, his views on race can be reconstructed by fleshing out the implica-tions of his linear historicism and comparing and contrasting it with the views of his colleagues and peers. As I demonstrated in Chapters 1 and 2, most scholars at the turn of the century subscribed to the recapitulational view that the stages of sociological growth corresponded with the psychological stages of child development, and that these earlier, childlike forms still existed in the world in the form of primitive tribes. Dewey was no exception. "To under-stand the origin and growth of moral life, it is essential to understand primi-tive society," James Tufts stated in *Ethics*, the textbook he coauthored with Dewey. "It is beyond question that the ancestors of modern civilized races lived under the general types of group life which will be outlined, and these types of their survivals are found among the great mass of peoples today."[12] Accordingly, as Dewey wrote Clara Mitchell in 1895, "practically all stages of civilization are *now* presented somewhere on earth's surface [emphasis in the original]."[13] Again, in *School and Society* Dewey argued that geography "presents the earth as the enduring home of the occupations of man."[14] That is, to Dewey, the world was like a living museum to previous and current stages of racial development, which could be arranged hierarchically along a single continuum. University of Chicago laboratory school teacher Lauren Runyon translated this historicist approach to the curriculum into a comparative pedagogy wherein the more civilized (White) societies were not merely different, but ethically superior to the less civilized non-White cultures. She explained, "In getting land from the Indians the same methods were used that have prevailed through the ages when a people with superior weapons and brains, in sufficient number, meet an inferior people."[15] Perhaps Dewey's coauthor, Tufts, stated the view most clearly: "Primitive societies suggest a way of living and view of life very different from that of the American or most Europeans." Who exactly were these primitive societies? Once again Tufts provided a succinct answer to this question; the primitive form of ethics was best exemplified by "the so-called totem group, which is found among North American Indians, Africans, and Australians, and was perhaps the early form of Semitic groups."[16] These primitive groups, it was believed, had survived into the modern world and thereby provided a rare window into the earlier phases of Western culture.[17]

The leading social scientists of the day also subscribed to racialist views of social progress. The idea that non-White societies and American minorities were socially deficient permeated the thoughts and policies of virtually every scholar of the day. For example, despite his pragmatic historicist and antiformalist views, one of Dewey's University of Chicago colleagues, economist Thorstein Veblen, subscribed fully to the sociocultural evolutionary view that the historical world (that is, the Western world) evolved from savagery to barbarianism to civilization along a linear hierarchical path. In fact, it was central to the argument of *The Theory of the Leisure Class.* In this classic text he argued that the pecuniary class was a direct result of "the barbarian temperament" that had been genetically retained from an earlier time. Veblen demonstrated how inherited instincts from the racial past could be redirected toward more modern and civilized means. Veblen's theory of cultural evolution was based upon a specific heredity theory identifying three basic European ethnic types: "The dolichocephalic-blond, the brachycephalic-brunette, and the Mediterranean." Each group could be further divided into the "peacable" and "predatory" variants, which were the result of self-selection and breeding during the savage stage of social evolution. The ethnic groups of the present day, he argued, were variants of these primitive racial types. Specifically, the leisure class was a product of the predatory variant that had never fully progressed past barbarism. "The man of the hereditary present," Veblen explained, "is the barbarian variant, servile or aristocratic, of the ethnic elements that constitute him."[18] Thus the undesirable aspects of the modern life were unfulfilled potentials from previous social stages. While Dewey never subscribed to Veblen's idea that social traits and ideas were passed on biologically, he nevertheless believed that the world could be subdivided into different linear stages of civilization based on how far they had socially evolved. Also, as I stated earlier, Dewey agreed with Veblen's idea that traditional education was a by-product of outdated, class-based European culture.

Racial hierarchy also informed the views of one of Dewey's Columbia University colleagues, influential sociologist Franklin Giddings, whose Spencerian positivism stood in contrast to the pragmatic historicism of Veblen and Dewey. While Veblen viewed economic differentiation as the driving force within society, Giddings considered ethnic differentiation as the most significant factor; it was also the biggest threat to democracy: "You cannot have freedom, liberty, democratic representative government, or anything of that kind, if you have a highly heterogeneous population." Nevertheless, despite their disagreement over the explanation for the evolving modern society, Veblen and Giddings agreed that modern cultures were the result of racial differentiations that had taken place early in the evolution of man. According to Giddings, "the beliefs and customs of civilized peoples contain many survivals of beliefs and practices that still exist in full force in savage communities. These indicate not only that the civilized nations have developed from savagery, but that existing savage hordes are in a stage of arrested development, and therefore approximate the condition of primitive man."[19] Likewise, theories of racial hierarchy also informed the thoughts of sociologist and international expert on the education of minorities Thomas Jesse Jones, who had studied under Giddings at Columbia University. But Jones took a more moderate view than his mentor because he believed that all races could be brought up to speed, but one had to respect the biological and social restraints they inherited.

According to Jones in his overview of the social studies program at the Hampton Institute, Blacks and American Indians were at present inferior races; they were unfortunate, but innocent, victims of history. Through no fault of their own they had been left behind in an earlier stage of human development while the cultures of Europe continued to progress beyond them. Reformers needed to be patient because Indians and Blacks had "suddenly been transferred from an earlier form of society into a later one without the necessary time of preparation." Jones explained that "natural evolution from one social stage to another requires time."[20] As a result, exposing these minority students to an academic curriculum would be futile and wasteful because they had not socially evolved far enough to make use of such knowledge and responsibility. Employing Giddings's "law of sympathy," Jones argued that social groups would emulate one another in proportion to the quantity and intensity of a particular trait found in the group. "An appreciation of this law of sympathy," Jones insisted, "contributes greatly to a knowledge of all race divisions."[21] This theory of sympathy was reinforced by one of the most influential books of the 1890s and 1900s, French sociologist Gabriel Tarde's *The Laws of Imitation*. In this study Tarde asserted that "society may . . . be defined as a group of beings who are apt to imitate one another," an argument that reinforced not only the views of Giddings, but also those of leading social scientists James Mark Baldwin, Josiah Royce, William I. Thomas, and George Herbert Mead.[22] Dewey, in contrast, downplayed imitation as a major factor in social development. As we shall see in the next chapter, although Dewey recognized the significance of Tarde's imitation-suggestion theory in launching the subfield of social psychology, he asserted that individuals just happen to arrive at similar outcomes when faced with similar contexts and situations. Imitation possibly played a small part in the process, but ultimately the imitated traits had to be confirmed by each individual. Thus, for Dewey, imitation was contingent, not deterministic.

According to Jones, however, imitation via the law of sympathy explained why the limitations of the Southern Blacks he educated were greater than those of Northern Blacks. The law of sympathy acted more intensely upon them because there was a greater concentration of Blacks in the South and a greater intensity of historical persecution. Likewise, the law of sympathy explained why Indians who left the reservations achieved a higher level of civilization than those who remained. The Dawes Act of 1887 funded the removal of many Indians from their homes and the forced enrollment in boarding schools. Over the objection of conservative critics, who doubted that the Indians could ever be civilized, thousands of Native Americans were stripped of their names, clothes, customs, and languages and placed in boarding schools such as Jones's Hampton Institute at public expense. Only complete immersion in civilized culture, it was believed, could undo hundreds of years of savagery. As Dewey explained in *Democracy and Education* in a passage that seemed to support such policies, education provides the individual the "opportunity to escape from the limitations of his social group in which he was born, and to come into living contact with a broader environment."[23] Similarly, Jones concluded that based on the law of sympathy, progress occurred only when certain members of the race were isolated from the rest, so they would not regress back to their earlier forms. This was why progress was such a slow, incremental process. This historical narrative of differentiated racial development not only informed the policy of what to teach the Indian and Black student, but also constituted the substance of the curriculum. Jones explained:

> The study of [the] stages in the development of the social mind and character is of great value to the pupil in that it gives him confidence that the present condition of his people is merely a stage and not a permanent condition; in that it enables him to

recognize the weaknesses of his people the more readily, especially those faults, usually overloaded in eagerness to develop the economic side; and in that it calls his attention to the highest stage toward which he must strive to educate his people, by correcting their faults and encouraging their virtues.[24]

Sadly, Jones was not exaggerating when he claimed that his minority students internalized his presented narrative of racial hierarchy. "The red people they are big savages," one Indian student explained in an essay, "they don't know nothing. . . . The white people they are civilized." As another Hampton student explained, "The Caucasian is the strongest in the world. The semi-civilized have their own civilization, but not like the white race."[25] Thus the hierarchical history of linear social progress was not only used as a means of social policy, but it also served as a foundation for race-specific pedagogy at the Hampton Institute.

Because Dewey never specifically addressed the education of American minorities until 1909, we can never really know his views on the topics and policies of his colleagues. Yet we can ask the following question: If Dewey had African American and/or Native American students at the Dewey School, would they have had to compare degrees of civilization of racial groups like the Hampton students did? The answer is likely, yes. In fact, as we have seen, the Dewey School students directly engaged in such activities when studying the interaction of American Indians and White settlers. I am not suggesting that Dewey subscribed entirely or specifically to the views of any one of the scholars above, nor did he endorse the policies of forced assimilation. Instead I am simply suggesting that major American scholars generally shared Dewey's ethnocentric views of linear social development, but, for the most part, did so in much more explicitly racialist and racist ways. The curriculum Dewey implemented at the University of Chicago laboratory school was indeed ethnocentric and implicitly racialist, as we have seen, but there were many more deterministic versions of the recapitulation theory available. Nevertheless, during the 1890s and 1900s Dewey was firmly embedded in the moderate social deficiency camp outlined above and not yet in the interactionist, pluralist camp of Boas and Du Bois. To determine exactly how Dewey's linear historicism fit into these biopsychological theories, we have to revisit Dewey's specific views on neo-Lamarckianism.

BIOLOGY AND RACE

Although it may seem somewhat counterintuitive, neo-Lamarckianism was for most a more racist view than Darwinism because neo-Lamarckians used the theory to suggest that White ancestors had gradually acquired and strengthened their mental faculties over time and that these acquired mental abilities became part of the biological inheritance of the Northern European races. As Jones outlined above, the neo-Lamarckian view made the ability of non-White races to catch up with Whites in the short term seem unrealistic. In addition, many Christians clung to the theory of acquired characteristics because it left room for a divine force driving evolution, whereas Darwinians suggested that the human race (and the White man's ascendancy to the top of it) was merely the result of chance, not divine guidance. So by the turn of the century, the first step in overcoming biological determinism was to reject neo-Lamarckianism and to accept a view that social environment played an equal, if not greater, role in the formation of culture. Dewey took this step as early as 1898 in his essay on evolution and ethics:

> We do not need to go here into the vexed question of the inheritance of acquired characteristics. We know that through what we call public opinion and education certain forms of action are constantly stimulated and encouraged, while other types are as constantly objected to, repressed, and punished. What difference in principle exists between this mediation of the acts of the individual by society and what is ordinarily called natural selection, I am unable to see. In each case there is the reaction of the conditions of life back into the agents in such a way as to modify the function of living. [26]

Dewey argued that the debate between neo-Lamarckians and Darwinians was irrelevant because once man developed associated forms of living, education and innovation so permeated and transformed the context of man that they inevitably mediated the individuals' socialization to the existing environment. "If we personify Nature," Dewey insisted, "we may say that the influences of education and social approval and disapproval in modifying the behavior of the agent, mark simply the discovery on the part of Nature of a shorter and more economical form of selection than had previously been known." In other words, the social environment as constructed by the evolutionary history of man mediated and thereby partially controlled, which traits were "naturally selected," making the distinction between natural and social selection completely arbitrary. Education broadly conceived, Dewey insisted, was the selective force of evolution, not the passive "fit" to the environment. Dewey thus publicly denied the significance of acquired characteristics—a significant point he shared when he first addressed the National Negro Conference in 1909.[27]

Dewey's brief speech delivered a simple, uplifting message to his African American audience that day: the scientific community had largely rejected neo-Lamarckianism. For example, Dewey's Chicago colleague William I. Thomas suggested in 1907 that "the characteristics of body and mind acquired by the parent after birth are probably not inherited by the child." Sociologist Carl Kelsey explained more assertively in 1903, "We know pretty definitely today that acquired characteristics are not passed on from generation to generation."[28] While Dewey held this view early on, it was the aforementioned empirical work of biologist August Weismann (see Chapter 2) who was most effective at convincing others to abandon this widely accepted theory. Recall that Weismann had cut off the tails of laboratory mice only to observe that their offspring had grown full-length tails. Wiesmann, an ultra-Darwinian, used his experiment to confirm that natural selection was the only force that drove evolution.

In particular, the rejection of acquired characteristics challenged two biological laws necessary for Haeckel's biological recapitulation theory: terminal addition and condensation. The former referred to the biological idea that evolutionary features were added to the end of the ontogenetic sequence, and the latter referred to the related idea that earlier stages of ontogenetic growth were condensed or deleted to make room for the additional stages. Weismann's experiment, which challenged both these ideas, was also reinforced by the rediscovery of Mendelian genetics in 1900. Simply put, according to Mendel's famous study on peas, inherited genes of individuals (recessive or dominant) either did or did not appear in their offspring; genes did not gradually blend and/or strengthen over time through acquired or habits and traits.[29] Mendelian genetics implied that a new gene could bring about a change at any and all stages of growth, and that the change was not merely added to the end of the ontogenetic sequence, but rather replaced existing traits altogether. Herbert Spencer, whose social scientific view was largely dependent upon the inheritance of acquired characteristics, argued furiously against Wiesmann in public debate during the 1890s, but with no empirical evidence to back him up, Spencer's view eventually lost out by the turn of the century.

Nevertheless, to many the acceptance of Darwinianism underscored by Mendelian genetics confirmed that the biological traits of the different races were fixed, or at least were established so long ago that there was little point to intervening in the natural order. The non-White and inferior White races, some argued, were simply not mentally equipped to deal with the modern world. In other words, most Darwinians were still racist, despite their rejection of acquired characteristics. Such a view added fuel to the emerging eugenics movement and to the fear that racial catastrophe was inevitable unless society curtailed the reproduction and immigration of undesirable groups. However, there was another, more optimistic way to interpret the new discovery. Columbia University education professor William Bagley explained in

1908 that "the principle, now almost conclusively established, that the characteristics acquired by an organism during its lifetime are not transmitted by physical heredity to its offspring, must certainly stand as the basic principle of education."[30] Bagley celebrated the abandonment of neo-Lamarckianism because it pushed social environment and education to the forefront of explanatory factors. While heredity could serve as a potential limitation to certain individuals and groups, education was a more powerful liberating force that could bring any student up to speed. This, in essence, was Dewey's message to the National Negro Conference.

"It was for a long time the assumption . . . that acquired characteristics of heredity, in other words capacities which the individual acquired through his home life and training, modified the stock that was handed down," Dewey explained to his African American audience, "[but now] it is reasonably certain that the characteristics which the individual acquired are not transmissible." To some, Dewey continued, this was discouraging news because it meant that the intellectual training people accomplished in their lifetime was not passed on to their offspring; each generation would have to start from scratch. However, Dewey assured the audience, one must distinguish between "mental culture from the standpoint of the individual and mental culture from the standpoint of society." Instead, the rejection of neo-Lamarckianism should be "very encouraging because it means, so far as individuals are concerned, that they have fair and free social opportunity." The new doctrine confirmed that "there is no inferior race, and the members of a race so-called should each have the same opportunities of social environment and personality as those of the more favored race." Nevertheless, despite the "slight" differences among races, Dewey explained, there are indeed "very great" differences among individuals.[31] These individual differences are the factors to which educators and policy makers should be most attuned. So Dewey did not dismiss the significance of heredity outright, nor did he deny that certain individuals were culturally deficient. Instead, he tried to separate the idea of culture from being inherently or biologically attached to particular groups and races, and substituted a generic "mental culture from the standpoint of the individual" that every individual with access to modern society could achieve. Significantly, he confirmed that the cultural differences within racial groups were more significant than the differences across racial groups.

He developed these ideas further in *Democracy in Education*. In his classic 1916 text Dewey had shifted his terminology regarding inherited impulse, which he now referred to as native activities and aptitudes. Dewey again directly attacked the idea that "heredity somehow means that past life has somehow predetermined the main traits of an individual, and that they are so fixed that little serious change can be introduced into them." He emphasized the importance of environment and education in redirecting, but not fully overcoming, the limitations of inheritance. The "native activities" of students, he insisted, were a "basic fact. . . . In this sense, heredity is a limit of education." He confirmed that it was wasteful to try "to make by instruction something out of an individual which he is not naturally fitted to become," but admonished that teachers should not use this as an excuse to dismiss certain students altogether.[32] So education and social environment (which in Dewey's evolutionary scheme were essentially the same thing) were the primary means of becoming socialized to the existing culture, but they were not the only force affecting the child's growth. Native activities and aptitudes also played a role. Therefore, biological inheritance was a limiting, but not a determining, factor in the socialization to the culture.

So what exactly did Dewey mean by culture? Conveniently, he defined the term specifically for an entry in the *Cyclopedia of Education* in 1911. He defined *culture* as "the habit of mind which perceives and estimates all matters with reference to their bearing on social values and aims." Dewey contrasted his definition with the elitist, Germanic definition of *culture* as the "purely external polish and refinement, a mark of invidious class distinction." Dewey's definition was clearly intended to be a more democratic view than the traditional, conspicuous-consumption or leisure-class approach—it suggested that culture was a way of approaching the world thoughtfully and reflectively by creating products and ideas that were valued by the entire society, not merely the elites. However, these products and ideas also had to contribute to the growth of the social environment. "In other words," Dewey asserted, "manual and industrial activities at once acquire a cultural value in education when they are appreciated in light of their social context, in their bearing upon social order and progress."[33] That is, culture was something one acted upon and with, not something one mentally acquired. It was generic, shared, and accessible to all; it was an evolving, but organic, holistic social activity. Above all, for Dewey, culture did not venerate the old; it had to contribute to the progress of "the new."

Dewey insisted that his definition of *culture* appreciated the contingent nature of knowledge and denied that culture was the unraveling of a latent potential. For example, in an essay Dewey wrote critiquing Herbert Spencer, he criticized the influential theorist because his philosophical system "discounted . . . all individual contingencies, all accidents of time and place, personal surroundings and personal intercourse, new ideas from new contacts and new expansions of life."[34] Dewey's philosophy, in contrast, recognized that there was no predetermined path toward an idealized culture; instead all cultural knowledge was the result of contingent new ideas that furthered the social occupations of the race. While Dewey's definition of *progress* recognized the open-ended nature of emerging knowledge, it was entirely based upon the interaction of "new contacts" and "new expansions of life." As a result, allegedly "old," "primitive," "savage," and "barbarian" forms of life had nothing to contribute to progress, other than to be studied as prior steps toward the present. For Dewey, culture was not a variety of contingent outcomes, but only those outcomes on the vanguard that contributed to the progress of the entire human race.

Based on Dewey's view of culture, we can make some summary remarks about Dewey's early and middle views on race. Dewey subscribed early and consistently to the idea that the development of the child corresponded with the development of Western civilization, which just happened to have the most advanced culture. I say "happened to have" because it is important to note that Dewey did not believe that Western society was inherently or necessarily superior to non-Western culture (nor did it contain latent potentials), but rather that it was contingently superior because social evolution just happened to have placed it at the forefront of "social order and progress." Nevertheless, Dewey's associates such as Laura Runyon and James Tufts used the cultural superiority of Western society to ascribe ethical and cultural inferiority to non-Western societies, which Tufts specifically identified as the (non-White) Africans, North American Indians, and aboriginal Australians. Dewey clearly agreed that primitive societies represented earlier forms of living, which Western society had moved beyond. These primitive societies had culture, but they had it to a lesser degree than the adults of modern society and the advanced students at the Dewey School, who had been taught to progress to more qualitatively complex and socialized forms of understanding.

Because Dewey conceived of culture as singular and linear, all of the world's societies and social occupations (past and present) were subsumed within his historicist definition of the term. Consequently, there were no "cultures," only "culture"; there were not alternative, equally valid forms of living, there was only a linear, hierarchical continuum of social occupations that just happened to end with modern Western society on top. Regarding the biological inheritance of different races, Dewey was an early opponent of the inheritability of acquired characteristics, and he openly professed his belief that no races were biologically inferior. However, as I have argued throughout, his linear historicism still led him to the belief—which he shared with the vast majority of his peers—that the cultures of Africans, African Americans, Native Americans, and aboriginal Australians were socially deficient by the contemporaneous standards of the modern civilized world.

CRITIQUES OF EUROCENTRISM

Although Dewey's racial views were less ethnocentric than the hereditary determinism of Herbert Spencer, Ernst Haeckel, G. Stanley Hall, and Franklin

Giddings, there were alternative theories available at the time, specifically the innovative work of anthropologist Franz Boas, who began to question the assumptions of linear evolutionary anthropology as early as the 1880s. Boas was a pioneer in his method of fieldwork in which he investigated specific cultures on their own terms, thus laying the foundation for the pluralist cultural anthropology that later emerged. During Boas's ethnographic study of Eskimos, he directly questioned the Eurocentric definition of culture then in place:

> I often ask myself what advantages our "good society" possesses over that of the "savages.". . . The more I see their customs, the more I realize that we have no right to look down on them. . . . We have no right to blame them for their forms and superstitions which may seem ridiculous to us. We "highly educated" people are much worse relatively speaking.[35]

Boas's study of the Eskimos questioned the idea that these alleged "savages" were somehow less happy, productive, or ethical than their "civilized" cultural descendents. He questioned whether the Eskimos were truly deficient in any way. By 1887, after his ethnographic study of the Bella Coola Indians of the Pacific Northwest, Boas confirmed "the fact that civilization is not something absolute, but that it is relative, and that our ideas and conceptions are true only so far as our civilization goes." Boas reasoned, in a statement confirming Dewey's historicism, "The physiological and psychological state of the organism at a certain moment is a function of its whole history." Boas was the first social scientist to use "cultures" in a relational sense and the first to employ the term in the plural.[36]

In 1904 Boas offered a critique of evolutionary anthropology and its specific relation to education. Beyond the practical value of the discipline to those who work with foreign races, Boas explained, the educational importance of anthropology "is its power to make us understand the roots from which our civilization has sprung"—an assertion with which Dewey would have wholeheartedly agreed. However, beyond this, Boas suggested that studying foreign and primitive cultures (as cited above) could "impress us with the relative value of all forms of culture, and thus serve as a check to an exaggerated validation of the standpoint of our own period, which we are only too liable to consider the ultimate goal of human evolution, thus depriving ourselves of the benefits to be gained from the teachings of other cultures."[37] In his groundbreaking study *The Mind of Primitive Man,* Boas convincingly attacked the "logical fallacy" that Europe "represents the highest racial type"—the very assumption upon which Dewey's historicist "repeating the race experience" curriculum was based.[38]

Thus Boas asserted the radical idea that each civilization offered alternative, equally valid forms of living and culture. Although the Dewey School curriculum explored the roots of present civilization through social occupations, its function was primarily to validate and inform the present period, not to appreciate the lessons other cultures had to offer on their own terms. It was a scheme of accumulation, incorporation, advancement, and hierarchy, not equivalence. The particular sequence of lived experiences was central to Dewey's pedagogy. In fact, in his textbook on teaching history, Dewey's colleague at Columbia University Henry Johnson drew directly upon Boas's classic text to dismiss the culture epoch/recapitulation theory altogether.[39] Johnson also cited the work of William I. Thomas, who in his *Source Book for Social Origins* asserted, "I have no doubt myself that this theory of recapitulation is largely a misapprehension." In this text, Thomas even quoted Dewey to dismiss the recapitulation theory outright, arguing that "the savage is not a modern child, but one whose consciousness is not influenced by the copies set in civilization."[40] As Dewey explained when he revisited the culture epoch theory again in 1911, "In short the child is not, educationally speaking to be led *through* the epochs of the past, but is to be led *by* them to resolve present complex culture into simpler factors, and to understand the *forces* which have produced the present [italics in the original]."[41] That is, pedagogically speaking, the past could serve as a series of experiments to demonstrate how the race arrived at the present, but not necessarily as a way to idealize Western civilization.

For Thomas and Dewey, education and environment were more significant than inherited impulse in explaining the disparity between the savage and civilized mind. But they never questioned the cultural disparity itself. Therefore, Thomas and Dewey shared the belief that the psychical potential of the savage and civilized mind were the same. The primitive and modern man differed only in their cultural and social inheritance—the civilized being superior to the savage. Ultimately, Dewey's view on the savage mind in his early and middle years was transitional and moderate. He was aligned with Thomas in his view that the savage mind had a nonactualized potential to achieve higher levels of civilization, but did not go so far as to suggest, as Boas had, that savage societies (such as aboriginal, African, and Native American) actually had something to offer civilized ones. Boas's more radical idea of cultural equivalence did not inform the curriculum of the Dewey School in any way.

Another significant challenge to the theoretical ethnocentrism of the Dewey School curriculum came from W.E.B. Du Bois. After earning his degree from Harvard, the prominent Black scholar studied in Germany and was impressed by European high culture and Victorian morality. He originally bought into the German historicist views of race and embraced cultural refinement and moral education as the primary means of social uplift. However, while recognizing the social deprivation of his race, in 1897 he also defiantly declared in a speech on "The Conservation of the Races" (cited previously in this chapter) that the American Blacks had something to contribute to Western society and should not be dismissed outright. More importantly, he insisted that Blacks needed to preserve their cultural traits: "It is our duty to conserve our physical powers, our intellectual endowments, our spiritual ideals; as a race we must strive by race organization, by our race solidarity, by race unity to the realization of that broader humanity which freely recognizes differences in men, but sternly deprecates inequality in their opportunity of development."[42] Du Bois expounded this idea in an article on "Strivings of the Negro People," in which he first employed the term "double-consciousness" to describe the feeling he had of recognizing his own intrinsic worth while simultaneously internalizing how others perceived him as Negro—a perception "which yields [the Negro] no self-consciousness, but only lets him see himself through the revelation of the other world . . . this sense of always looking at one's self through the eyes of others, of measuring one's soul by the tape of a world that looks on in amused contempt and pity."[43] Du Bois articulated a social psychological idea—which could be found in the work of James Mark Baldwin and George Herbert Mead—that self-conception was a function of how others viewed you. Social identity, according to Du Bois, was relational and dynamic, not biological and static.

Du Bois's discontent with the hierarchical view of social ethics grew as the century progressed, and by 1920 he developed an outright disdain for the kind of ethnocentric historicism embodied by the Dewey School curriculum. In his book *Darkwater* he asserted that racism was "not based on science," nor was it "based on history, for it is absolutely contradicted by Egyptian, Greek, Roman, Byzantine, and Arabian experience; nor is the belief based on any careful survey of the social development of men of Negro blood today in Africa and America." Du Bois concluded that racism was simply the result of "passionate, deep-seated heritage, and as such can be moved neither by argument nor fact."[44]

Indeed, as the evidence accumulated, the cultural and biological inferiority of African Americans became harder for progressives to defend. However, the cultural deprivation of Blacks was no longer a pressing concern for most White reformers in the wake of the First World War when Du Bois published his pointed critique of racism. A far more significant issue was how to absorb and educate the waves of White, non-Anglo-Saxon immigrants flooding American shores, and more significantly, how to quickly create a transracial American culture in preparation for the First World War. Intellectual historian Axel Schafer identified an important distinction progressive reformers made between Blacks and immigrants during these years. "The progressive conception of social ethics subordinated the black experience to white American's cultural conception of the new immigrants," Schafer explains. "This created a framework for judging the social and cultural potential of blacks and for excluding them from full participation in society."[45] As we shall see, Dewey's cultural views on immigrants both embodied and challenged the pervasive view of the time.

THE GREAT WAR, IMMIGRATION, AND AMERICANIZATION

Dewey reconsidered the significance of culture during the First World War because the conflict had thrust the issues of assimilation, nationalism, and Americanization to the forefront of the minds of most American scholars. As usual, Dewey put his own stamp on the controversies of the day, but his originality has been somewhat exaggerated. In particular, three related themes that characterized Dewey's work during this time were shared with other intellectuals and policy makers. The first theme was that the war underscored a break from the intellectual roots of German thought in America. Dewey viewed the militarism of the Germans as a direct consequence of their cultural and philosophical background. For Dewey and many others, American culture stood in stark contrast to the German one. The second theme was that although the war necessitated the rapid acculturation of immigrants, the process should not emulate the Prussian model of forced assimilation to a single cultural type. Rather, the American process of acculturation had to reflect the exceptionality of the American experience. Dewey and others insisted that the cultures of the different immigrant groups had to be assimilated to one another rather than to one generic type. The third theme was that the linear germ theory narrative of institutional development, which posited that American institutions were carried from the Greeks and Romans to the Teutons to the Anglo-Saxons to the Americans, had to be replaced by a aesthetic-pluralist narrative of cultural assimilation. Dewey and others argued that all immigrant groups had something to offer to the transracial democratic culture, not just those with Anglo and Teutonic roots.

During the second half of the nineteenth century, the German educational system was the envy of the world. Thousands of American scholars had studied at German universities and had transplanted hierarchical theories about the superiority of Western culture to American schools. Accordingly, many reformers insisted that the United States emulate the German curriculum and methods. However, by the First World War this had undergone a rapid change because Germany was now viewed as an enemy and an international threat to democracy. The nation that had once been viewed as the pinnacle of free and enlightened thought was now viewed as narrow-minded, imperialistic, and excessively bureaucratic. For example, in 1909 education professor William Bagley admired that in a single century education had transformed Germany "from the weakest to the strongest power on the continent of Europe," yet by 1918 Bagley no longer had praise for the nation. He now considered Prussianism "a disease, a moral lesion which has cut away every sentiment of decency and humanity, which has eaten from the social mind the spiritual and moral values of life, which has glorified the material and left the brute supreme."[46]

The most significant critiques of the formerly admired German system were Dewey's *German Philosophy and Politics* and Veblen's *Imperial Germany and the Industrial Revolution*. Both works were published in 1915 and criticized the Germans' excessive emphasis upon veneration of state and considered German imperialism as a natural outgrowth of its idealistic philosophy and bureaucratic efficiency. As Dewey explained the next year in *Democracy and Education*, "Under the influence of German thought in particular, education became a civic function and the civic function was identified with the realization of the ideal of the national state. The state was substituted for humanity; cosmopolitanism gave way to nationalism. To form the citizen, not the 'man' became the aim of education."[47] It was specifically in the context of his critique of the German system that Dewey issued one of his most popular, influential, and enduring statements: "A democracy is more than a form of government; it is primarily a mode of associated living, of conjoined communicated experience."[48] Thus Dewey clarified his own definition of *democracy* in relation to what it was not. As intellectual historian Morton White explains, "Both Veblen and Dewey had been trained in German philosophy and both were products of the generation which had looked with scorn upon British empiricism. For this reason their critical comments on German thought in 1915 . . . mark an important turn in twentieth-century American thought."[49] In light of the First World War, it was no longer appropriate to proclaim the superiority of German culture and its educational system. This forced American scholars to define American exceptionality as post-European.

In fact, the Americanization process was self-consciously aimed at defining itself against the Prussian system of militarism, forced assimilation, and efficiency. P. P. Claxton, head of the U.S. Bureau of Education, asserted in 1918, "Americanization can come only through teaching. We must win the mind and heart of the people for the country and its institutions and ideals. This cannot be done by force or compulsion. Americanism can never be obtained through the process of Prussianism."[50] Royal Dixon, vice-president of the League of Foreign-born Citizens, also warned against emulating the German system: "In the terrible name of efficiency, the thing for which Germany lost her soul," many Americans were also catering "to the crass demands of the business world."[51] For these leaders, assimilation needed to transcend mere economic socialization; it needed to include cultural elements as well.

Nevertheless, Americanizing immigrants with public funds was still an unpopular idea among many constituents, and so leaders crafted their rationales carefully to appeal to all groups; defining the United States against its enemy, Germany, was a useful rhetorical device. However, these leaders sincerely recognized that assimilating foreign-born workers from across the globe in a democratic manner represented a historically unique effort—it would need to be done thoughtfully and deliberately.

Franklin Lane, Secretary of the Interior, proclaimed: "The test of democracy is in our ability to absorb [the immigrant] and incorporate him into the body of our life as an American." By 1920, Lane considered the job of incorporating American Indians and Blacks into the fabric of American society a largely completed, but still ongoing, process. "The Indian we feel we are responsible for as a Nation, and we give him an education—a most practical one," he explained, and "the Negro . . . is slowly, very slowly coming into that knowledge . . . of developing into a growing national asset—the knowledge of the way of making a living."[52] Having educated the preexisting American minorities, who were metaphorically perceived of as savage extensions of the frontier itself, American educators were now ready to conquer the internal frontier of urban immigrants. This was a uniquely American task and consequently one that required uniquely American content and methods. Dewey confirmed repeatedly in his essays and books written during the First World War that the United States was exceptional and needed to move beyond its European roots.

Despite Dewey's rejection of biologically based theories of race, when approaching the immigrant problem, most other reformers did not fully transcend biological racialist thinking. "Race consciousness is in the blood, and no injection of Americanism will be able to get it out of the system," Peter Roberts explained. Roberts was considered a leader in Americanization and was hired as a consultant by factory owners to help assimilate their foreign workers, who in some cases made up 50% of the workforce. To Americanize correctly, Roberts insisted, one must appreciate the historical backgrounds of each race. "The Jew and the Pole have long been without a country," he explained, "but in no people is the race consciousness more pronounced. The Irish had little self-determination, and yet no immigrant people in the United States have clung more tenaciously to race consciousness." [53]James Tufts confirmed this racialist view in 1908 in the *Ethics* text he coauthored with Dewey: "One difficulty in the English administration of Ireland had been this radical difference between the modern Englishman's individualistic conception of property and the Irishman's more primitive conception of group or clan ownership."[54] Accordingly, to recognize these intellectual and cultural deficiencies, Roberts suggested creating different programs to meet the needs of each group. "The peoples of southeastern Europe," he explained, "are most teachable and receptive; they do not profess to know all that is worth knowing about democracy, . . . this is not the case with many immigrants coming from northern Europe."[55] Along with many others, Roberts believed that immigrants with European blood would be able to take to democracy much quicker than other groups. By this, he meant that they would understand how to balance willfully their own selfish interests with those of the common good. They would be able to demonstrate informed self-restraint in the face of unlimited freedom. However, breaking down the inherited racial traits of the other groups, especially those from Southern and Eastern Europe, demanded a more intense process. There was a perception that these groups were more likely to resist Americanization by clustering together in urban settlements.

Dewey directly targeted these cultural cliques and supported a vision of Americanization in which each group contributed to the greater fund of American culture. Roberts agreed with Dewey that by appreciating the cultural heritage of the entire human race, the immigrant would see how counterproductive his selfish behavior actually was to his own long-term goals. Americanization meant the adoption of the American ideals of cooperation and the rejection of class, foreign, and provincial interests. Roberts concluded that ignorance, especially illiteracy, was the greatest threat to democracy. The two greatest contributing factors to this ignorance were specifically "the negroes and the foreign born." Overcoming their ignorance, Roberts believed, would usher in a more rational, harmonious society for both native and foreign born. "When race prejudice as well as illiteracy, narrowness as well as ignorance, class consciousness as well as class indifference are banished," Roberts argued, "the foreigners will be happier."[56] He, like most progressive reformers, believed that freedom came through self-restraint and education.

How did the subject of history fit into this new mandate to Americanize immigrants? There were a variety of approaches, although all of them corresponded to a large degree with the linear, ethnocentric historicism of the Dewey School. A textbook on citizenship written by Milton Bennion, dean of the School of Education at the University of Utah, continued to employ the germ theory narrative of institutional and racial hierarchy. He argued, "The political inheritance of modern Europe and America is derived mainly from three sources: Hebrew law, Roman law, and Teutonic customs and ideals of political life."[57] The United States was the final depository of these ideas. This view came directly from popular world history textbooks like Philip Van Ness Myers's, in which the author explained how Christianity "has been the most potent factor in modern civilization." Myers depicted his Eurocentric world history as dramatic competition among races. At the beginning of the Middle Ages the "Celts were in front of the Teutons," and "the Slavs were in the rear of the Teutonic tribes," while "the Arabians were hidden in the desert" and "the Mongols and Turks were buried in central Asia." However, despite their initial limitations, the Teutons "had personal worth . . . because of their free independent spirit, of their unbounded capacity for growth, for culture, for accomplishment, the future time became theirs." According to Myers (whose text remained in use until the 1920s), the Teutons were the only race of modernity and progress. The superiority of Northern European culture was the direct result of these long-term historical developments, or the actualization of a latent potential of the institutional germ they carried from the forests of Germany to England to the United States.[58] Thus Bennion and Myers both clung to the old teleological definition of culture that Dewey attacked in his essay on Spencer as well as to the idea of latent potentials, and thus they ascribed the highest form of culture to certain racial groups who carried the institutional germ with them through time.

Royal Dixon presented an alternative to the germ theory narrative, one that looked a lot like Dewey's emerging pluralism. In his text *Americanization*, Dixon demanded reform in state and national laws to make naturalization an easier process. Like Dewey, he directly recognized the poor working conditions of many immigrants and insisted on improvements. Unlike Bennion, he did not suggest that foreigners had to suppress their native instincts to become American. On the contrary, he believed that the unique racial characteristics of each group had something to offer the nation. It was precisely this multiethnic background that gave the United States its uniqueness. "The poem of the Swiss, the Bulgar, the Armenian, the poem of the Russian Jew, the Scandinavian," Dixon argued, "each of these epic inheritances must contribute to the sentiment, the historical justification of our country."[59] The new America, he continued, would only be united when it transcended the Teutonic germ theory outlined by Bennion and Myers and rewrote its own history as the cumulative experience of all White immigrant groups:

> That which is needed most of all for the welding together of the aesthetic-spiritual interests, which are the common interest of all the races, and hence the one line of pursuit for native and alien minds, is some educational system in the teaching of history which will do away with the accumulated, confusing mass of mere annual events from ancient to recent times, and will cut through all ages, as it were, in cross sections to trace, discover the evolution of America.[60]

Dixon proposed that the histories of each (White) ethnic group be traced through time for the artistic and spiritual contributions each one made. Dixon's history was still Eurocentric, but differed in its emphasis. First, it stressed the blending of all Western cultures, not the mere adoption of the "civilized" Anglo-Saxon one. Second, it suggested that the native and the recently arrived foreigner were products of the same historical narrative of aesthetic-spiritual interest—what he called "the epic American conscious-ness." His emphasis on the artistic achievements of the races, instead of their institutional and intellectual developments, made it easier to construct such a "welded" historical view. Third, Dixon explicitly objected to the kind of nar-rowly conceived utilitarianism of Snedden and Bennion, but he agreed that schools needed to address citizenship directly. "By nourishing the spiritual consciousness of the American in this patriotic method," he argued, "the way lies open to training the political consciousness of the young man in such a manner that civics as a study would be no fruitless instruction."[61] In Dixon's view the germ theory narrative did not serve the purpose of instill-ing patriotism, especially because it glorified the Teutonic Germans who were now American enemies. On the other hand, the new patriotic world history, Dixon believed, would lead to improved racial relations between aliens and immigrants.

When Dewey wrote a series of essays on culture and immigrants dur-ing the war, he was doing so in the context of the reconceptualization of American culture described by Dixon and other scholars and policy makers cited above. Although Dewey had always rejected the germ theory narrative because it implied a static Germanic form of culture that contained a latent potential that could only be actualized from within by a certain race, he still insisted on American exceptionality. Although Dewey's definition of culture was contingent and transcended specific races and nations, he still placed American-European intellectual culture at the forefront of progress. This idea was based on the three assumptions outlined above: that American intel-lectual history had moved beyond its German roots; that the voluntary and slow cultural assimilation of immigrants was necessary; and that, as Dixon had outlined, American culture should be grounded in its transracial and international exceptionality.

NATIONALIZING EDUCATION

In 1916 Dewey argued that democracy would "fall to pieces" if schools did not do their part to assuage "divisions of interests, class, and sectional ideas." Dewey outlined two forms of nationalism he thought should be fostered in the United States by carefully distinguishing his American brand of na-tionalism from the European. The first American form of nationalism, he explained, "was interracial and international in its makeup" and constituted a "unity created by drawing out and composing into a harmonious whole the best, the most characteristic which each contributing race and people has to offer." This was fully consistent with Dewey's definition of *culture* as those attributes that contributed to the new and progressive growth of mankind. He encouraged the mixing of cultures, but only so that the best traits from each could contribute to the greater, transracial fund of progress. "The way to deal with hyphenism [German-American, Jewish-American, and so on]," Dewey explained, "is to welcome it, but, to welcome it in the sense of extracting from each people its special good, so that it shall surrender into a common fund of wisdom and experience what it especially has to contribute. All of these surrenders and contributions taken together create the national spirit of America." Dewey's second form of nationalism reinforced his notion that the hyphen should "connect" rather than "separate" Americans from one another. "The other point in the constitution of a genuine American nationalism," Dewey explained, "is that we have been occupied during the greater part of our history in subduing nature."[62] This was an indirect reference to progressive historian Frederick Jackson Turner's "frontier thesis"— the idea that American democratic foundations could be attributed not to the Teutonic germ, but rather to the availability of free land, which throughout American history had served as a safety valve for immigrant and marginalized groups.[63] Jackson had first presented his influential thesis in 1893 in Chicago the year before Dewey arrived. The thesis confirmed Dewey's conviction that society, if it was to move forward, must continue its ability to subordinate the environment through the creation of more generic, transracial knowledge (even though Turner's actual theory did not address minorities). Thus Dewey's second form of nationalism restrained him from arriving at a fully pluralist view, because it still reflected Dewey's linear, ethnocentric definition of culture outlined above. Dewey was placing his old and new definitions of culture side by side: one definition that was diverse and interactional, and one definition that was generic and necessarily progressive. Precisely how Native American and African American cultures fit into this nationalism scheme was not addressed. They clearly represented earlier forms of living and thus had little to offer to the transracial culture, nor did they contribute to the subordination of the environment. Therefore, according to both of Dewey's definitions of culture, Blacks and Indians were socially deficient.

Pragmatic philosopher Horace Kallen put forth a view similar to Dewey's in his 1915 essay "Democracy Versus the Melting Pot." Like his contemporaries, Kallen contrasted his views against the cultural aggressive imperialism of Russia and Germany. He did not want to see America go down the same course of forced assimilation. Instead, Kallen suggested, "'American civilization' may come to mean the perfection of 'European civilization,' the waste, the squalor, and the distress of Europe being eliminated—a multiplicity in a unity, an orchestration of mankind . . . so in society each ethnic group is the natural instrument, its spirit and culture are its theme and melody, and the harmony and dissonances and the discords of them all make the symphony of civilization."[64] Kallen's vision did not necessarily support social mobility; instead, it suggested that all Americans accept and celebrate their role, to play the metaphorical instrument they were given to the best of their ability. The acceptance of all types, instead of the movement toward a single type, was what made America exceptional.

Kallen's view was transitional because he accepted that the characteristics of racial types were fixed, but he wanted to remove these groups from a limited hierarchical view. In other words, he did not go as far as Boas and Du Bois had gone in arguing that all cultures had something to teach one another. Rather, they each contributed to a larger homogenized American culture, which no single culture owned. In a letter to Kallen, Dewey expressed his approval of his "Melting Pot" essay. "I quite agree with your orchestration idea," Dewey explained, "but upon condition we really get a symphony and not a lot of different instruments playing simultaneously. I never did care for the melting pot metaphor, but genuine assimilation to one another—not to Anglo-Saxondom—seems to be essential to an America."[65] Again, although Dewey rejected the idea of the White Protestant as the archetype of culture, like Kallen he did not fully commit to the pluralist view (even though he did move beyond Kallen in recommending cultural "assimilation to one another"). Instead, Dewey confirmed his linear historicism of open-ended inquiry toward progress, a democratic, assimilating process that would lead society toward the generic and/or objective view.

However, Dewey denied the necessity of maintaining cultural diversity, as Du Bois had suggested. Any antisocial or self-serving clique was counterproductive to this evolutionary process, Dewey explained in *Democracy and Education*, because "its prevailing purpose is the protection of what [the clique] has got, instead of reorganizations and progress through wider relationships." Dewey argued that such a tendency could be seen in "savage tribes" who have "identified their experience with rigid adherence to their past customs."[66] Because Tufts had elucidated in their coauthored *Ethics* text that he considered native, Black, and Indian populations as "savage," many readers of the time would likely have read the term as if Dewey were referring to these groups.

In Dewey's *Schools of To-Morrow*, in a passage likely written by his daughter Evelyn, the coauthors enthusiastically described the civics program implemented in the schools of Gary, Indiana—a system that, according to the Deweys, had successfully found the right balance between respecting native limitations and developing thoughtful citizens. Instead of using textbooks, the Gary students engaged in mock political campaigns and built furniture from scratch. The effects of the functional civics curriculum in the industrial town were believed to have a double value, because not only were immigrant students informed about practical citizenship, but their parents were also educated. In a somewhat condescending tone, the Deweys explained, "[Immigrant] parents, learn nothing of the laws until they break them, of public health until they endanger it, nor of social resources until they need something; . . . it is very important that their children have some real knowledge on which to base a sounder judgment."[67] Immigrants, the Deweys believed, were naturally suspicious of government and authority until their children taught them otherwise. This rather dismissive view of immigrant attitudes and culture—likely written by Evelyn—does not exactly reinforce the orchestra metaphor Dewey endorsed above. Rather, it reflected the liberal prejudices and beliefs of the time.

Ultimately, heading into the First World War Dewey was a moderate on the issue of nationalism and racial differentiation. Like many of his peers, Dewey still believed that primitive cultures were culturally deficient, that members of these communities who were not exposed to new environments were consequently deficient, and that these individuals might be further inhibited by their inherited native aptitudes and activities. However, Dewey seemed to make a distinction, as most progressives did, between immigrant White groups and non-White cultures. The former could contribute to the emerging interracial and international fund of knowledge, but the latter could not. Dewey's linear historicism, which was slowly moving in a less ethnocentric direction, would be reconstructed in the years to come as he embraced a more interactionist and pluralist view. But first he had to reconstruct the very pragmatic historicism that was preventing him from embracing the idea of cultural equivalence.

Chapter 6

MUTUAL ADJUSTMENT
TO ONE ANOTHER

O VER THE COURSE of the first two decades of the twentieth century
Dewey gradually reconstructed his views of culture and race. That
is, he subtly but significantly revised his cultural views from a linear,
hierarchical one that subsumed all societies past and present within a single
narrative of progress (as expressed by the Dewey School curriculum) to a
pluralist view that recognized the necessity of interaction among diverse, but
equivalent, ways of living. Dewey's transformation was the result of both
internal and external developments. The debunking of neo-Lamarckianism
and the rediscovery of Mendelian genetics pulled the rug out from under the
proponents of biologically based recapitulation theory. Dewey was never a
neo-Lamarckian, and he never believed in the biological differentiation of racial and ethnic groups. However, he still arranged his laboratory school curriculum as a linear historical reenactment of the stages of race history that he
attempted to coordinate with the emerging native capacities and interests of
the child, which were biologically based. Thus the complete abandonment of
the recapitulation theory by biologists and psychologists must have cast some
doubt on the appropriateness of the curriculum Dewey constructed at his famous laboratory school. Furthermore, the positive reception of the behavior
psychology of Edward Thorndike and Dewey's former student John Watson
underscored the significance of observable, immediate reinforcements in the
lifetime of the individual and shifted attention away from long-term biological and cultural-institutional explanations of mind and behavior. In reference
to nonexperimental strands of his field, Watson exclaimed in 1909, "Damn
Darwin. The Neo Darwinians and Neo Lamarckians, etc. are in a worse hole
than psychologists." Watson insisted that the future of the field resided in his
mechanistic behaviorism, not the structionalist and functionalist approaches
of the German and Chicago schools. As Watson later recalled, "I never knew
what [Dewey] was talking about then, and unfortunately for me, I still don't
know."[1] Indeed, Thorndike and Watson's behavioral approach was easier to
communicate to teachers than Dewey's instrumentalism. By 1912 Watson

was confident that "any careful investigator in experimental education will have to be an animal psychologist. . . . We just have to give . . . educationists time for this to soak in."[2] By the First World War, educators had largely validated Watson's prophetic boast. Specifically, most psychologists abandoned attempts to link the biologically inherited instincts of individuals with the social inheritance of cultures, and instead focused on immediate environmental factors and stimuli.[3] In fact, after *Democracy and Education* Dewey would never again address the culture epoch theory. Instead, he shifted his attention toward the more immediate environmental influences of culture and social psychology.

After 1916 Dewey became less concerned with the emerging instincts of young children and focused more attention on adolescents and adults. In one sense, his interests simply progressed in accordance with the aging students of the Dewey School from the third stage of "consciousness of organization itself" to the fourth stage of "consciousness of calling or function." But on another level, his focus shifted in response to the emerging concerns of the broader fields of education and social science outlined in the last two chapters. Overall, as evolutionary biology became less of an issue for educators, the more immediate conditions outlined by social psychology, behavioral psychology, and cultural anthropology grew in significance. As a result of this important paradigm shift, Dewey reconsidered his philosophical views on the necessity of a diverse, pluralistic environment for actualizing potentials. This corresponded with Dewey's visit to the foreign nations and cultures of China and Japan. Dewey's complete immersion in foreign, non-Western societies challenged his presiding views of culture and race.

PLURALISM AND SOCIAL PSYCHOLOGY

In the 1890s social psychology had gained a significant following among social scientists in the wake of two figures: American psychologist James Mark Baldwin and French sociologist Gabriel Tarde. Both figures had made "imitation" a central component of their respective schemes. In 1901 leading sociologist Charles Ellwood proclaimed that of all the psychological and sociological theories, Tarde's imitation theory was the most "widely accepted and most in the public eye."[4] Accordingly, Dewey's colleague and friend George Herbert Mead explained—in language echoing Du Bois's notion of double-consciousness—"The work of writers influenced by Gabriel Tarde shows that the self exists only in relationship with other selves and cannot be reached except through other selves."[5] Although Mead did not endorse Tarde's "imitation-suggestion" theory outright, he nevertheless confirmed the pervasiveness of the imitation idea on the emerging field.

Dewey also confirmed the significance of Tarde and Baldwin in his entry on "imitation" for *A Cylopedia of Education*. "Largely under the influence of Tarde," Dewey explained in 1914, "imitation was made the chief, if not sole, category of social psychology." Dewey agreed more with "Baldwin's account" of imitation that man "is dealing with the various processes by which one person arrives at a community of beliefs and ideas with others," but Baldwin had not gone far enough in appreciating the interactional nature of socialization.[6] What appeared to be similar behavior brought about by imitation, Dewey reasoned, was actually similar habitual and socially mediated responses to the same cultural environment. Like so many of Dewey's intellectual targets, Tarde and his followers had imposed a teleological scheme upon an interaction after the fact without recognizing how individuals arrived at an imitated social position for their own reasons. "What is called the effect of imitation," Dewey later explained, "is mainly the product of conscious instruction exercised by the unconscious confirmations and ratifications of those with whom one associates."[7]

Furthermore, for Dewey, imitation was inherently conservative if not accompanied by some means of progress and reform, an aspect that Tarde and Baldwin had not fully appreciated. Dewey added to imitation another important factor, which would become crucial to his later pluralist views on culture, the necessity of diversity of viewpoints. "The intellectual and moral progress of the human race," Dewey insisted, "has come through first tolerating and then encouraging divergencies and diversities of thought."[8] That is, progress occurred when individuals of diverse backgrounds and thoughts aligned with a similar idea through imitation, not passively but actively by consciously realizing that their own viewpoint aligned with the imitated idea. Thus individuals arrived at the imitated social perspective through the means of their own perspective. To put it in more Darwinian terms, the native capacities of the individual as mediated by the social contents of the mind, realized its inchoate potential by "fitting" some of its cultural ideas to the environment, while other native capacities either were incorporated within the new activity or lived on to contribute further to the plurality of the environment.

The idea of applying the Darwinian notion of natural variation to the thoughts, viewpoints, and cultures of the present could be traced to William James. But Dewey, having arrived at his pragmatic historicism through Hegel, had emphasized the movement toward convergent, generic, and objective knowledge. As the twentieth century progressed, Dewey began to emphasize and appreciate the other side of the equation. In other words, Dewey recognized the necessity of pluralism for achieving a meaningful unity. As it emerged during the beginning of the twentieth century, *pluralism* was the view that the world was multidimensional. As outlined in the last chapter, Boas and Du Bois subscribed to this view in the final decade of the nineteenth century, but there is little evidence to connect Dewey directly to either of these figures before the 1910s. William James, however, was an immediate and direct influence on Dewey, and he too expressed the pluralist viewpoint.

James was a cognitive pluralist—his application of the Darwinian concept of natural variation and selection. Competing ideas emerged in consciousness, and the one that best fit the needs of the emerging problem won out. Thus a pluralism of ideas was a necessity for progress. In a 1903 letter to James, Dewey implored him to "state your Plurality as a matter of historic significance as well as the universal unity" and recognized that James's "Plurality as it now stands is aesthetic rather than logical."[9] That is, Dewey wanted James to recognize that historical progress was a necessary outcome of pluralistic interaction and that current problems organically contained the historical solutions of the past. James later explored the philosophical implications of his pluralism: "Everything is many directional, many dimensional, in external relations. . . . No one point of view or attitude commands everything at once in a synthetic scheme . . . the pluralistic universe is . . . more like a federal republic than like an empire or a kingdom."[10] In this 1908 quotation, James expanded his pluralism to suggest that multiple ideas could adequately "fit" and explain a problem. Therefore, a full understanding of an issue required viewing it from multiple angles.

Likely influenced by James as well as the other factors listed above, Dewey slowly began employing a more pluralistic language in the mid-1910s. "A modern society is many societies more or less loosely connected," he explained in Chapter 7 of *Democracy and Education*. "The intermingling in the school of youth of different races, differing religions, and unlike customs creates for all a new and broader environment." In his classic text Dewey insisted that democratic man associated "in all kinds of ways and for all kinds of purposes . . . in a multitude of diverse groups," which created "varied and free points of contact with other modes of association." Such "back and forth play" and "diversity of stimulation" among the cultural groups were essential to bringing forth novel ideas that would contribute to progress.[11]

At approximately the same time that Dewey began using the term "associated form of living" to describe democracy, he began referring to "cultures" in the plural—first in *Democracy and Education* and again that same year (1916) in his essays on "Nationalizing Education" and "Education and Culture." In the first essay Dewey insisted that there was a danger in refusing to accept "what other cultures have to offer" and in trying to accept one component of culture as the "pattern to which all other strains and cultures are to conform."[12] In the second essay Dewey insisted on the importance of liberating modern society from the "class cultures of the past."[13] Likewise, in *Democracy and Education* Dewey demanded that a reformation of education required that "the ideas and ideals which are inherited from older and unlike cultures" be reevaluated.[14] It is not likely that Dewey consciously started using "cultures" in the plural, but it is, nevertheless, very suggestive that the term suddenly appeared in 1915–1916, when he began reconsidering the necessity of pluralistic interaction. By 1915 Dewey even accepted the label of "pluralist," but only after some coaxing by a peer.

Scudder Klyce, a former naval officer and eccentric independent scholar, wrote a lengthy letter to Dewey in April explaining how he planned to use Dewey in a philosophical research project he was currently working on. As he bluntly informed Dewey in a letter, "you are an infinite pluralist, explicitly; Kant was one, James was one: . . . most scientists are very vaguely but actually pluralists."[15] After reflection upon Klyce's description of his pragmatic position, Dewey replied with the following revelation:

> I . . . have everywhere made prominent that the only end or aim of education is capacity for more education, or widening and refining the scope of perception of meanings. I have also identified this, as extended all the way around, with a democratic society. The further I go the more I see that I have become a confirmed infinite pluralist. I simply can't get monism with any reality . . . twenty years ago it would have met me. But I am grateful for having the *infinite* part of the pluralism made obvious. I find plenty of places where I had criticized certain things and the principle of the criticism is that the things involved a finite pluralism, but I had never generalized it. While I don't have occasion here to use the words, having the thing formulated consciously increases my confidence.[16]

In this remarkable letter Dewey seems to have discovered three significant things. First, Dewey admitted that 20 years before—that is, when he first put his pen to paper to describe his pedagogical vision for the Dewey School to Clara Mitchell in the winter of 1895—he was in essence a "monist." In the letter to Klyce he suggested that what he had been critiquing as "latent potentials," was actually the idea of finite pluralism—the Spencerian notion that all was moving toward a predetermined, static essence. Although Dewey never subscribed to the idea of a predetermined essence, as I showed in Chapters 1 and 2, he had for many years identified the modern world as moving toward a more "generic" and/or "objective" social consciousness. By 1915 he no longer believed this, at least not in these terms. Second, having realized this transformation, Dewey reconsidered the long-term goals of his pragmatic historicism. Dewey had been so occupied with the immediate educational and logical implications of his theory that he had not given ample attention to what the actual end point of his scheme would be. Of course, for Dewey, there was no end point; growth led to more growth and reconstruction led to more reconstruction. His historicism was, indeed, infinite. Perhaps, at this point, Dewey realized fully that his historicism was not leading to a more socialized, more generic and scientific future; it was not necessarily leading anywhere. Third, he adopted the term *pluralism* as an alternative description of his approach. If we follow the first and second realizations to their logical conclusions, then we can see that cultural pluralism and diversity were absolute necessities for infinite reconstruction. They were the very material from which infinite reconstruction would come. In appreciation of these insights, Dewey had a copy of his new book *Essays in Experimental Logic* sent to Klyce, and Dewey thanked him for influencing his thinking on the topic. Dewey's acceptance of "infinite pluralism" can be seen in an important essay on social psychology in which he not only endorsed some of his emerging ideas, but also subtly reconstructed some of his older ones.

In 1916 Dewey was asked to speak to the American Psychological Association on the occasion of their 25th anniversary, and he chose the topic of social psychology because he considered the subdiscipline as offering the most promise for the future of the field, which by 1916 was moving in a more behaviorist direction. Dewey argued that psychologists should approach the mind from a "pluralistic basis: the complexity and specific variety of the factors of human nature, each operating in response to its own highly specific stimulus, and each subject to almost infinite shadings and modulations as it enters into combination and competition with others." Accordingly, Dewey defined *mind* as the "reorganization of original activities through their operation in a given environment. It is formation, not a datum; a product, and a cause only after it has been produced." Essentially endorsing the functionalist approach to psychology—but stripped of its somewhat outdated genetic and historicist baggage—Dewey underscored the significance of social and cultural environment on mental development. He subtly denounced the excessively genetic or comparative approaches of social psychology of the 1890s (perhaps, including his own approach to curriculum at the Dewey School), saying: "That anything which may properly be called mind or intelligence is not an original possession but is a consequence of the manifestation of instinct under the conditions supplied by associated life in the family, the school, the market place and the forum, is no remote inference from speculative reconstruction of the primitive mind." In other words, the mind was not merely a deductive distillation to its essential, pristine form—or what he called the misguided idea of "progressive unfolding of original potencies latent in a ready-made mind." Instead, it was the product of native tendencies (or what he once called interests and instincts) realized in the plurality of associated living—a conclusion, he insisted, that was "confirmed by the development of specific beliefs, ideas and purposes in the life of every infant now observable."[17] Dewey stated forcefully a conviction that he had always held, but which now had immediate consequences for the education of minorities: that social environment trumped biological inheritance.

To combat further the potentially deterministic approach of behaviorist psychology, which was associated with intelligence testing and eugenics, Dewey addressed it directly. Regarding the "behaviorist movement" of Thorndike and McDougall, Dewey insisted, "It radically simplifies the whole problem by making it clear that social institutions and arrangements, including the whole apparatus of tradition and transmission, represent simply the acquired transformation of original human endowments."[18] In other words, behaviorism correctly focused on interactions. However, by focusing solely on the relationship between stimuli and responses and reinforcements and punishments, it reduced the social world to only these immediate factors, without accounting for how these factors were permeated with the social inheritance of the race (recall the savage and the invention of the bow and arrow from Dewey's review of Ward's book). For Dewey, the most significant factor in explaining the development of the mind, especially as his "infinite pluralism" was emerging, was the interaction among different social ideas. Change for the individual occurred "in connection with interaction with new elements in its surroundings."[19]

For example, in 1915 Dewey declared, "Science is always a plurality of diverse interacting and changing existences."[20] Two years later, in reference to the evolution and growth of the individual, Dewey wrote that "the organism is in and of the world, and its activities correlated with those of other things in multiple ways . . . these connexions [sic] are of diverse kinds. . . . *In this sense,* pluralism, not monism, is an established empirical fact [italics in the original]." Drawing upon and citing the pluralism of James, Dewey continued, "Empirically, then, active bonds or continuities of all kinds, together with static discontinuities, characterize existence. . . . Experience is an affair of facilitations and checks, of being sustained and disrupted, being let alone, being helped and troubled, of good fortune and defeat in all the countless qualitative modes which these words pallidly suggest."[21] The reconstruction of knowledge that occurred as a result of these interactions was dependent upon a diversity of native capacities emerging from the individual, as well as a plurality and heterogeneity of ideas in the social environment.

Dewey's pluralistic view of society and culture was best and most fully on display in Chapter 7 of *Democracy and Education,* one of the most original and influential passages he ever wrote. In it Dewey outlined the necessity of diversity to democracy and progress. "The realization of a form of life in which interests are mutually interpenetrating, and where progress, or readjustment, is an important consideration," Dewey explained, "makes a democratic community more interested . . . in deliberate and systematic education." Because democratic citizens ultimately had to rule themselves instead of depending upon the traditional ruling elite and its prescribed knowledge, they not only had to be informed about the present situation, but they needed the tools to envision a better future. According to Dewey, such a progressive vision was dependent upon the ability for ideas and attributes to be "mutually interpenetrating," and an educational system that fostered and modeled these ideals.

The Dewey School had not done this. While the school was indeed set up as an embryonic community reflective of the larger social world, its focus was on social occupations based upon Dewey's old linear view of culture, whereas the vision he outlined in Chapter 7 of *Democracy and Education* was based upon his new pluralistic view. In theory, the vision outlined by Dewey would require a diverse student population within the school and classroom. An education that broke down "barriers of class, race and national territory," Dewey insisted—in a rare instance of clearly using "race" in a pluralistic way instead of in reference to the broader "human race"—would lead to the liberation of a greater diversity of personal capacities which characterize a democracy." Dewey concluded, "only diversity makes change and progress." [22]

In summary, social psychology became a central component of Dewey's thought between 1915 and 1917 as pluralism and interactionism became more significant aspects of his historicism, particularly as they related to potentiality. He explained, using the metaphor of an apple: "To say that an apple has the potentiality of decay does not mean that it has latent or implicit within it a causal principle which will some time inevitably display itself in producing decay, but that its existing changes (in interaction with its surroundings) will take the form of decay, if they are exposed or subjected to certain conditions not now operating upon them." That is, the apple did not contain the finite pluralism of decay; rather, its decay was contingent upon the interaction of the apple with the particular environment producing decay. Yet Dewey still maintained elements of his linear historicism when he concluded: "Potentiality thus implies not merely diversity, but a progressively increasing diversification of a specific thing in a particular direction."[23]

Let's say, for the sake of argument, that this particular thing was a savage. Dewey would argue that the savage contained within him the potential to achieve civilization as long as he interacted with a heterogeneous social context through education. Yet after this process the savage's contingent transformation would lead to his individual heterogeneity, but it would also lead to the loss of his primitive way of life. The savage lifestyle, by being absorbed in the civilized one, would diversify the internal state of the now-civilized savage, but at the same time the loss of his savage lifestyle would homogenize the social environment. In other words, if the whole world moved toward the Western standard of civilization, then it would inevitably deprive itself of the diversity necessary for growth and reconstruction. Pluralism could not be infinite, unless a plurality of cultures was accepted and maintained. Thus Dewey began to appreciate the necessity of preserving the social-psychological elements of culture that could contribute to a heterogeneous context, including non-Western cultures. Dewey realized that the potential of the individual and society was dependent upon a diverse environment wherein new cultural combinations and interactions could take place. Appropriately, Dewey's cultural pluralism further emerged when it interacted with a new

context—the allegedly less civilized nations of China and Japan, to which
Dewey traveled in 1919.

DEWEY VISITS AND EVALUATES THE ORIENT

On sabbatical leave from Columbia University in 1917 Dewey decided to
visit Japan, where he was asked to deliver some lectures. Later, he was convinced by some of his former students to visit and speak in China as well.
He ended up staying in China for 2 years. During his visit the May Fourth
Movement erupted in which over 3,000 students protested the decision of
the Versailles Peace Conference to transfer German concessions in Shantung
to Japan. Dewey was excited by the prospects of the movement, which likely
inspired him to extend his stay.[24] Nevertheless, Dewey clearly approached the
people of Japan and China through a lens of cultural deficiency and largely
viewed his job as enabling the Chinese educational reformers to bring about
Western-style reforms (to be fair, this is what many Chinese and Japanese
reformers hoped as well). In fact, Tufts and Dewey's *Ethics* textbook had
specifically identified China and Japan at a lower level of civilization than the
West: "At a somewhat higher stage of civilization [than the totem group of
Africans and Native Americans]," Tufts explained, "the invisible members
of the group are the departed ancestors. ...This ancestor worship is a power
to-day in China and Japan, and the tribes of the Caucuses."[25] Thus Dewey
approached the Asian nations with his ethnocentrism intact, but his infinite
pluralism in the forefront of his mind. His brief stay in Japan helped to reinforce his ethnocentrism, but his extended stay in China had a more profound
and lasting effect on his views. China presented an opportunity for him to
contemplate and confront these competing views of culture.

His grieving wife Alice accompanied Dewey on his trip; their son Morris
had recently passed away in Italy. Alice was a proponent of racial and cultural equality. Upon departing from Kyoto, Japan, Alice succinctly wrote her
children: "Certainly these people have a nobility of character which entitles
them to race equality."[26] Dewey himself was not as empathetic. The Japanese,
he dismissively wrote his friend Albert Barnes, "have a childlike and almost
touching eagerness to be thought of well—especially as they are still new to
their membership in Western civilization to be sure." Dewey identified an
irritability of all foreigners in Japan, which he himself felt and attributed to
"seeing and feeling things done in a way that is foreign to one's own inbred
habit—a mere clash of cultures—accentuated by the fact that outwardly there
is much resemblance [note Dewey's use of cultures in the plural again]."
But he also attributed the irritability of foreign visitors to the deficiencies of
the Japanese people, to their excessive politeness and their failure to criticize

themselves and others—a trait he attributed to "a survival of the mutual distrust of enemies from the feudal period."[27] Regarding race, he noted, "They discriminate more against the Chinese than we do against them."[28] Dewey offered some broader sociological generalizations of the Japanese as well.

Psychologically the Japanese were "communistic . . . or marked by social solidarity." Intellectually they were "not an individualistic people—they like to conform, and are very sensitive, as said, to disapproval by others." Morally, they were "more individualistic than we are." Dewey concluded that the Japanese lacked "social glue," and so he sardonically commented, "In spite of our fifty races we are in many ways a more unified people than these with their single homogenous race."[29] What the Japanese were lacking, although Dewey did not directly identify it, was an appreciation for a democratic and associated form of living. Dewey essentially dismissed Japanese culture as not far enough developed, as clutching too tightly to their traditional communal forms of living. That is, like Europeans, Dewey believed that the Japanese had to first develop Western-style institutions and dispositions before they could create the kind of international and interracial worldview he envisioned for the United States and the rest of the world. At the same time he identified a "clash of cultures" as a notable aspect of his experience. Thus we can see his old linear ethnocentric and newer pluralistic definitions of culture commingling as he tried unsuccessfully to wrap his mind around the Japanese experience. Were the Japanese and Western forms of living "to assimilate to one another," or were the Japanese to transcend their outdated form of life and accept the more modern transracial-transnational one? Dewey did not directly address this issue in his letters, but it seems likely that, as he left Japan, he would have argued for the latter. He had a lot more time to contemplate this dilemma in China.

Upon arriving in China, the Deweys observed communal behaviors similar to the Japanese. "I had found the human duplication of the bee colony in actual working order," Alice joked to her children. "China is it, and in all particulars lives up to the perfect socialization of the race. Nobody can do anything alone, nobody can do anything in a hurry."[30] Yet the more time Dewey spent there, the more he gained admiration for the rich history of its people and the complexity of its sociological and anthropological aspects. The more Dewey tried to describe the Chinese culture with his preconceived notions, the more he appreciated the relative and contingent nature of culture itself. By the end of the transformative trip Dewey had gained a greater respect for the cultural difference of the Chinese people, a difference he could simply describe in terms of his ethnocentric linear historicism. That is, Dewey could not simply place a country so vast, populous, and ancient on a single continuum of cultural development with Western Europe and the United States as the final cultural destination. Chinese politics had to be "understood in terms of itself," Dewey insisted in a position that would have been unthinkable 20 years earlier, "not translated over into classifications of an alien political morphology. . . . China can be understood only in terms of the institutions and ideas which have been worked out in its own historical evolution."[31] Dewey translated his more nuanced cultural perspective directly to his recommendations for educational reform.

The overriding theme of Dewey's essay on "American and Chinese Education" was that Western approaches to the topic would need to be translated into forms that would be palatable to the Chinese and sensitive to their unique cultural position. Drawing upon his firsthand experiences, Dewey explained, "In wanting a transformation of their country, the Young Chinese have no thought of a Westernized China, a China which repeats and imitates Europe or America. They want Western knowledge and Western methods which they themselves can independently employ and sustain in a China which is itself and not a copy of something else." Although Dewey recognized and respected the cultural norms of the Chinese, he was not proposing a cultural exchange of ideas. In other words, he was not arguing on behalf of "assimilation to one another" or "mutually interpenetrating" of ideas as he did for American immigrant groups. Instead he suggested a one-way transaction. Nevertheless, Dewey approached the Chinese with a degree of humility and cultural sensitivity that was missing when he departed from Japan. He skillfully articulated the position of "other" by placing himself in their cultural shoes. Chinese educational reformers were, Dewey recognized, "profoundly resentful of all efforts which condescendingly hold up Western institutions, political, religious, educational, as models to be humbly accepted and submissively repeated." He suggested that the useful cultural lessons he acquired abroad needed to be passed on to future reformers. "China does not need copies of American colleges, but does still need . . . well trained foreigners who are capable of understanding Chinese needs, alert, agile, sympathetic in their efforts to meet them."[32]

A close reading of Dewey's position on China reveals three things. First, Dewey recognized that the Chinese did not necessarily see the West as inherently superior, and they actually resented such a suggestion. Second, Dewey realized that the rich, complex history of China could not simply be ignored when adjusting to Western ways; European methods, ideas, and institutions would have to undergo some kind of a transformation to meet the needs of the Chinese people. Third, despite his nuanced and semipluralistic take on cultural transmission, Dewey still believed that the future of China resided in the adoption of Western ideas. Thus, to a large extent, Dewey continued to conceive of the nation in terms of linear cultural distance from the West, a concept revealed in the title of his essay "What Holds China Back?"

Dewey had come a long way in reevaluating his ethnocentric historicism, but he had not come as far as W.E.B. Du Bois in insisting upon the necessity of preserving cultural differences instead of merely recognizing them, nor had he come as far as Franz Boas in suggesting that the Chinese potentially had something to teach the Westerner. Ultimately, Dewey's recognition of Japanese and Chinese racism toward each other and the rest of world, along with his realization that they, in fact, had distinct cultures, would have a lasting effect on his views on race. His travels to the East challenged, but did not entirely overturn, his linear historicism, and reinforced his emerging interactionist views of culture and race.

RACE AND EDUCATION REVISITED

Dewey addressed race most fully and explicitly in a 1922 essay titled "Racial Prejudice and Friction," which was first delivered as a speech to the Chinese Social and Political Science Association. In it he revealed a new perspective on the topic that had been in gestation since 1915. In addition to Dewey's emphasis on social psychology, his reconsideration of the significance of environmental interaction for actualizing potentials, and his transformative travels to Japan and China, Dewey revised his views on culture and race in response to changes within the field of anthropology itself. Specifically, Dewey reconsidered the significance of the field of cultural anthropology as practiced by Franz Boas and William I. Thomas. While the changes that occurred were subtle and traces of his ethnocentrism remained, Dewey took significant steps toward a cultural pluralist position, which he revealed in his essay on race prejudice

Dewey biographers Steven Rockefeller and Alan Ryan both attribute a change in Dewey's cultural perspective to Boas. However, with a few exceptions, there is little evidence directly connecting the two. In a course syllabus for "Types of Philosophical Thought" (1922) Dewey briefly cited Boas's *Mind of Primitive Man* in support of the significance of social environment on cultural evolution.[33] Boas and Dewey reportedly cotaught a seminar at Columbia University at one time, but testimony regarding the existence of this class is secondhand, and Dewey never mentioned it in his writings or correspondence.[34] One notable exception to the lack of evidence linking the two scholars is a 1916 letter Boas wrote Dewey addressing how he methodologically would approach a study of ethics. Dewey, who was serving on the editorial board of *International Journal of Ethics*, solicited Boas's advice about what a scientific study of ethics would look like. Boas responded with a viewpoint that potentially challenged the linear historicist approach outlined by Dewey and Tufts in their popular *Ethics* text. Boas wrote, "One of the most important problems that I think should be solved in order to gain a satisfactory basis for ethical studies is the question of how far, in cultural types that have grown up independently of our own, distinctive ethical concepts occur."

Boas suggested the detailed comparative study of "some people where distinct social standards may be observed" such as "one of the tribes of British Columbia," the Crow Indians, and "an investigation of African proverbs." Boas hypothesized that such a study would likely confirm his conviction that "instinctive, ethical tendencies are the same everywhere where social factors do not exert a disturbing factor."[35]

Boas's approach challenged Dewey's linear historicism in three ways. First, Boas used the term *cultural types,* implying a diversity of equivalent forms of ethical living that could not be arranged hierarchically. Second, Boas refrained from using the terms *savage* or *primitive* in reference to the premodern cultures. Dewey, in contrast, used *savage* in reference to hunter-gatherer cultures numerous times in *Democracy and Education*, published the same year as this letter. Third, methodologically Boas conceptualized "ethics" in nonhistoricist terms, as something that emerged in diverse forms as it developed independently in different cultures and locations. To study the topic adequately, Boas suggested, cross-cultural analysis was necessary, not to see how ethics evolved over time within a single linear scheme, but rather to see how ethics manifested itself differently in different cultural environments.

We do not have Dewey's response to Boas's letter. However, it is likely that Dewey read his own views into Boas's position—that is, Dewey likely believed that Boas supported his convictions that social environment trumped biological inheritance and that a study of many cultures was necessary to discover the generic aspects of ethics. Many years later, Dewey referred Boas's book *The Mind of Primitive Man* to another scholar with this description of it: "Boas doesn't believe in what a graduate student, after taking some anthropology courses called the solipsistic Theory of Cultures, but he does come out strong in what may be called "Cultural Relativity."[36] This comment can be interpreted a couple of ways. In one sense, Dewey recommended Boas's classic text to a colleague and thereby, to a certain extent, endorsed its message. On the other hand, by putting "cultural relativity" in quotation marks, he seemed to be distancing himself from Boas's position. Dewey often had to defend his pragmatism from accusations of relativity, and so he probably did not want to be affiliated with the term. Ultimately, Boas's influence on Dewey was ambiguous and difficult to determine, but his views likely reinforced Dewey's movement toward interactional pluralism.

The influence of William I. Thomas on Dewey, however, was much more direct and easier to trace. Dewey's admiration for Thomas was first expressed in a letter in 1898 in which he proclaimed, "Mr. Thomas, to my mind, is without any doubt opening a distinct new field in Sociology . . . he will at once command recognition as a pioneer in a most important direction." According to Dewey, Thomas's work represented "the attempt to discover concrete laws of social growth through the application of modern psychological methods to historical material."[37] Recall that Thomas's impact on Dewey's savage mind essay was so great that he considered it a "joint contribution." Like Dewey, Thomas combined sociological, psychological, and anthropological elements into functionalist theory of cultural and racial development.

Also like Dewey, Thomas was an early proponent of the significance of cultural environment on social inequality. Despite the increasing popularity of Dewey's ideas, adherents of biological determinism continued to consider functional environmentalism (often associated with Tarde's imitation-suggestion theory) as misguided. For example, in 1901 leading sociologist Charles Ellwood insisted that socialization of minorities was "at every turn limited, controlled, and modified by a series of instinctive impulses which have become relatively fixed," a point exemplified by "the negro child, [who] even when reared by a white family under the most favorable conditions, fails to take on the mental and moral characteristics of the Caucasian race." The reappearance of "voodooism" and "fetishism" in Southern Blacks, Ellwood argued, confirmed that biological inheritance exerted a powerful force upon individuals that could not be completely overcome by social forces and education.[38] In an essay on "The Mind of Woman and the Lower Races" Thomas rebuked Ellwood's view. He insisted that "difference in natural ability is in the main a characteristic of the individual, not of the race or of sex." Thomas cited an important laboratory study of the mental traits of men and women by Helen Thompson, arguing that differences among the sexes were due more to social influences than to their intellectual potentials. "Differences in intellectual expression are mainly social rather than biological," Thomas concluded, "dependent on the fact that different stages of culture present different experiences to the mind, and adventitious circumstances direct the attention to the different fields of interest."[39] Drawing upon his extensive ethnographic readings, his own empirical work, and no doubt the pragmatic historicism of his friend Dewey, Thomas reached an iconoclastic conclusion about the cultural value of Western civilization. As early as 1907 Thomas suggested the radical Boasian idea that women and the so-called inferior races could potentially contribute to Western culture by contributing to a diverse, pluralist environment:

> The instinct to belittle outsiders is perhaps at the bottom of our delusion that the white race has one order of mind and the black and yellow races have another. It is certain at any rate, that our civilization is not the highest type possible . . . the participation of woman and the lower races will contribute new elements, change the stress of attention, disturb the equilibrium, and force a crisis which will result in the reconstruction of our habits on more sympathetic and equitable principles. Certain it is that no civilization can remain the highest if another civilization adds to the intelligence of its men the intelligence of its woman.[40]

In this passage Thomas in essence suggested the position of infinite pluralism years before Dewey fully appreciated and embraced the position. There is no direct evidence suggesting that Dewey read these specific essays, but there is evidence of intellectual contact between Dewey and Thomas and expressions of their mutual admiration. So it is more likely that Dewey was influenced by Boas-via-Thomas than that he was influenced directly by Boas. In fact, Dewey's position of emphasizing the importance of environment on development and the benefits of cultural interaction, while maintaining a degree of linear historicism, was much closer to Thomas's position than Boas's when Dewey wrote his race prejudice essay in 1922. In fact, the argument Dewey presents in this essay are almost identical to the views Thomas presented in his various essays on race and race prejudice in years before.

As early as 1904 Thomas asserted, "Race prejudice is an instinct originating in the tribal stage of society, when solidarity in feeling and action were essential to the preservation of the group."[41] By 1912 Thomas had become a leader in racial social psychology. In a 50-page article cataloging the mental capacities of immigrants and Negroes, Thomas drew on the empirical work and theories of Tarde, James, Boas, Du Bois, Dewey, and many others to establish the fact that "individual variation is of more importance than racial difference." Despite the progressive nature of Thomas's views, he still subscribed to the linear historicist view of cultural distance. That is, he argued in a somewhat neo-Lamarckian manner that time was needed for the less established races to adjust to the "crisis" of the new environment before "a modification of structure" could take place. "The Negro, for instance, had not been properly prepared for freedom," he explained in language echoing Thomas Jesse Jones. "Enthusiasts for Negro and peasant emancipation did not foresee the loss of control involved in the disturbance of old habits, nor make a proper allowance for the time elements involved in education into new habits."[42] Thus Thomas presented a position that looked a lot like Dewey's. Racial disparity was an outcome of historical oppression and social standing, which could eventually be overcome by education and enhanced environmental exposure. However, such a transformation would take time and required "a modification of structure." Thomas even suggested the radical idea that when the cultural transformation did eventually bring equality to women, immigrants, and minorities, these oppressed groups could potentially contribute to and improve upon the existing dominant culture. This, in essence, was the argument of Dewey's essay "Racial Prejudice and Friction," the fullest exploration of race he ever attempted.

Like Thomas, Dewey attributed race prejudice to biological and social inheritance, to "biases that originally spring from instincts and habits which are deep set in our natures." As he did in 1909, Dewey insisted that "race is an abstract thing; according to science it is largely a mythical idea, since all peoples now powerful in the world are highly mixed."[43] So if scientists had determined that race was a social construction largely correlated with nationalism and social inequality, why were people still racist? Dewey traced racial prejudice to an instinctual sense of abhorrence that historically emerged when different tribes and groups first encountered one another. The habitual instinct to resist and fear someone different was embedded in the nature of individuals and fostered by threatened social groups. For example, Dewey explained, Anglo-Saxons first resisted the Irish, then the Chinese, then the Southern Europeans, before they eventually drew accustomed to each culture. And the group that was previously discriminated against became the most active in opposing the next group; for example, the Irish were the most vigilantly prejudiced against the Chinese. Prejudice, Dewey argued, was an unreflective response, not the application of the intellect. However, the prejudice instinct could be overcome through continued exposure to alternative cultures and reflective thinking.

In the essay, Dewey again used "cultures" in the plural, pointing to his newer conception of the term, but he still had not entirely transcended his ethnocentric historicism of its original definition. The world was still characterized by a linear narrative of social progress. "The simple fact of the case is that at present the world is not sufficiently civilized to permit close contact of peoples of widely different cultures without deplorable consequences," Dewey admonished. "This deficiency of civilization is much more than a personal matter; it may be and is readily overcome in many individual cases."[44] Significantly, in this passage, Dewey defined *civilization* not as the ability to understand and contribute to industrial development as he had earlier, but rather as the ability to tolerate and assimilate multiple cultures. This was both a refutation of his earlier Eurocentric definition of *culture* and simultaneously an affirmation of culture as a means of developmental distance. As Dewey further explained, using the term *types of culture* for the first time (perhaps borrowing the term from Boas), the authentic adjustment of cultures to one another would be a difficult and drawn-out process:

> Racial discrimination is a bad thing, but an indiscriminate reaction against it may also be a bad thing. For as I have tried to bring out, the question is not primarily one of race at all, but of the adjustment of different types of culture to one another. These differences of culture include not only differences of speech, manner, religion, moral code . . . but also differences of political organization and habits and national rivalries. What is called race prejudice . . . is a product and sign of the friction which is generated by these other deep-seated causes.[45]

Dewey concluded that the unavoidable, yet difficult, solution to the problem of racial friction was "mutual adjustment to one another."[46] While espousing this culturally pluralist, interactionist view, Dewey also endorsed the outright restriction of immigrants to the United States in order to give the world "rest and recuperation." Dewey argued that the First World War had put an unnatural stress on the nation, and postwar society was not the best context to test his "mutual adjustment" proposal. Heeding the advice of Dewey and many others, the U.S. Congress passed the Immigration Restriction Act in 1924, which drastically reduced the immigration of Jews and other undesirable groups into the United States (Dewey's pluralist friends, Boas and Kallen, were both Jewish). This policy would have dire consequences in the 1930s when Germany started persecuting its Jews, many of whom hoped to immigrate to the United States for refuge.

Overall, the "Racial Prejudice" essay reflected Dewey's change of cultural perspective from a linear, Eurocentric view of culture to a transactional, infinite pluralistic one. But, like Thomas, Dewey proposed that "mutual adjustment to one another" required time. However, it was not a matter of letting one culture catch up with the other that required time, as his earlier linear historicism implied, but rather a matter of allowing the cultural groups to interact slowly and intrinsically with one another so as to derive the best aspects of each from one another. Such a process required a constant replenishing of fresh cultural insights, ideas, and contributions. This was the application of pluralistic interactionism to the associated living of democratic society. Nevertheless, it should be noted that Dewey again failed to state explicitly whether African Americans and Native Americans had the "types of culture" to which the White groups should adjust. In contrast, Thomas had specifically identified these oppressed groups in his characterization of racial diversity. By 1922 it was likely that Dewey included these groups in this scheme as well, but he never stated it outright. For example, later that year in an essay on inferiority and superiority, Dewey wrote, "Inferior races are inferior because their successes lie in different directions, though possibly more artistic and civilized than our own."[47] Thus Dewey implied that so-called inferior groups could "possibly" have artistic cultural contributions to make. In a 1923 essay on schools and social consciousness, Dewey suggested in Boasian language that "we need a curriculum in history, literature and geography which will make the different racial elements in this country aware of what each has contributed," as well as inspire "feelings of respect and friendliness for other nations and peoples of the world."[48] Again, these passages suggest the significance of cultural diversity, but never explicitly identify Native American and African American cultures as potential contributors to the transnational and transracial associated form of culture Dewey outlined.

Drawing upon his new pluralistic interactionist approach, Dewey also revisited his educational views. Dewey's new perspective on culture and interactional metaphysics was reflected in a trilogy of essays published in 1922 for the *New Republic* on education as religion, engineering, and politics. In contrast to Dewey's numerous writings on education in the 1890s when he was trying to align the psychological growth of the child with the sociological growth of civilization, these essays did not contain any references to genetic psychology or linear historicism. It was almost as if the University of Chicago laboratory school had never existed. Rather than trying to proselytize reformers with his earlier ideas, Dewey called for a pluralistic spirit of experimentation and humble tinkering. What teachers and educators needed above all else in the world of infinite pluralism, Dewey proclaimed, was a "creatively courageous disposition."[49]

Dewey pointed out that most educators tended to approach the topic from an inherently contradictory position. On the one hand, they espoused a religious faith in the power of education to transform individuals and society through "deliberate direction in the formation of human disposition and intelligence," yet they simultaneously blamed the failure of students on "some intrinsic defect or some outer chance which has unaccountably entered in and deflected our correct procedure to a bad outcome." Both positions viewed the world in absolute, rather than contingent, pluralistic terms. Instructors would never discover a perfect method, Dewey insisted, because education, if properly conceived, was an evolving endeavor that constantly reconstructed its methods to meet the emerging needs of a transforming society. Dewey insisted that no one method could ever be effective for the "complexity and diversity of human beings," yet nevertheless the quest for scientific methods must continue. But science could only enhance the art of teaching by recognizing the pluralistic, interactional nature of reality—by recognizing "through ways of understanding human nature in its concrete actuality and of discovering how its various factors are modified by interaction with the variety of conditions under which they operate."[50] Those who attempted to establish "definitive, usable, educational directions out of the new body of science," Dewey concluded, "[were] pathetic."[51] Contingency, experimentalism, and diversity should not only characterize the field, but it should embody its method and content as well. The pluralistic world demanded a "discriminating intelligence," not an "undiscriminating mental habit." In a rejection of (or an organic natural growth out of) his laboratory school curriculum, Dewey demanded that current and political events be directly addressed in the classroom, lest students "enter upon the responsibilities of social membership in complete ignorance that there are any social problems, any political evils, any industrial defects."[52] The modern world required a full, authentic description and analysis of its existing state including its political issues, something his original educational approach never explicitly addressed. Perhaps Dewey's new nonlinear historicist approach to knowledge and education was best summarized in *Democracy and Education* when he succinctly wrote "that the educational process has no end beyond itself . . . the educational process is one of continual reorganizing, reconstructing, transforming."[53]

Dewey's subtle shift during this period could be explained easily by stating that his interests evolved from psychology to anthropology via social psychology—or a shift from internal to external factors of growth. However, this is too simplistic because Dewey had always been interested in all these fields. Rather, the discipline of anthropology shifted from a linear, Spencerian interest in how the cultures of the world could be arranged hierarchically to a Boasian interest in how to explore most accurately the differences among them. Likewise, the discipline of psychology shifted from an interest in the biological evolution of mind to an interest in the impact of immediate social and behavioral contexts. Both fields became more descriptive and less prescriptive, more utilitarian and less theoretical, and more presentist and less genetic and linear. But most significantly, both fields became more interactionist. That is, they became less concerned with "essences" as deducted from the history of the thing and more interested in the nature of the immediate interactions among things of the present. Dewey, who in 1903 insisted that "the historical method is invading the business of education and is likely to be one of the most fundamental forces in directing its immediate future," by 1917 concluded that "the historic method . . . does not show man how his mind is to take part in giving these changes one direction rather than another."[54] As I have shown, Dewey was as much a driver of as a passenger in this paradigm shift. Despite the significance of these external influences, internal factors were significant as well. When confronted with his "infinite pluralism" by Scudder Klyce, Dewey embraced the term and began to employ the concept in subtle ways in his works. When corresponding with and about Franz Boas and William I. Thomas, Dewey recognized the innovative aspects of their sociological-anthropological ideas and how they supported his interactionist, pluralist view.

Chapter 7

THE ENVIRONMENT IS MANY, NOT ONE

THE INTELLECTUAL AND SOCIAL world after the First World War was fundamentally different from the one before it. In light of these changes Dewey reevaluated and expanded his earlier views. The horrific and senseless violence of the First World War undermined the optimistic view that Euro-American culture was necessarily evolving toward a more enlightened, advanced future. Social scientists no longer believed that history was itself the driving force of progress. This underscored the divergence of social scientists and historians that had been taking place for nearly 2 decades. In particular, younger social scientists viewed the historicist theories that had formerly occupied the disciplines as too metaphysical and imprecise. Instead, they gravitated toward more measurable theories of social control, turning the field in a more quantitative, positivistic, and presentist direction. In this context, the Stanford-Binet intelligence test, which was first used for sorting purposes during the war, offered a promising alternative to the qualitative racial and historicist theories of the previous generation. Under the guise of scientific objectivity, the culturally neutral idea of "intelligence" rationalized racial inequalities, at a time when Franz Boas's cultural anthropology was emerging as an alternative to evolutionary anthropology.[1] The popularity of intelligence testing promised to usher in scientific rationality to the classroom by sorting students into their predetermined social roles, which were based "objectively" on intelligence and not on race. In other words, many social scientists simply switched out one form of scientific-based racism for another. Yet cracks were forming in the intellectual foundations of racism, and many were following Dewey's lead in questioning the innate inferiority of any groups.

In particular, the year 1924 marked a significant turning point in the history of American education and intellectual culture regarding race. The passage of the Immigration Restriction Act slowed the influx of foreigners onto American shores to a trickle. However, the children of the earlier waves of immigrants were entering the school system in greater numbers, and as Dewey had predicted, policy makers debated how to best approach these students. On the one hand, some argued that the cultural differences of these students should be celebrated. The idea of cultural pluralism found an influential following as many of the students of Dewey and Boas espoused the celebration of cultural difference. For example, in 1924 Horace Kallen first published the term *cultural pluralism* in his book *Culture and Democracy in the United States*. That same year Bruno Lasker demonstrated in his groundbreaking book *Race Attitudes in Children* how racial stereotypes were socially learned, not biologically inherited, as many had believed. The ascendancy of behavioral psychology provided additional support for the significance of social environment on racial attitudes. As John Watson boasted in *Behaviorism*, also published in 1924, "Give me a dozen healthy infants, well-formed, and my own specified world to bring them up in and I'll guarantee to take any one at random and train him to become any type of specialist I might select—doctor, lawyer, artist, merchant-chief, and yes, even a beggar man and thief, regardless of his talents, penchants, tendencies, abilities, vocations, and race of his ancestors."[2] Thus Watson insisted that hereditary instincts and impulses were not at all deterministic; conditioning and environment could explain everything. Kallen, Lasker, and Watson's studies deemphasized the biological aspects of race and racism and cast prejudice as irrational and socially learned. This opened the door for a more pluralist approach to race and culture.

Taken together, these studies demonstrated that the cultural contents of mind were linked directly to its immediate environment, and, therefore, racial prejudice was something that was learned, not innate. That is, racial prejudice was historically contingent, socially acquired, and environmentally conditioned. Drawing on Kallen and Watson's research, Rachel DuBois launched a successful educational program aimed at recognizing the cultural gifts of the recently arrived immigrant groups.[3] Thus Dewey's arguments about the plasticity of the human mind turned out to be prophetic and influential to a generation of social scientists and educators. Even though Dewey disagreed with the epistemological assumptions of mechanistic behaviorism, the approach reinforced his ideas about the importance of environment on the development of racial attitudes and culture. However, unlike Watson and his followers, Dewey never abandoned inherited impulse as a factor in the formation of culture. For Dewey, all knowledge originated with inherited impulses and native activities. But in Dewey's new interactional, pluralistic vision the mind actively shaped this impulse through a plurality of possibilities to forge temporary alliances with the pluralistic, socially mediated environment. This new concern was reflected in his book *Human Nature and Conduct*.

HUMAN NATURE AND CONDUCT

Human Nature and Conduct was published in 1922 and grew out a set of lectures Dewey delivered at Stanford University in 1918 before he departed for Japan and China. The most striking thing about the text is not what it argues, but instead what it does not. The book does not make a single reference to the psychological stages of growth that played such a central role in his early and middle works. However, as I will show, the book did make several explicit references to his linear historicism, and Dewey still regarded impulse as a central component of his philosophy. Primarily concerned with the social nature of morality, *Human Nature and Conduct* reflected Dewey's post-1916 concern with the lateral, pluralistic, and interactional reconstruction of experience as and while it was being experienced. Although this new concern did not necessarily contradict his earlier interests in the historic social occupations of man and the emerging instincts of the child, it placed more emphasis on the present and made greater use of social psychology. In fact, the subtitle of the book was *An Introduction to Social Psychology,* and the general objective of the book was to outline the significance of social environment in shaping conduct, without dismissing the significance of human nature altogether. The primary focus, Dewey explained in the preface, was on the "interaction of biological aptitudes with a social environment."[4] He was also trying to forge a middle path between the behavioral psychology of Thorndike and Watson and the psychoanalysis of Sigmund Freud, whose work had grown in popularity among some American psychologists. Dewey even employed some Freudian language such as *sublimation* and *suppression* in his discussion.

Drawing on the language of linear historicism, in *Human Nature and Conduct* Dewey again referred to the significance of a civilized social environment for democratic living. Accordingly, he outlined the deficiency of savage and barbarian cultures. "A savage can travel after a fashion in a jungle," Dewey explained in what seemed to be direct reference to contemporaneous African and aboriginal populations, "[but] civilized activity is too complex to be carried on without smoothed roads." Dewey's distain for the superstitions of savage groups was clear. While the savage's belief in magic "may be natural and spontaneous, it is not innocent. It obstructs intelligent study of operative conditions and wastes human desire and effort in futilities." But at the same time Dewey was careful not to dismiss the savage outright because his ethical theory relied heavily on the incorporation of the moral innovations of previous social groups. "Even a savage custom may be reasonable in that it is adapted to social needs and uses," Dewey explained. He even suggested that civilization is "only skin deep" and "a savage persists beneath the clothes of a civilized man." But these savage customs were inadequate for the scientific world, because modern institutions demanded a more complicated approach. These modern institutions, he continued, "reconstruct. . . . They open up new avenues of endeavor and impose new labors. In short, they are civilization, culture, morality." At the end of a chapter on the plasticity of impulse, Dewey outlined his view of the savage clearly and succinctly. Some view "the savage as a wild man," while others "view savages as bondsman of custom . . . governed by many inflexible tribal habitudes in conduct and ideas." Dewey's own position lay in a combination of these two conceptions. "Strict conformity and unrestrained wildness intensify each other," he insisted. "Within civilization, the savage still exists. He is known in his degree by oscillation between loose indulgence and stiff habit." That is, both habit and inhibition created savagery because both forms did not incorporate the social mediations of the present in a manner that led to growth toward a more inclusive, socialized experience. For Dewey, the savage and civilized man both experienced the same impulses, but the civilized man drew upon his social environment to translate these impulses into civilized habits. Dewey explained exactly how this process took place. There were three ways an impulse could be satisfied. It could find "surging, explosive discharge"; it could be sublimated, "that is, become a factor coordinated intelligently with others in a continuing course of action"; or it could be "suppressed." The first and third reactions were the signs of "immaturity, crudity, savagery," but the second was the sign of civilization. Thus interaction of impulse with a culturally mediated environment was the central mode of education and growth.[5]

Pluralistic interaction was a central concern of *Human Nature and Conduct*, and his discussion of the concept represented the most original ideas he presented in the book. "The problem of social psychology is not how either the individual or collective mind forms social groups and customs," Dewey argued, "but how different customs, established interacting arrangements, form and nurture different minds." Dewey was pointing to the limitations of both the individual approach of behavioral psychology and the sociological group approach of Tarde's imitation-suggestion theory. Neither approach focused adequately on the interaction among instinct, environment, and culture. Because the native stock of instincts "is practically the same everywhere," Dewey insisted, the native differences between cultures had been exaggerated. Dewey listed the Patagonians, Greeks, Sioux Indians, Hindus, Bushmen, and Chinese as evidence of the strength of acquired habits, "not the growth of customs in terms of instincts." In a rare instance, Dewey specified some of the acquired habits (some might say, stereotypes) of different cultural groups:

The wholesale human sacrifices of Peru and the tenderness of St. Francis, . . . the practice of Suttee and the cult of the Virgin, the war and peace dances of the Comanches and the parliamentary institutions of the British, the communism of the southsea islander and the propriety and thrift of the Yankee, the magic of the medicine man and the experiments of the chemist in his laboratory, the non-resistance of Chinese and the aggressive militarism of an imperial Prussia; . . . the countless diversity of habits suggested by such a random list springs from practically the same capital stock of native instincts.[6]

Dewey argued—in a statement that perhaps summarized the entire book—that "the thing we need to know is how native stock has been modified by interaction with different environments." The importance of interaction had led anthropologists to study and appreciate the centrality of primitive man as a component of "progress and reform."[7] Cultural interaction guided how native tendencies and impulses were turned into habits.

Another important contribution of *Human Nature and Conduct* was Dewey's discussion of *deliberation*. By deliberation, Dewey did not mean discussion among several individuals but rather the analogous process wherein the individual discussed and explored competing options within his or her own mind. Deliberation, he explained, was a "tentative trying out of various courses of action. . . . It flies toward and settles upon objective situations not upon feelings." Deliberations were sparked by "confusion and uncertainty in present activities." At first glance, it is not clear how Dewey's notion of deliberation differed from the generic steps of reflective thinking outlined in *How We Think*. But if we view his discussion of deliberation in the broader context of his genetic psychology, then we can see that deliberation was the highest stage of reflective thinking. It addressed the construction of new knowledge, not merely the rediscovery of existing knowledge. "The action of deliberation . . . consists in selecting some unforeseen consequence to serve as a stimulus to present action," he explained. "It brings future possibilities into the present scene and thereby frees and expands present tendencies." Dewey's emphasis on the knowledge and situation of the present reflected his newfound interest in the plurality of immediate experience. But this process assumed a mastery of the linear knowledge of the past.[8] For those at the highest level of consciousness, who were at the vanguard of knowledge construction in their own life and in the history of the race, it was deliberation, not merely reflective thinking, that guided their actions and experience. Modern men and women engaged in deliberation. In contrast, savages merely engaged in a primitive form of reflective thinking.

Deliberation grew out of pluralistic interaction, and Dewey portrayed interaction as a critical component of his infinite pluralism. "We are not caught in a circle; we traverse a spiral in which social customs generate some consciousness of interdependencies, and this consciousness is embodied in acts which in improving the environment generate new perceptions of social ties, and so on for forever," he explained. "The interactions are forever there as fact, but they acquire meaning only in the desires, judgments, and purposes they awaken." That is, the constant recombination of individuals with different experiences and ideas interacting with one another led to continual reflection, deliberation, and growth. Dewey quoted William James at several significant points in the book, and so James's idea of an active mind seeking and creating meaning in a pluralistic universe provided a foundation for Dewey's investigation of exactly how this took place. "The formation of habits of belief, desire, and judgment is going on at every instant under the influence of the conditions set by men's contact, intercourse, and associations with one another," he argued in his concluding chapter. "This is the fundamental fact in social life and in personal character."[9] This passage reflected Dewey's concern with present experience and with how imagination was employed to envision and generate the new knowledge of the future. Experiment came after and grew out of imagination; judgment grew out of experience.

In summary, Dewey's new vision was messier and less linear than the historicist scheme he had outlined prior to the First World War. Dewey now argued that the knowledge of higher cultures was not inherently better than that of the past, but rather it simply better met the needs of its own context and conditions. Once students had reached the fourth stage of the "consciousness of calling"—that is, the stage of science, democracy, and associated living—then they were ready to forge new knowledge as adults by contributing to the discourse of the present. As Dewey explained in *Human Nature and Conduct,* knowledge represented "adjustment *of* the environment, not merely *to* it [italics in the original]." For Dewey, however, the environment was not fixed; instead the "the environment is many, not one; hence will, disposition, is plural."[10] Adopting the cognitive pluralism of James, Dewey focused his attention on the pluralistic construction of experience in the present. His new approach was both a critique of mechanistic behaviorism and an elaboration of the significance of environment on the formation of the individual and social dispositions.

DEMOCRATIC EDUCATION ABROAD

In striking contrast to the esoteric and highly theoretical discussions in *Human Nature and Conduct,* in 1924 Dewey wrote perhaps his most practical work on education, "Report and Recommendation upon Turkish Education." Invited by the Minister of Public Instruction of Turkey, Dewey spent 2 mon, hs touring the nation and issued a specific set of prescriptions for establishing a national education system for the emerging democracy. Dewey's vision for Turkey was comprehensive and ambitious. Although there were no new ideas in the work, he expressed his educational ideas clearly, candidly, and free of philosophical jargon. In addition, he demonstrated a newfound respect for local conditions and for encouraging a plurality of educational approaches to meet these conditions. His ambitious goal for the nation was "the development of Turkey as a vital, free, independent, and lay republic in the full membership of civilized states." To move from an earlier to a later stage of social development, Dewey insisted, the Turkish citizens must "develop traits and dispositions of character, intellectual and moral, which fit men and women for self-government, economic self-support and industrial progress." Dewey outlined specifically what democratic traits he had in mind, "namely, initiative and inventiveness, independence of judgment, ability to think scientifically and to cooperate for common purposes socially."[11] With the development of these traits the benefits of learning would be spread to all Turkish citizens, not just its intellectual and ruling classes.

Drawing on his idea of the school as a social center, Dewey's vision for the Turkish school was tied closely to local needs and conditions. He insisted that Turkish health centers be coordinated with educational development because the two were closely related. In addition, the importance of extra-curricular activities for students needed to be emphasized so that "youth who do not attend school are brought into games and sports and instructed therein" and so that "material reaches their parents and the members of the community in which the school is located."[12] In addition to health centers and libraries, he recommended the construction of local playgrounds and the facilitation of outdoor sports.

Dewey insisted that the Turkish teachers and administrators learn from the experiences of others, and so the first thing he recommended for the Ministry of Public Instruction was that it translate educational literature and research from other nations and make the circulation of these materials a priority. In accordance with the social center idea, Dewey emphasized the importance of a flexible educational system that could adapt to local conditions and economies. He warned the Ministry against producing "too uniform a system of education, not flexibly adapted to the varying needs of different localities, urban, rural, maritime, and to different types of rural communities, different environments and different industries, such as pastoral, grain-growing, cotton, fruit, etc." He insisted that the central ministry not only allow for diversification, "but promote it, and even insist on it." Dewey's allegiance to democratic pluralism was on full display. "The central Ministry should stand for unity, but against uniformity and in favor of diversity," he explained. "Only by diversification of materials can schools be adapted to local conditions and needs and the interests of different localities be enlisted." Accordingly, Dewey recommended that the teaching of Turkish history and geography should be connected with local conditions and histories, just like his teachers at the University of Chicago laboratory school had done by designing their curriculum around the development of the city of Chicago. In the section on elementary schools Dewey even suggested that "in parts of the country where parents hesitate to send their children at certain periods of the year because their labor is needed on the farm, the dates of the opening and closing the schools could be so fixed as to hold the children for the leisure time." In the elementary schools, Dewey explained, the curriculum should be agricultural or industrial "according to the customs of the locality." Dewey emphasized flexibility in pedagogical approach, curriculum, and scheduling in order to bring the disparate parts of the county under a single system.[13]

Dewey also expressed his discontent with the specialization of teachers and the resulting balkanization of the curriculum. This problem was not unique to Turkey; it was also true of Europe and the United States. He complained that the subdivision of subjects led to the arbitrary isolation of each subject from one another and its isolation from actual life. He also found it inefficient for teachers to travel from school to school teaching their specific subject expertise instead of teaching multiple subjects in a single school. "The great weakness of almost all schools, a weakness not confined in any sense to Turkey," he concluded "is the separation of school studies from the actual life of children and the conditions and opportunities of the environment." To remedy some of these problems, Dewey insisted on the adequate training of Turkish teachers at normal schools by offering courses specifically in pedagogy and also by allowing them paid sabbaticals to travel abroad to Europe and America to study other teachers and schools in democracies. He emphasized the importance of attracting and retaining teachers with adequate pay. He bluntly remarked that effective teachers will not be attracted "upon starvation wages." He also pointed out the importance of having teachers live close to the schools in which they taught, so they could foster relationships with the community and appreciate the specific needs of each locality.[14]

Compared with his cultural analysis of China, Dewey's assessment of Turkey was far more assured for a number of reasons. First, Dewey was specifically invited to tour the country for the sole reason of issuing recommendations for the reforming nation. Dewey's trip to China, on the other hand, was conducted mostly through universities, not through the Chinese government. Second, unlike China, Turkey itself was embarking on an explicit effort to modernize and secularize its country after a major military defeat. Third,

Dewey seemed to be less concerned that Turkey's history and culture would serve as a barrier to change because it already had a recent history of reform. As a result, Dewey's recommendations for Turkey were frank, specific, and intended to have an immediate impact. However, Dewey did not comment on whether or not he thought his ideas would ever actually be implemented. Others had a more pessimistic view. For example, the U.S. Ambassador to Turkey commented in a letter to his superior that Dewey was "leaving with a rather pessimistic view of the future of education in Turkey." The ambassador commented that the Turkish Minister of Education was incompetent, autocratic, and not interested in taking the advice of the American advisor who "was foisted upon him by his predecessor." The ambassador concluded that the effects of Dewey's visit would be "nil."[15] However, there is evidence to suggest that Dewey's visit to Turkey made some impact. In 1926 a Turkish educator on the Council of Education, Avni Basman, wrote Dewey informing him that they had put together a syllabus for elementary schools based on two Deweyan principles: first, "three grades studies are unified in a topic which is named 'life-knowledge' (Lebenskunde) including nature study, home geography and history, in other terms, the study of the relations of child to his natural and social environment," and second, "the subject matter is divided into project units which are to be rearranged and modified according to the requirements of the localities of schools in which they are to be worked out."[16] Basman was enthusiastic about the syllabus and hoped that the experiment would be used as a basis for reform across the entire nation. In addition, a few years later Dewey's *Democracy and Education* was translated into Turkish.

In a letter to his children Dewey made a few superficial comparisons between Turkey and China, remarking on the cooler nights in Turkey and availability of melons and tea in both nations. However, he made few comments on the character and characteristics of the Turkish people. Dewey published four essays in the *New Republic* while in Turkey, which mostly addressed specific political issues. Just as with China, Dewey expressed his respect for the people and specific history and culture of Turkey, but still conceptualized its culture in terms of deficiency along a single continuum of development. "Any marked change in the present regime of Turkey, other than its own natural evolution, would be a calamity from the standpoint of all those who have philanthropic and educational interest in the country," he insisted. "For it would signify an arrest of a movement which is in the direction of progress and light."[17] Dewey's language of "arrest," "progress," and "evolution" toward "light" reveal his historicist view of culture as taking place along a single, linear path toward democracy. But his appreciation for the specific context and history of Turkey also demonstrate his recent respect for pluralistic interaction. Putting these ideas side by side led to a paradox, which he specifically recognized as such. Turkey's leaders, Dewey wrote, "wish that Turkey be Europeanized in their own way and for their own benefit . . . an incredible paradox, of which the mingling of old and new in [Turkey] is but a symbol."[18] The paradoxical nature of Turkey trying to emulate European ways yet doing so in a way that preserved the nation's culture and history fascinated Dewey. Since he conceived of culture in transnational terms, Dewey tolerated and encouraged the different approaches to modernization, but was a harsh critic of those ideas he thought were barriers of progress and growth. But how did Dewey determine what was a barrier and what was a mere cultural adaptation? He never fully explored this issue because, conveniently, Dewey's culture also happened to be White, Western, and European. In other words, unlike W.E.B. Du Bois, Dewey never had to experience the "double-consciousness" of being part of a culture that Western civilization had allegedly left behind. Dewey's former student, Hu Shih, however, discussed this very paradox in a letter to Dewey in 1926, which touched on many of the themes Dewey considered in Turkey

Dr. Hu had studied philosophy under Dewey at Columbia University and then taught at Peking National University in China. He had played a major role in arranging Dewey's lecture tour in China in 1920–21. Dr. Hu's philosophical work considered how to adapt and assimilate new, Western ideas—which inevitably led to a better, more enlightened life—while at the same time respecting the cultural uniqueness and contributions of his own Chinese culture. This was the very dilemma with which W.E.B. Du Bois had struggled in *The Souls of Black Folk*. How does a non-White scholar navigate and reconcile a "double-consciousness" in a world in which White, Western values represented the state of the art, but at the same time found little use for the ideals and values of the non-Western culture? Both Hu and Du Bois had studied with and appreciated the best that Western culture had to offer, but both of these scholars had to explain these ideas to non-White audiences—something Dewey rarely had to do.

In the letter to Dewey, Dr. Hu related a story about a speech he had recently delivered in which he expressed his disappointment that "China never came into a real understanding and appreciation of the modern world and its civilization," and argued that China needed to rationalize its beliefs and ideas to "humanize and socialize our institutions." After delivering the speech, Hu was approached by a "Hindoo" student who asked why he was denigrating his own culture and venerating Western civilization. As a modernist, Hu saw no value in premodern ways. As a result, he dismissed the Hindu student as backward and conceited. He used the opportunity to reflect on the arrogance of his own people and the unwarranted faith in their own non-Western cultures. "You are quite right in saying," he explained, paraphrasing Dewey, "that 'the Indians of position always gives one the impression of an element of pose' . . . what you called the 'peculiar Oriental point of view of deeper wisdom.'" Hu then elaborated in the margin: "The same psychology explains what you see in China, Mexico and Turkey." That is, Hu seemed to have solved the paradox of double-consciousness by denying that there was a paradox at all. Western culture was indeed more developed and superior to the Oriental ones. "It has taken me some time to completely get rid of this stage of 'orientalism,'" Hu explained to Dewey as if orientalism was a disease. However, having overcome these initial limitations, he discovered how Western civilization was "highly capable of satisfying the spiritual demands of mankind while at the same time ministering to its material needs." Hu created a pragmatic philosophy that applied the rational, scientific thinking of the Western world but also incorporated the spiritual aspect of his own Chinese culture. However, Hu also pointed out to Dewey the "lack of a consciously critical philosophy on the part of the Western world of its own civilization." Hu explained how he resented those Westerners who looked to the East to provide a spiritual aspect of philosophy that they lacked because they failed to recognize the spiritual potential of Western science and civilization.[19]

Hu argued that science, if properly conceived, could liberate the mind of both Chinese and Western cultures. "So you see, my dear professor," Hu concluded to Dewey, "I have become more Western than most of the Westerners!"[20] That is, by approaching Western culture from outside of its cultural tradition and then following its implications to their logical conclusion, Hu argued, he had appreciated the full potential of what civilization had to offer. Like Dewey, Hu conceived of culture in transnational terms, and, also like Dewey, he believed that the entire world could be placed upon a single continuum of development. Hu concluded that provincial Westernization and "orientalism" were both prior stages toward a more enlightened transnational future. Thus Hu resolved his double-consciousness by casting both Western and Eastern cultures in linear historicist terms and constructing a new definition of culture that moved beyond them both.

In conclusion, Dewey's trip to Turkey created much less cognitive dissonance than his trip to China and Japan had. This was likely because during his visit to Turkey Dewey was specifically cast as a Western authority and educational expert, not as a mere visitor and observer like he was in China and Japan. But this was also because he was better equipped to deal with the Turkish culture. Dewey's revised philosophy involved a greater appreciation for pluralism and the contextual, interactional nature of knowledge application. Therefore, Dewey began to conceive of education in more international terms, which, ironically, provided him with confidence in the universal applicability of his ideas while at the same allowing him to gain greater respect for local contexts and cultures. However, unlike Dr. Hu, Dewey never struggled with how to reconcile a premodern culture with a modernizing one that considered premodern culture as deficient. Dewey never had to reconcile this paradox because he happened to be part of the transnational, interracial modern world of science and progress. Dewey did not experience double-consciousness because he happened to be White and European, the culture that happened to be the most "advanced." Turkey, Dewey concluded, simply needed to become more like the West, but, paradoxically, it needed to do so on its own terms.

DEWEY REVISITS HIS EDUCATIONAL PHILOSOPHY

In *Human Nature and Conduct* Dewey identified the overtly political implications of a democratic education, something he had failed to do in his earlier works, even *Democracy and Education.* "To say that the welfare of others, like our own, consists in a widening and deepening of the perceptions that give activity its meaning, in an educative growth," he explained "is to set forth a proposition of political import."[21] That is, by believing that education had the power to transform not only the individual but also society, educators were political whether they wanted to be or not. Envisioning and working toward a better future was a political act. Prior to the First World War Dewey had mostly steered clear of political stances. There were, of course, political implications to his positions on vocational education and cultural pluralism, but he rarely took explicit political stands. However, after the war he took clear public positions against the American inclusion in the League of Nations because of its exclusion of Germany and Russia, and he offered enthusiastic support for the unsuccessful international legal movement to outlaw war. In addition, in 1924 he supported the Progressive Party candidate for president, Robert La Follette. This new focus on political issues inspired him to revaluate his own view on the place of social issues and politics in the public school curriculum.

While at the University of Chicago, Dewey identified the significance of history and geography throughout his writings on education and, as I have shown, history played a central role in organizing the curriculum at his laboratory school. *Democracy and Education* had separate chapters specifically on the significance of history and geography, in which he outlined how these subjects fit into his broader genetic and linear historicist schemes. However, prior to the war Dewey never mentioned anything about addressing political issues or current events in the classroom. In fact, Dewey's failure to endorse current events in the classroom prior to 1923 put him somewhat at odds with the proponents of the social studies.

The social studies as a coherent educational reform movement began with the publication of the report of the Committee on Social Studies in 1916. The report cited Dewey's work repeatedly in justification of the new scope and sequence of history and social sciences courses it recommended. While Dewey had no direct relationship to that committee (or to the larger Commission on the Reorganization of Secondary Education of which it was a part), his colleague and friend James Harvey Robinson was an influential member of the social studies group. One major suggestion that the committee issued was the creation of an interdisciplinary senior capstone course called "Problems of Democracy." As its title suggested, the class was designed to center on enduring public issues and current events, topics Dewey had never explicitly endorsed. However, in a significant but overlooked essay Dewey published in 1923, "The School as a Means of Developing a Social Consciousness and Social Ideals in Children," Dewey fundamentally revised his views on how to teach history, geography, and social studies in relation to citizenship. In particular, he seemed to have finally thrown his weight behind the social studies movement by outlining the significance of addressing current events and politics in the classroom.

In the essay Dewey recognized that social and educational conditions had changed. He praised schools for the excellent work they had done in "uniting and bringing together the exceedingly heterogeneous elements of our population," specifically, for "bringing children of different religions, of different traditions, of different races, and of different languages together, and for a certain number of hours a day having them in contact with each other in common play, study and work." As result of such schooling, Dewey asserted, children of different ethnic and religious backgrounds had "grown more like each other." However, Dewey was dismayed by what he saw as growing intolerance in recent years. In a rare recognition of the overt racism of the South, Dewey denounced the "racial intolerance" of the Ku Klux Klan. However, he did not see this as a specific symptom of the social and economic conditions of the South, but rather as a broader "spirit of suspicion and fear" that was gripping the entire nation. In a distasteful metaphor considering that the KKK were torturing and murdering African Americans in the South, Dewey charged many writers of having "put on a kind of intellectual and moral white robe and hood to conceal their purposes" like the KKK. In accordance with his essay on race prejudice a year earlier, Dewey attributed this suspicion to an impulse that transcended race and religion. "It is not at all a racial and religious matter," he insisted, but rather the suspicion of other was a "desire, an intellectual desire, to find out what other people are thinking and believing." Dewey attributed racism to a lack of social development, or a failure to achieve "the international phase of social consciousness." [22]

To combat this suspicion, intolerance, and distrust, Dewey proposed two specific educational objectives. First, he argued that students would need to develop an "interracial and international" mind based in "international friendship, amity and good will." In an apparent endorsement of Rachel DuBois's cultural gifts educational program, Dewey argued that we "need a curriculum in history, literature and geography which will make the different racial elements in this country aware of what each has contributed and will create a mental attitude toward other people which will make it more difficult for the flames of hatred and suspicion to sweep over this country." Second, Dewey suggested that social class divisions and conflicts be discussed openly with students. Overall, he insisted, "our instruction in history and geography and our social studies [the first time Dewey used the term *social studies*] in general should be intellectually more honest, they should bring students into gradual contact with the actual realties of contemporary life." The students at the Dewey School had studied the social conditions of the present in a broad sense, but they had not studied current events or specific social conditions. Dewey was now stating that students should indeed study the present.[23]

As Dewey explained in another essay published that year, there were three things that American public schools should explicitly address to prepare them for the postwar interracial and international phase of social consciousness. To be "good citizens in the broadest sense," Dewey explained, politics should be addressed directly in the classroom and teachers should have the courage to do so. "The political aspect is an important one, and one that is increasingly important for the public schools of the country to emphasize." He implored teachers to move beyond the mere mechanics of how government worked and address the specifics of the larger social problems facing the nation. Dewey recognized that there would be resistance to evaluating American society critically with students, but, he insisted, teachers were not taking on their full responsibility if they failed to do so. Teachers should not take sides on political and social issues, but rather they should provide a forum in which the facts could be explored and considered. He even suggested that teachers would gain greater respect in their local communities if they became more engaged with the social realties surrounding them. "We need to develop in the coming generation a much more discriminating judgment about political problems and plans," he reasoned, "if our public schools are going to train our people so that they will really make our democratic experiment a complete and adequate success." The second aim of schools, Dewey explained, was to provide students with the skills to enter the American workforce in ways that they found fulfilling. As Dewey had explained at length in previous works, the schools should approach all subject matter as vocational because this would organically combine traditional and industrial subject matter into a single course of study that would equip all students, regardless of class or projected occupation, with the intellectual tools to socialize to, as well as critically evaluate, the social world. "To take people on the basis of class divisions," Dewey reiterated, "is against the democratic idea of society." Dewey's third aim was to educate students to make better use of their leisure time. Sounding a bit cantankerous (he was 64), Dewey complained that "too many people of the community, especially the young people, are concerned with having a 'good time.'" Instead, Dewey stated, "Students should be educated to appreciate higher forms [of entertainment]." If schools explicitly addressed these three aims, Dewey concluded, then they would succeed in meeting the social purposes of schools.[24]

Dewey's new emphasis on specific current events and issues was a logical outgrowth of the sense that he and many intellectuals had after the First World War that Americans had been duped into supporting the war effort. Many believed that had the U.S. citizens been more informed, reflective, and critical about entering the alleged "war to end all wars," then they could have approached the conflict and its aftermath with greater insight and reserve. Perhaps no text captured the tension between an increasingly complex world and an apathetic and ignorant citizenry than journalist Walter Lippman's *Public Opinion*. Lippman's provocative book argued that most Americans did not have the knowledge or inclination to distinguish the comprehensive and objective facts from subjective opinions. As result, the American citizenry largely made their political decisions based on limited knowledge, stereotypes, short-term irrationalism, and emotion. To remedy the issue, Lippman argued that experts should be organized to collect objective data and provide it for administrators and executives. Guided by science, these experts would rise above the subjectivity and irrationalism of local and emotional politics. Lippman's emphasis on the expert over the average citizen struck many as undemocratic, but his view was fully in line with progressive administrative thought.

Dewey had great respect for Lippman and was somewhat sympathetic to his argument. However, Dewey clung to his belief in democratic means and reiterated his faith in education as a means of creating an informed, responsible citizenry. "The enlightenment of public opinion still seems to have priority over the enlightenment of officials and directors," Dewey rebutted in a review of Lippman's book. "Democracy demands a more thoroughgoing education than the education of officials, administrators, and directors of industry." Dewey believed that the citizenry should be made aware of the objective facts, particularly in relating news events "to a continuing study and record of underlying conditions." True democracy was extremely difficult, Dewey admitted, because "this fundamental general education is at once so necessary and so difficult of achievement"[25] What Dewey learned from Lippman and the aftermath of the First World War was that learning the long-term social-industrial history of the race was indeed significant, but that these trends needed to be linked explicitly with present issues and events. This essentially was the position of social studies educators like Harold Rugg, who had broken ranks with many professional historians over the role of chronological history in the schools. While not exactly endorsing the theme-based or issue-based approach to social studies instruction professed by Rugg, Dewey nevertheless threw his support behind a progressive curriculum that celebrated cultural difference and explicitly examined contemporary political events. This constituted a significant addition, if not revision, to his earlier writings on education.

EDUCATION AND INDIVIDUALITY
IN A NEW ENVIRONMENT

Prior to the First World War Dewey had written extensively against the dual system of education, in which separate academic and industrial educational tracks would be created and maintained. Since the war a new threat to democracy had emerged: intelligence testing. Just as he had done with vocational education, Dewey did not denounce the movement outright, but rather evaluated it in light of the broader goals of democratic education. He approved of the use of IQ tests for "intimate and intensive inquiry into individualized abilities and disabilities," but was opposed to applying them at large and making broad generalizations about the entire student population. He accepted that certain individuals were superior and inferior in certain contexts and domains, but denied that an overall intelligence existed. He viewed intelligence testing as part of the larger utilitarian approach to education proposed by David Snedden and his followers: "The movement is on a par with the movements to make instruction more efficient while retaining that notion of teaching which emphasizes the receptively docile mind instead of an inquiring and pioneering purpose." Intelligence, Dewey argued, was not innate and fixed. Rather, it was "an acquired matter, due to opportunity and experience." He concluded by explaining, "The most limited member of the populace has potentialities which do not now reveal themselves and which will not reveal themselves till we convert education by and for mediocrity into an education by and for individuality."[26]

For Dewey, the issue of intellectual superiority and inferiority was fundamentally philosophical because the idea of innate intelligence aligned with the outdated idea that he had been attacking for 30 years—namely, that things, peoples, and races had predetermined essences and/or static potentials. Instead, success was an outcome of interactions with social contexts that allowed the individual to achieve his or her potentials. "At present superior races are superior because of their own conspicuous achievements," he insisted, not because of an innate, hereditary, and/or genetic advantage that destined them to greatness. In fact, Dewey bluntly asserted, "The idea of abstract, universal superiority and inferiority is an absurdity." Although useful in some situations, all intelligence tests did was arbitrarily determine a set of acquired traits deemed useful by those in power and then identify the individuals who, largely through forces out of their control, already possessed those traits. Intelligence testing reinforced misguided ideas of predetermined superiority, mediocrity, and inferiority, and it also ignored the significance of educational process, context, contingency, and growth. More sinister, Dewey alleged, intelligence testing was a way to reinforce social inequalities by denying certain individuals the opportunity to fulfill their potentials and express their creativities. This was undemocratic: "Democracy will not be democracy until education makes it its chief concern to release distinctive aptitudes in art, thought and companionship." Dewey called for an education that valued qualitative diversity and the fostering of individual strengths and talents.[27] In other words, he argued on behalf of cultural plurality.

However, Dewey was not merely endorsing indulgence and self-fulfillment as the only objectives of education. Often accused of placing too much emphasis on the expression of the individual by allowing the student to essentially run wild, Dewey outlined specifically what he meant by individual freedom in education in a 1922 essay, "Individuality in Education." This essay marked another important turning point for Dewey, because it represented the first time he began to respond to his critics and correct some of the progressive educators who implemented misguided reforms in his name. "Trying to stand for freedom in dealing with teaching," Dewey complained, "I have found that I have been considered by many as upholding the doctrine 'that children should do exactly as they please.'" Dewey sought to clarify three specific shortcomings of the excessive emphasis on individuality. First was the undue emphasis on "bumptiousness, conceit, or self-assertion." Students were using individuality as a means of asserting themselves through unnecessary argumentation or knee-jerk contrarianism. Instead, Dewey suggested that multiple methods and approaches should be tolerated, but they should all ultimately arrive at the same answer. "Individuality really means a certain originality of method." Second, he objected to the excessive attention to physical freedom at the expense of intellectual freedom. The student should not be permitted to run wild and at random; rather, "he has to have enough physical activity to see that his ideas are made definite and precise." Finally, Dewey objected to Madame Montessori's emphasis on social isolation. Montessori was an Italian educator who believed that children learned best through spontaneous self-development. In contrast, Dewey believed that learning was social and so students must be taught to cooperate and engage in educational activities collectively. Dewey insisted, "The more you have real social unity the more diversity, the more division of labor, and the more differentiation of operations there is."[28]

In summary, Dewey continued to define education as primarily a social endeavor. But he also began to clarify his position on the significance of individuality because Dewey's new pluralistic approach emphasized that individual expressions were necessary to diversify the social environment. Only then could progress and growth take place. As a result, he opposed sorting students based on intelligence tests because such a practice denied them the opportunity to actualize their individual potential. By being tracked into a particular path, students would be deprived of many possible social and cultural interactions. On the other end of the spectrum, excessive physical freedom and self-expression would not allow students to realize their potential either. This was because students' self-actualization required their subordination of the social environment by learning to engage in socially meaningful activity. Therefore, self-fulfillment required others. Teachers could only fulfill the full potential of the individual by allowing the greatest number of social interactions in a pluralistic, democratic environment. Intelligence testing and self-indulgence greatly narrowed the number of potential interactions and were therefore undemocratic. In addition, an understanding of the current social conditions was a prerequisite for Dewey's form of social intelligence. For this reason, his post-1922 pedagogy placed more emphasis on the study of current events and issues. His new emphasis on present and immediate conditions reflected, or even incorporated, the approach of most social scientists of the period. Dewey's pluralistic interactionalism allowed him to both adapt his approach to multiple conditions and contexts and also continue to emphasize the expression and fulfillment of the individual.

TRUE TO HIS OWN PHILOSOPHY, by 1924 Dewey had reconstructed his owns views on evolution, race, culture, and education to meet the needs of a changing world. The emphasis of his newer ideas—pluralism and interaction—did not immediately replace the old ones—ethnocentrism, genetic psychology, linear historicism. Rather, they coexisted, each appearing in slightly different forms depending on its interaction with the particular problems and particular contexts that brought them forth. He retained his historicism and the significance of mental development, but the exact sequence of the stages of growth became less important and the social means of making the most of the present educational environment became more significant. There were no sudden ruptures or revelations in his intellectual career. Growth was gradual. New ideas organically emerged out of old ones. Problems were never fully solved, as much as he simply got over them. Dewey's dilemma of how to reconcile evolution, education, democracy, and race was never fully resolved; he merely moved on to new aspects of the dilemma. He was as much part of his changing context as he was contributor to it; his ideas were as much his as they were others'. But this transformation was significant because the post-1924 Dewey was one who could, in good faith, be relevant to the postmodernist world. For this reason, scholars who have revived or reconstructed Dewey for today's world—including African American scholars—have appropriately relied almost exclusively on the texts he authored after this important turning point.

Perhaps the most telling depiction of Dewey's transformation appeared in Dewey's forward to the 1930 edition of *Human Nature and Conduct*. In it Dewey outlined specifically how the "rise of anthropology and allied sciences" drew him to the "pervasive and powerful influence of what anthropologists call culture in shaping manifestations of every human nature subject to its influence." This allowed him to appreciate how "diversity operates to create different attitudes and dispositions in the play of ultimately identical human factors." He hoped that his book placed "due emphasis upon the power of cultural habitude and trend in diversifying the forms assumed by human nature."[29] Through reflection, deliberation, and experience, the individual resolved tensions of an emerging problem or issue as long as the solution continued to accomplish the task. Such a vision of mind required both a plurality of ideas and a plurality of cultures in the environment, upon which the reconstruction of experience could draw its innovations and growth.

The texts that Dewey published after 1924 reflected his new concerns with cultural interaction, local context, political deliberation, aesthetics, and immediate experience. To philosophers, the books and essays Dewey published late in his life are his most enduring and significant. He wrote prolifically in his later years, so it would take another book to do justice to his post-1924 works. Dewey published *Experience and Nature* in 1925, *The Public and Its Problems* in 1927, *The Quest for Certainty* in 1929, *Art as Experience* in 1934, *Logic: A Theory of Inquiry* in 1938, *Freedom and Culture* in 1939, and *Knowing and the Known,* coauthored with Arthur Bentley, in 1950. Dewey continued to write about education in his later years, although mostly through brief essays and editorials on current issues. He supported the unionization and professionalization of teachers and encouraged progressive experimentation in schools. He continued to support the teaching of social issues in the classroom. He joined the Progressive Educational Association (PEA) and served as its honorary president. He engaged in discussion with the Social Frontier group at Teachers College and published several articles in its journal. However, he introduced few new educational ideas, and his discussions became increasingly more abstract and detached from the day-to-day reality of classroom instruction. The one exception was his small book *Education and Experience*, published in 1938 and first presented at the annual meeting of the PEA.

In *Education and Experience* Dewey hoped to distance himself from some of the pedagogical follies associated with his name and also to update his educational views. In the book Dewey also distanced himself further from the linear historicism and genetic psychology of his early career. In its place

Dewey outlined the significance of growth as the "exemplification of the principle of continuity," and interaction as the "second chief principle for interpreting an experience in its educational function and force."[30] Dewey's explicit identification of interaction as a major component of his educational philosophy demonstrates how he revised his pedagogy in a more pluralistic direction after 1916. Interaction as a crucial component of present experience became a greater focus in all of his later works.

DEWEY IN THE
POSTMODERN WORLD

D
EWEY'S STRUGGLE TO reconcile evolution, education, democracy, and
race was the central focus of this study. Through repeated reconsideration of the relationship among these ideas, by 1916 Dewey had
reconstructed his views in a way that is more palatable to the minds of the
twenty-first century. Yet his early and middle works remain as monuments to
Dewey's linear cultural views and ethnocentric historicism. So, how do we
reconcile the pre-1916 and post-1916 Deweys?

There are three ways to do so. The first is to do as many scholars have
done: recognize the alleged "discontinuity" between Dewey's early and later
educational and cultural writings and demonstrate how he recognized the
shortcomings of his earlier views and then corrected them when his later
interactional-pluralist views were further explored. According to this view,
Dewey's later ideas negate and/or update his former ones. Or similarly, his
later views implicitly addressed the shortcomings of his earlier ones. For example, in his overview of Dewey's writings and correspondence on race, Michael Eldridge argues that "One committed to a multicultural society will
find some help in John Dewey's direct statements on race; he or she will
find greater assistance in Dewey's more general social and political thinking
and overall philosophical approach." However, those "wanting Dewey to be
a moral hero," Eldridge concludes, "are embarrassed by some of Dewey's
statements on and actions in regard to racial matters."[1] Thus Eldridge recognizes the limitations of Dewey's specific work on race, but argues that a comprehensive look at his philosophy, particularly his later works, can overcome
his specific "embarrassments" on the issue. These embarrassments include
Dewey's failure to denounce lynchings and Jim Crow laws directly, his casual
use of the term *nigger* in a letter to his son, his failure to respond to W.E.B.
Du Bois's repeated requests for a contribution on race for his periodical *Crisis*, his opposition to the cultural autonomy of Polish Americans, his and
his daughter's praise for the segregated schools of Gary, Indiana, and, most
conspicuously, his repeated use of the term *savage* in reference to non-White

hunter-gatherer societies. However, Dewey's racial accomplishments include being a founding member of the National Association for the Advancement of Colored People (NAACP), his early and explicit denouncement of bio-logical-based racial discrimination and the doctrine of the transmission of acquired characteristics, his attack on latent potentials and Spencerian social statistics, his defense of the African American sharecropper Odell Walker, and his later espousal of pluralistic-interactional cultural views.[2]

Appropriately, most proponents of recovering Dewey's pragmatism for the twenty-first century have recognized both his embarrassments and ac-complishments on race, but specifically have found his post-1916 social and political views conducive to the postmodern, multicultural world. For exam-ple, African American scholar Eddie Glaude "is not convinced that [pragma-tists'] failure to address white supremacy philosophically constitutes an un-forgivable moral failing" and ultimately suggests that Dewey's "pragmatism can help suggest some of the more challenging dimensions of contemporary African American politics."[3] Glaude, like most scholars, draws upon Dewey's works written after the period covered in this book. Likewise, leading Dewey educational scholars draw mostly upon Dewey's later philosophical works and self-consciously reconstruct his educational views for the present day by drawing lightly and selectively upon or (even ignoring) Dewey's pre-1916 works.

The problem with this approach is that Dewey never explicitly denounced any of his earlier writings on education. In fact, he contributed an introduc-tion to Katherine Camp Mayhew and Alice Camp Edwards's *The Dewey School* in 1934 in which he essentially defended the linear historicist curriculum he developed at the University of Chicago laboratory school. These scholars are more interested in constructing a Dewey for use in the twenty-first century (and they do so successfully) than they are in recovering his original mean-ing. This is the fundamental difference between a philosophical and historical approach to the subject.

The second way to reconcile the early and later Dewey is to describe the pluralist Dewey of his later works like *Art as Experience* and then impose this later Dewey onto the earlier one by ignoring the linear ethnocentrism of the Dewey School and the specific curriculum and principles he worked out there. This has been the method employed most commonly by educational philosophers, who tend to overemphasize continuity in Dewey's work at the expense of his intellectual development and growth. The problem with this approach is that it abstracts a theory of education from his works that are not really about education and ignores how Dewey actually set up a specific school and curriculum at the University of Chicago, which, as I have demon-strated, were permeated with genetic psychology and linear historicism. In-versely, recent critics of Dewey's ethnocentrism such as Shannon Sullivan and

Frank Margonis have projected the pre-1916 views onto his entire career.[4] As a result they fail to recognize how Dewey's views evolved significantly during these years. Therefore, both those who praise and those who critique the adequacy of Dewey's views on race often take an ahistorical approach by imposing a philosophical consistency upon all of his works. As a result, they fail to recognize how his ideas evolved significantly during his long career.

The third way, I suggest, is a genetic one. A genetic psychological approach to Dewey's philosophy neither views his shift in interest as discontinuity nor glosses over how his earlier views contradicted his later ones. Instead, it demonstrates that a shift in consciousness is an unavoidable outcome of social and personal growth that must take place in a particular linear sequence even though later stages necessarily incorporate (through contradiction) earlier stages.[5] If we accept, as Dewey did, that each stage does not contain a latent potential for further stages, but rather just happened to have occurred in a particular sequence because history happened to have unraveled that way, then we can escape the cultural imperialist baggage of genetic psychological approaches. Dewey's post-1916 work reflected the growth in Dewey's own thinking as he progressed from an interest in how children became critically socialized to the existing world to an interest in how adults formulated political positions and created new useful knowledge. As a result, his philosophical interests progressed from a linear modernist ethnocentrism to a postmodernist phase of psychological and sociological development. Dewey's later position did not negate the previous one; rather, it incorporated it. Dewey's own evolving philosophy from linear ethnocentrism to interactional pluralism reflected the emerging stages of the individual and race that all societies and individuals must progress through.

If we conceptualize each stage as a "closeness of fit" between the individual and the mental demands of his or her social context, instead of as a necessary linear sequence, then we can avoid the elitism and ethnocentrism of historicist theories of development. In fact, genetic psychologists drawing on the Deweyan tradition such as William Perry, Lawrence Kohlberg, and Robert Kegan have abandoned the sociological pretensions of genetic theory, but still assert that humans develop through universal, sequential stages of mental development. Kohlberg even demonstrated empirically how his moral developmental scheme can be applied to non-Western individuals and cultures. So Kohlberg recognized and attempted to correct for the inherent cultural bias of developmental schemes such as Dewey's. These genetic psychologists agree with Dewey that each higher stage allows the individual to do more things psychologically than the previous one; yet, like Dewey, they do not ascribe inherent superiority to those who are at a higher stage. Again, growth is simply a matter of fitting the psychological stage to the mental demands of the social and cultural environment. Self is a product of psychological-sociological interaction, not a matter of "proper" development. In other words, in this book I have argued that Dewey's early philosophy was ethnocentric because it incorporated and reflected the cultural beliefs of his time. However, his scheme did not necessarily need to be Eurocentric. In fact, psychologists such as Kohlberg and Kegan, who both cite Dewey, have demonstrated how easily his ideas can be updated for the postmodern world.

However, the developmental psychologists cited above are more concerned with form than content. That is, they see cognitive development as the primary aim of education and the transmission of specific content as merely a means toward that end. In contrast, Dewey (or at least the pre-1916 Dewey) viewed form and content as equally important. Dewey never intended that his vision be used for justification of any educational experience that merely led to growth. Instead, growth had to be directed through and by the content of the lived experiences of the past in a particular sequence. That is, the stages of sociological and psychological growth as demonstrated by the history of the race provided both the descriptive and prescriptive elements of Dewey's curriculum by describing the reflective thinking process at any given stage and pointing to the higher stage toward which the student should be directed. Each stage of development represented a particular level of thinking and a particular body of content as dictated by the history of the race. Subject matter was both the form and content of the present and higher level.

Ironically, by reading Dewey in the context of the early twentieth century, I recovered a component of his thinking that could potentially make his ideas even more relevant to the concerns of the twenty-first century. Because we now live in an educational climate that values the acquisition and assessment of specific discipline-based content and skills, teaching generically for reflective thinking is no longer an adequate educational objective. Educators must now teach both reflective thinking and specific subject matter. Dewey's educational vision can allow us to do so. If we appreciate that Dewey argued not only for meaningful educational experiences, but specifically for those experiences that led students through the history of the social occupations of the human race, then we are provided with a specific set of criteria for selecting and organizing subject matter. We simply ask ourselves, how and in what sequence did our racial ancestors originally discover the subject matter and processes we now take for granted? Likewise, if we appreciate that Dewey argued not only for encouraging reflective thinking and growth, but specifically for leading students through the prescribed developmental stages of understanding of the human race, then we are provided with a specific road map for teaching and assessing critical thinking. Once again, we simply ask ourselves, in what sequence and in what context did the intellectual discoveries of the past originally take place? Dewey argued that form and content needed to be taught simultaneously in the same way that the race originally discovered them.

Regarding standardized testing, Dewey would obviously be opposed to the way most tests present content as ready-made and abstract—facts and processes to be memorized and regurgitated, but in no way linked to the problems and contexts that historically engendered them. Dewey's curriculum successfully overcame this by situating the learning of all subject matter in the context of real-world occupations such as cooking, gardening, and woodworking. The underlying scheme for the Dewey School curriculum was to repeat the race experience in a sequential way that united the form and content of the present world by presenting it in the context from which it originally (that is, historically) emerged. This was a brilliant solution to an enduring problem of how to organize content. However, the shortcoming of such an approach was that students at the Dewey School did not learn the abstract symbols of the modern world (that is, the three Rs) until the race had actually done so. In practice this meant that Dewey School students did not learn how to read and write until the equivalent of the race had done so (i.e., the third year). I think even today's most progressive educators would be uncomfortable with waiting until second or third grade to introduce students to letters, words, and numbers, despite their abstract nature. In this sense, Dewey's vision is out of sync with what we now know about the development of literacy and numeracy, but this part of his curriculum can be updated rather easily by condensing the early part of his curriculum. When stripped of its ethnocentric baggage, there is still tremendous potential in approaching subject matter as an outcome of historic discovery. Revising and updating the curriculum in light of present needs was a fundamental part of Dewey's pedagogy.

Notes

Introduction

1. George Dykhuizen, *The Life and Mind of John Dewey* (Carbondale: University of Illinois Press, 1973); Robert Westbrook, *John Dewey and American Democracy* (Ithaca, NY: Cornell University Press, 1991); Steven Rockefeller, *John Dewey: Religious Faith and Democratic Humanism* (New York: Columbia University Press, 1991); Alan Ryan, *John Dewey and the High Tide of American Liberalism* (New York: Norton, 1995); Lawrence Cremin, *Transformation of the School: Progressivism in American Education, 1876–1957* (New York: Knopf, 1961); Herbert Kliebard, *The Struggle for the American Curriculum, 1893–1958*, 2nd ed. (New York: Routledge. 1995); Louis Menand, *The Metaphysical Club: A Story of Ideas in America* (New York: Farrar, Straus, and Giroux, 2001).

2. John Dewey, *The Child and the Curriculum* and *The School and Society*, 10th ed. (1902 and 1900; Chicago: University of Chicago Press, 1969), 48.

3. John Dewey, "Contributions to *A Cyclopedia of Education* (1911)," in *Middle Works*, vol. 6: 399.

4. John Dewey, *How We Think* (1910; Mineola, NY: Dover, 1997), 160.

5. John and Evelyn Dewey, "*Schools of To-Morrow*" (1915), in *Middle Works*, vol. 8: 369–370.

6. John Dewey, *Democracy and Education: An Introduction to Philosophy of Education* (New York: Free Press, 1916), 217.

7. Katherine Camp Mayhew and Alice Camp Edwards, *The Dewey School: The Laboratory School of the University of Chicago, 1896–1903* (New York: Appleton-Century, 1936), 98–99.

8. William James to John Dewey, 28 September 1902 (record 00746), in *The Correspondence of John Dewey*, vol. 1, 3rd ed., ed. Larry Hickman (Carbondale: Center for Dewey Studies, Southern Illinois University, 2005, CD-ROM).

9. In particular, the following were very informative: William Watkins, *The White Architects of Black Education: Ideology and Power in America, 1865–1954* (New York: Teachers College Press, 2001); Axel R. Schafer, "W.E.B. Du Bois, German Social Thought, and the Racial Divide in American Progressivism," *Journal of American History* 88 (December 2001): 925–949; James B. McKee, *Sociology and the Race Problem: Failure of a Perspective* (Urbana: University of Illinois Press, 1993); Dorothy Ross, *The Origins of American Social Science* (New York: Cambridge University Press, 1991) and Dorothy Ross (ed.), *Modernist Impulses in the Human Sciences, 1870–1930* (Baltimore: Johns Hopkins Press, 1994); Robert Richards, *Darwin and the Emergence of Evolutionary Theories of Mind and Behavior* (Chicago: University of Chicago Press, 1987); John M. O'Donnell, *The Origins of Behaviorism: American Psychology, 1870–1920* (New York: New York University Press, 1985); Peter Bowler, *The Eclipse of Darwinism: Anti-Darwinian Evolution Theories in the Decades around 1900* (Baltimore: Johns Hopkins University Press, 1983); Stephen Jay Gould, *Ontogeny and Phylogeny* (Cambridge, MA: Belknap, 1977);

George Stocking Jr., *Race, Culture and Evolution: Essays in the History of Anthropology* (Chicago: University of Chicago Press, 1968).

10. Thomas Jesse Jones, *Social Studies in the Hampton Curriculum* (Hampton, VA: Hampton Institute Press, 1908), 4.

11. David Saville Muzzey, *An American History* (New York: Ginn, 1911), 619–620.

12. John Dewey to Clara Mitchell, 29 November 1895 (record 00272), in *Correspondence*, vol. 1.

13. Dewey, *The Child and the Curriculum* and *The School and Society*, 19.

14. Laura Runyon, "The Teaching of Elementary History in the Dewey School" (masters thesis, University of Chicago, 1906), 55.

15. Ibid., 47.

16. John Dewey, "Racial Prejudice and Friction" (1922), in *Middle Works*, vol. 13: 253.

17. John Dewey, "Individuality, Equality, and Superiority (1922)," in *Middle Works*, vol. 13: 295.

18. See note 9.

19. Thomas S. Kuhn, *The Essential Tension: Selected Studies in Scientific Tradition and Change* (Chicago: University of Chicago Press, 1977), xii.

20. Dewey, *Democracy and Education*, 18.

21. Morton White, *Social Thought in America: The Revolt against Formalism* (New York: Oxford Press, 1947), 12.

22. Dipesh Chakrabarty, *Provincializing Europe: Postcolonial Thought and Historical Difference* (Princeton, NJ: Princeton University Press, 2000), 7.

23. On Tarde's influence on social scientists see Ruth Leys, "Mead's Voices: Imitation as Foundation; or the Struggle Against Mimesis" in *Modernist Impulses in the Human Sciences 1870–1930*, ed. Dorothy Ross (Baltimore: Johns Hopkins University Press, 1991), 213.

24. John Dewey and James H. Tufts, "Ethics (1908)," in *Middle Works*, vol. 5: 25, 26.

25. Scudder Klyce to John Dewey, 4 April 1915 (record 03511), in *Correspondence*, vol. 1.

26. Richard Rorty, *Contingency, Irony, and Solidarity* (New York: Cambridge University Press, 1989), xiii. There is a rich, contentious literature on the definition(s) of *historicism*. For a recent, readable summary see F. R. Ankersmit, "Historicism: An Attempt at Synthesis," *History and Theory* 34 (October 1995): 143–161. Morton White contrasts his definition with Karl Popper's narrower meaning of *historicism*—the idea that the evolution of society is governed by transcendent and prophetic laws of progress (i.e., Comte, Marx). Both definitions refer to the centrality of the past as the raw data from which to extract useful knowledge, but they differ in their views on the ontological and epistemological value of the means of progress. In White's pragmatic definition, historical movement toward progress is believed to exist historically within the past and present, while in Popper's positivistic definition the laws of progress are believed to exist ahistorically beneath the past and present. Rorty's historicism denies the existence of any movement toward progress whatsoever. Instead, Rorty's ironic historicism refers to acceptance of the relativism, contingency, and context-boundedness of all knowledge. Historicism, for Rorty, is simply the open-ended "redescription" of history. As I will demonstrate, prior to 1916 Dewey was neither a positivistic historicist, nor an ironic historicist; he was a pragmatic historicist, which means that each successive stage of consciousness could be found within the social and biological inheritance of the race, not in any transcendent realm beneath it, and that the evolution of mankind was necessarily progressive toward a more generic, socialized consciousness. After 1916, his historicm starts to look more like the one described by Rorty.

Chapter 1

1. John Dewey to Alice Chipman Dewey and children, 11 April 1894 (record 00218), in *Correspondence*, vol. 1.

2. Neil Coughlan, *Young John Dewey: An Essay in American Intellectual History* (Chicago: University of Chicago Press, 1975); Dykhuizen, *Life and Mind*.

3. John Dewey, "From Absolutism to Experimentalism (1930)," in *John Dewey: The Later Works, 1925-1953*, vol. 5, 153.

4. Dorothy Ross, *G. Stanley Hall: The Psychologist as Prophet* (Chicago: University of Chicago Press, 1972).

5. Richards, *Darwin and the Emergence of Evolutionary Theories*, 522–524.

6. On the significance of Weissman's experiment, see Menand, *Metaphysical Club*, 382.

7. Stocking, *Race, Culture and Evolution*, 241–242.

8. G. Stanley Hall, "The New Psychology as Basis of Education," *The Forum* 17 (March–August 1894): 716.

9. John Dewey to William Torrey Harris, 4 December 1894 (record 00493), in *Correspondence*, vol. 1.

10. William T. Harris, "Editors Preface" in *The Psychology of Number and Its Application to Methods of Teaching Arithmetic* by James A. McClellan and John Dewey (New York: Appleton, 1895), ix.

11. Dewey to Alice Chipman Dewey and children, 25–26 August 1894 (record 00178), in *Correspondence*, vol. 1.

12. All of the quotations in this paragraph are from James A. McLellan and John Dewey, *The Psychology of Number and Its Application to Methods of Teaching Arithmetic* (New York: Appleton, 1895), 52, xiii, 57, 18.

13. H. B. Fine, "Review of The Psychology of Number and Its Application to Methods of Teaching Arithmetic, by James A. McLellan and John Dewey, International Education Series (1896)," in *John Dewey: The Early Works, 1882–1898*, vol. 5, ed. Jo Ann Boydston (Carbondale: Southern Illinois University Press, 1971), xxiii–xxiv, 189.

14. D. E. Phillips, "Number and Its Application Psychologically Considered (1897)," in *Early Works*, vol. 5: xxxvi–xxxvii.

15. John Dewey, "Remarks on the Psychology of Number (1898)," in *Early Works*, vol. 5: 189.

16. Dewey, "From Absolutism to Experimentalism (1930)," in *Later Works*, vol. 5: 157.

17. John Dewey, "The Theory of Emotions (1894)," in *Early Works*, vol. 4: 171.

18. Ibid.

19. Ibid., 174.

20. John Dewey, "Review of *Studies in the Evolutionary Psychology of Feeling* by H. M. Stanley, New York: Macmillan Co, 1895 (1896)," in *Early Works*, vol. 5: 360, 363.

21. Ibid., 366.

22. John Dewey to Alice Dewey and children, 9 September 1894 (record 00188), in *Correspondence*, vol. 1.

23. John Dewey, "Educational Ethics: Syllabus of a Course of Six Lecture-Studies (1895)," in *Early Works*, vol. 5: 297.

24. Howard Gardner, *The Mind's New Science: A History of the Cognitive Revolution*, (New York: Basic Books, 1987), 102.

25. Dorothy McMurry, *Herbartian Contributions to History Instruction in American Elementary Schools* (New York: Bureau of Publications, Teachers College, Columbia University, 1946), 30–40.

26. Charles DeGarmo, *The Essentials of Methods, A Discussion of the Essential Form of Right Methods of Teaching: Observation, Generalization, Application* (Boston: Heath, 1889). See also Sir John Adams, *The Herbartian Psychology Applied to Education* (New York: Heath, 1897) and Catherine Isabel Dodd, *Introduction to the Herbartian Principles of Teaching* (New York: Macmillan, 1898).

27. C. C. Van Liew, "The Educational Theory of Cultural Epochs: Viewed Historically and Critically," *The Yearbook of the Herbart Society for the Scientific Study of Teaching* (Chicago: Herbart Society, 1895): 113.

28. James Mark Baldwin, *Social and Ethical Interpretations in Mental Development: A Study in Social Psychology* (New York: Macmillan, 1897), 2.

29. G. Stanley Hall, "Moral Education and Will Training," *The Pedagogical Seminary* (1892): 88

30. Wilhelm Diesterweg, "Instruction in History," in *Methods of History*, ed. G. Stanley Hall (Boston: Ginn, Heath, 1883), 32–33.

31. See Charles McMurry, *The Elements of General Method: Based on Principles of Herbart* (New York: Macmillan, 1903), 82.

32. Van Liew, "Educational Theory of Cultural Epochs," 117–118.

33. Dewey, "Educational Ethics (1895)," in *Early Works*, vol. 5: 297.

34. Hall, "Moral Education," 72, 85.

35. William T. Harris, "Herbart's Doctrine of Interest," *Educational Review* 10 (June 1895): 73.

36. Charles DeGarmo, "Is Herbart's Theory Dangerous?" Letter to the Editor, *The Public-School Journal* 14 (May 1895): 514.

37. William T. Harris, "Reply to DeGarmo's 'Is Herbart's Theory of Interest Dangerous?'" *Public-School Journal* 14 (June 1895): 575.

38. John Dewey, "Interest in Relation to Training of the Will (1895)," in *Early Works*, vol. 4: 141, 124.

39. Ibid., 122.

40. Ibid., 148, 149; quotations taken from appendix to the essay.

41. Frank McMurry, "Interest: Some Objections to It," *Education Review* 6 (February 1896): 149, 152.

42. Harris, "Professor Dewey's Doctrine of Interest as Related to the Will," *Educational Review* 11 (May 1896): 489

43. William T. Harris, *Psychologic Foundations of Education: An Attempt to Show the Genesis of the Higher Faculties of the Mind* (New York: Appleton, 1902), viii–x, 8–9.

44. Harris, "Professor Dewey's Doctrine of Interest as Related to the Will," *Educational Review* 11 (May 1896): 489, 493.

45. W. E. Wilson, "The Doctrine of Interest," *Educational Review* 11 (March 1896): 256, 259.

46. Henry Tucker, "The Doctrine of Interest in the Social Sciences in the High School," *The History Teacher's Magazine* 3 (March 1912): 51, 52, 53.

47. Charles McMurry, *Elements of General Method*, 118–119.

48. John Dewey, "Review of Harris's *Psychologic Foundations of Education*" (1898), in *Early Works*, vol. 5: 372.

49. Harris, *Psychologic Foundations of Education*, viii.

50. Dewey, "From Absolutism to Experimentalism (1930)," in *Later Works*, vol. 5: 156.

51. Jane Dewey, "Biography of John Dewey" in *The Philosophy of John Dewey*, ed. Paul Arthur Schlipp (New York: Tudor, 1951), 9.

52. John Dewey to Clara Mitchell, 31 December 1895 (record 00277), in *Correspondence*, vol. 1.

53. John Dewey to Clara Mitchell, 29 November 1895 (record 00272) and 29 December 1895 (record 00276), in *Correspondence*, vol. 1.

54. John Dewey to Clara Mitchell, 29 November 1895 (record 00272), in *Correspondence*, vol. 1.

55. John Dewey, "Group IV: Historical Development of Inventions and Occupations"

(1900), in *Middle Works*, vol. 1: 222–223.

56. John Dewey, "Plan of Organization of the University Primary School (1895?)," in *Early Works*, vol. 5: 225.

57. Mayhew and Edwards, *Dewey School*, passim.

58. Dewey, *School and Society, in The Child and the Curriculum* and *The School and Society,* 158–159.

59. Menand, *Metaphysical Club*, 320.

60. John Dewey to Frank Manny, 26 May 1896 (record 00526), in *Correspondence*, vol. 1.

61. Albion Small, "Demands of Sociology upon Pedagogy," *Addresses and Proceedings: National Education Association of the United States* (1896): 177, 183. Small was working against a caricature of history instruction here. Certainly, even the Committee of Ten promoted more progressive methods than the ones he described.

62. Thorstein Veblen, *The Theory of the Leisure Class: An Economic Study of Institutions* (New York: Macmillan, 1899), 116.

63. Ibid., 392.

64. Ibid., 395, 398.

65. John Dewey to Joseph Dorfman, 27 January 1930 (record 09382), in *Correspondence*, vol. 3.

66. John Dewey to Alice Chipman Dewey and children, 11 April 1894 (record 00218), in *Correspondence*, vol. 1.

67. John Dewey to Clara Mitchell, 29 November 1895 (record 00272), in *Correspondence*, vol. 1.

68. Quoted in Menand, *Metaphysical Club*, 295.

69. Ibid., 313.

70. Ibid., 314.

71. John Dewey, "My Pedagogic Creed (1897)," *School Journal* 54 (January 1897), 77–80.

72. Ibid, 87, 89–90, 93, 95.

Chapter 2

Susan Blow to William Torrey Harris, 12 June 1896 (record 01247), in *Correspondence*, vol. 1.

2. Laura Runyon, "A Day with the New Education," *Chautauquan: Organ of the Chautauqua Literacy and Science Circle* 30 (1900): 589, 590.

3. Ibid., 591.

4. Ibid., 591.

5. John Dewey, "The University School (1896)," in *Early Works*, vol. 5: 440.

6. Runyon, "Teaching of Elementary History," 16.

7. Ibid., 27.

8. Ibid., 30, 32, 40.

9. Ibid., 43, 46.

10. Ibid., 19, 51.

11. See Richard Hofstadter, *Anti-Intellectualism in American Life* (New York: Knopf, 1963) and E. D. Hirsch, *Cultural Literacy: What Every American Needs to Know* (Boston: Houghton Mifflin, 1987).

12. Runyon, "Teaching of Elementary History," 57.

13. John Dewey to Clara Mitchell, 24 December 1895 (record 00276), in *Correspondence*, vol. 1.

14. Runyon, *Teaching of Elementary History*, 61

15. Ibid., 57, 47.

16. John Dewey, "Interpretation of the Savage Mind (1902)," in *Middle Works*, vol. 2: 39.

17. Ibid, 41.

18. Ibid., 52.

19. Ibid, 47n.

20. William I. Thomas, "The Gaming Instinct," *American Journal of Sociology* 6 (July–May 1901): 761, 762.

21. Dewey, "Interpretation of the Savage Mind (1902)," in *Middle Works*, vol. 2: 40–41.

22. John Dewey, "Review of Katherine Elizabeth Dopp, *The Place of Industries in Elementary Education*. Chicago: University of Chicago Press, 1903 (1903)," in *Middle Works*, vol. 2: 307–308.

23. Dewey, "Interpretation of the Savage Mind (1902)," in *Middle Works*, vol. 2: 48.

24. There is a small literature on how history was organized at the Dewey School, but the analysis is mostly descriptive and does not cast his curriculum in the context of evolutionary anthropology. See Leo Alilunas, "John Dewey's Pragmatic Idea about School History and the Early Application," *Social Studies* 41 (March 1950): 111–114; Charles Strickland, "The Child, the Community, and Clio: The Uses of Cultural History In Elementary School Experiments of the Eighteen-Nineties," *History of Education Quarterly* 7 (Winter 1967): 474–492; Eugene F. Provenzoi, "History as Experiment: The Role of the Laboratory School in the Development of John Dewey's Philosophy of History," *The History Teacher* 12 (May 1979): 373–382; Laurel N. Tanner, *Dewey's Laboratory School: Lessons for Today* (New York: Teachers College Press, 1997). See also Laurel N. Tanner, "The Meaning of Curriculum in Dewey's Laboratory School, 1986–1904," *Journal of Curriculum Studies* 23 (1991): 101–117. Tanner makes reference to Dewey's psychological stages but does not link them to his larger philosophy.

25. On the use and significance of Dewey's "circuit" metaphor see Menand, *Metaphysical Club*; Eric Bredo, "Evolution, Psychology, and John Dewey's Critique of the Reflex Arc Concept," *The Elementary School Journal* 98 (May 1998): 447–466; Ryan, *High Tide of American Liberalism*.

26. John Dewey, "Ethical Principles Underlying Education," in *The National Herbart Society for the Scientific Study of Teaching, Third Yearbook* (Chicago: Herbart Society, 1897). Reprinted as *Ethical Principles Underlying Education* (Chicago: University of Chicago Press, 1903), 18, 24.

27. Ibid., 21

28. Ibid.

29. Ibid.

30. Quoted in Kieran Egan, *Getting it Wrong from the Beginning: Our Progressive Inheritance from Herbert Spencer, John Dewey, and Jean Piaget* (New Haven: Yale University Press, 2002), 203.

31. G. Stanley Hall, "The Natural Activities of Children as Determining the Industries in Early Education II," *Journal of Proceedings and Addresses of the Forty-Third Annual Meeting of the National Education Association* (1904): 443.

32. Quoted in C.S. Parker, *A Textbook in History of Modern Elementary Education with Emphasis on School Practice and Relation to Social Conditions* (New York: Ginn, 1912), 413.

33. Dorothy McMurry, *Herbartian Contributions to History Instruction; Henry Johnson, Teaching of History in Elementary and Secondary Schools* (New York: Macmillan, 1916).

34. John Dewey, "Interpretation of the Culture-Epoch Theory (1896)" in *Early Works*, vol. 5: 247, 124, 250.

35. Ibid., 250.

36. Ibid., 48, 49, 53.

37. John Dewey to Clara Mitchell, 29 November 1895 (record 00272) and 22, 24, December 1895 (record 00275), in *Correspondence*, vol. 1.

38. Dewey, "Educational Ethics (1895)," in *Early Works*, vol. 5: 299.

39. John Dewey, "The Psychological Aspect of the School Curriculum (1897)," in *Early Works*, vol. 4: 165.

40. John Dewey, "Educational Psychology: Syllabus of a Course of Twelve Lecture-Studies (1896)," in *Early Works*, vol. 5: 311.

41. Dewey, "Interest in Relation to Training of the Will (1896)," in *Early Works*, vol. 5: 218.

42. John Dewey, "Pedagogy IB 19: Philosophy of Education, 1898–1899 (1900)," in *Early Works*, vol. 5: 339.

43. C. C. Van Liew, "Culture Epoch Theory," Letter to the Journal, *The Public-School Journal*: 546.

44. Ross, *Origins of American Social Science*; George W. Stocking Jr., *Victorian Anthropology* (New York: Free Press, 1987).

45. Ross, *Origins of American Social Science*, 53–97.

46. Lester F. Ward, *The Psychic Factors of Civilization*, 2nd ed. (New York: Ginn and Company, 1906), 2.

47. John Dewey, "The Bearings of Pragmatism upon Education (1909)," in *Middle Works*, vol. 4: 178.

48. Ibid., 178.

49. Ibid.

50. See Menand, *Metaphysical Club*; Bredo, "Evolution, Psychology, and John Dewey's Critique of the Reflex Arc Concept," 447–466; Ryan, *High Tide of American Liberalism* (New York: Norton, 1995); Coughlan, *Young John Dewey*.

51. John Dewey, "The Reflex Arc Concept in Psychology (1896)," in *Early Works*, vol. 4: 99.

52. Ward, *Psychic Factors of Civilization*, 4.

53. Ibid., 5.

54. John Dewey, "Review of *The Psychic Factors of Civilization* by Lester F. Ward. Boston: Ginn and Co., 1893; *Social Evolution*, by Benjamin Kidd. New York and London: Macmillan Co., 1894; *Civilization During the Middle Ages*, by George B. Adams. New York; Charles Scriber's Sons, 1894, and *History of the Philosophy of History*, by Robert Flint. New York: Charles Scribner's Sons, 1894 (1894)," in *Early Works*, vol. 4: 201, 206.

55. Ibid., 207, 208.

56. Ibid.

57. John Dewey, "Review of *Social and Ethical Interpretations in Mental Development: A Study in Social Psychology* by James Mark Baldwin, New York: Macmillan Co, 1897 (1897)," in *Early Works*, vol. 5: 417.

58. Dewey, "The Bearings of Pragmatism upon Education (1909)," in *Middle Works*, vol. 4: 179.

59. Ibid., 189.

60. Ibid.

61. Ibid., 190.

62. McLellan and Dewey, *Psychology of Number*, 18.

63. "Textual Commentary on School and Society," in *Middle Works*, vol. 1: 369.

64. Dewey, *Child and the Curriculum* and *The School and Society*, 20, 19, 53, 54.

65. Ibid., 19, 22.

Chapter 3

1. John Dewey, "Why Reflective Thinking Must Be an Educational Aim," in *John Dewey on Education: Selected Writings*, ed. Reginald D. Archambault (Chicago: University of Chicago Press, 1964), 253, 254.

2. Rorty, *Contingency, Irony, and Solidarity,* 101.

3. Dewey, "Ethical Principles Underlying Education," 27, 28.

4. Dewey, "What Psychology Can Do for the Teacher," in *John Dewey on Education,* 206–207.

5. John Dewey, "Remarks on the Psychology of Number" (1898), in *Early Works,* vol. 5: 188, 190, 191.

6. Dewey, "Educational Psychology: Syllabus," in *Early Works,* vol. 5: 311.

7. Dewey, "Pedagogy IB 19: Philosophy of Education," in *Early Works,* vol. 5: 331.

8. John Dewey, *The Child and the Curriculum* and *The School and Society,* 105.

9. Ibid., 106–107, 111.

10. Ibid., 115.

11. Ibid.

12. John Dewey, "Mental Development (1900)," in *Middle Works,* vol. 1: 215, 217.

13. John Dewey, *How We Think,* 30–33 passim.

14. Ibid., 33.

15. John Dewey, "Introduction to The Psychology of the Child Development by Irvin King," in *Middle Works,* vol. 2: 301.

16. Dewey, ""What Psychology Can Do for the Teacher," in *John Dewey on Education,* 206.

17. See Stocking, *Victorian Anthropology;* Stocking, *Race, Culture, and Evolution;* Ross, *Origins of American Social Science;* and Dorothy Ross, "Modernist Social Science in the Land of New/Old," in *Modernist Impulses in the Human Sciences,* ed. Dorothy Ross.

18. John Dewey, *The Child and the Curriculum* and *The School and Society,* 48.

19. Ibid., 20.

20. Dewey, "Contributions to *A Cyclopedia of Education* (1911)," in *Middle Works,* vol. 6: 399.

21. Dewey, "Review of Katherine Elizabeth Dopp (1903)," in *Middle Works,* vol. 2: 309.

22. Dewey, "Contributions to *A Cyclopedia of Education* (1911)," in *Middle Works,* vol. 6: 401.

23. John Dewey, "Some Stages of Logical Thought (1900)," in *Middle Works,* vol. 1: 151.

24. Ibid., 152, 154, 157, 159.

25. Ibid., 160, 161, 171.

26. Ibid, 169.

27. Ibid.

28. Dewey, "Plan of Organization of University Primary School (1895)" in *Early Works,* vol. 5: 224.

29. Mayhew and Edwards, *The Dewey School,* 328, 310.

30. Katherine Elizabeth Dopp, *The Tree-Dwellers: Age of Fear* (New York: Rand McNally Company, 1904), 9–10, 11.

31. Dewey, "Review of Katherine Elizabeth Dopp (1903)," in *Middle Works,* vol. 2: 308.

32. John Dewey, "The Influence of Darwinism on Philosophy (1909)," in *Middle Works,* vol. 4: 6, 7.

33. John Dewey, "Teaching Ethics in the High School (1893)," in *Early Works,* vol. 4: 61.

34. John Dewey, "Influence of the High School upon Educational Methods (1896)," in *Early Works,* vol. 4: 279.

35. Dewey, "Ethical Principles Underlying Education," 15.

36. Ibid., 21, 22, 23.

37. John Dewey, "Evolution and Ethics (1898)," in *Early Works,* vol. 5: 41.

38. Ibid., 46, 43.

39. John Dewey and James H. Tufts, "*Ethics* (1908)," in *Middle Works,* vol. 5: 3, 8–9.

40. Ibid., 14.

41. Ibid., 42.

42. John Dewey, *How We Think*, viii.

43. Ibid., 9, 72.

44. L.T. Hobhouse, *Mind in Evolution* (London, Macmillan, 1901), v, vi.

45. Dewey, *How We Think*, 62.

46. Ibid., 65, 137.

47. Ibid, 150.

48. Ibid., 71.

49. Ibid., 142.

50. Ibid., 22.

51. Dewey, *The Child and the Curriculum* and *The School and Society*, 16.

52. Richard Rorty, "Introduction (1986)" in *John Dewey: The Later Works*, vol. 8: xiv.

53. Dewey, *Democracy and Education*, 63.

54. John Dewey, "The Evolutionary Method as Applied to Morality" (1902), in *Middle Works*, vol. 2: 14.

55. Dewey, *Democracy and Education*, 159.

56. On the influence of *How We Think* on curriculum theorists, see Thomas D. Fallace, "Tracing John Dewey's Influence on Progressive Education, 1903–1951: Towards a Received Dewey," *Teachers College Record* (forthcoming).

57. Dewey, "The Influence of Darwinism on Philosophy (1909)," in *Middle Works*, vol. 4: 14.

58. John Dewey to William Torrey Harris, 14 April 1903 (record 00834), in *Correspondence*, vol. 1.

59. John Dewey to William Torrey Harris, 25 April 1904 (record 00936), in *Correspondence*, vol. 1.

60. Cornell West, *The American Evasion of Philosophy: A Genealogy of Pragmatism* (Madison: University of Wisconsin Press, 1989), 85.

Chapter 4

1. Survey cited in Richards, *Darwin and the Emergence of Evolutionary Theories*, 501.

2. Robert Richardson, *William James: In the Maelstrom of American Modernism* (New York: Houghton Mifflin, 2006), 432.

3. Henry Steel Commager, *The American Mind: An Interpretation of American Thought and Character since the 1880s* (New Haven, CT: Yale University Press), 100.

4. Dewey, *Democracy and Education*, 331.

5. John Dewey, "Democracy in Education (1903)," in *Middle Works*, vol. 2: 230, 231, 233.

6. John Dewey, "The School as Social Centre (1902)," in *Middle Works*, vol. 2: 80, 82.

7. Ibid., 82.

8. Daniel Rogers, *Atlantic Crossings: Social Politics in a Progressive Age* (Cambridge, MA: Belknap, 1998), 47.

9. John Dewey, "The School as Social Centre (1902)," in *Middle Works*, vol. 2: 84. 86. 87. 88.

10. Ibid., 90, 91, 92.

11. Ibid., 85–86.

12. John and Evelyn Dewey, *Schools of To-Morrow* (1915), in *Middle Works*, vol. 8: 208.

13. Ibid., 244, 260, 369–370, 391.

14. Ibid, 340.

15. Ibid, 351.

16. Randolph Bourne, *The Gary Schools* (New York: Houghton Mifflin, 1916), iii.

17. John and Evelyn Dewey, *Schools of To-Morrow* (1915), in *Middle Works*, vol. 8: 368, 370, 374.

18. William Bagley, "Editorial (1915)," in *Middle Works*, vol. 8: 466, 467.

19. John Dewey, "Letter to William Bagley and the Editorial Staff of *School and Home Education* (1915)," in *Middle Works*, vol. 8: 414.

20. John Dewey, "Some Dangers in the Present Movement for Industrial Education (1913)," in *Middle Works*, vol. 7: 103.

21. Ibid., 314.

22. John and Evelyn Dewey, *Schools of To-Morrow* (1915), in Middle Works, vol. 8: 404.

23. Lawrence Cremin, *American Education: The Metropolitan Experience, 1876–1980* (New York: Harper & Row, 1988), 545.

24. Denver Public Schools, *Social Science, Grades Seven, Eight, and Nine, Junior High School*, Course of Study Monograph, no. 3 (Denver, Co: Denver Public Schools, 1924), 138.

25. David Snedden, "Teaching of History in Secondary Schools," *The History Teachers Magazine* 5 (November 1914): 278.

26. Edward Thorndike and R. S. Woodworth, "The Influence of Improvement in One Mental Function upon the Efficiency of Other Functions," *Psychological Review* (May 1901): 250.

27. O'Donnell, *The Origins of Behaviorism*, 230. In fact, historian Robert Church's study of the early literature on educational psychology confirmed that the new generation of behaviorists not only ignored Dewey's social psychology, but also Snedden's attempts to link input-output psychology with broader social issues of efficiency and control. See Robert Church, "Educational Psychology and Social Reform in the Progressive Era," *History of Education Quarterly* 11 (Winter 1971): 390–405.

28. John Dewey, "The Relationship of Theory to Practice in Education (1904)," in *Middle Works*, vol. 6: 261.

29. Dewey, "Some Dangers in the Present Movement for Industrial Education (1913)," in *Middle Works*, vol. 7: 99, 100, 101.

30. John Dewey, "A Policy of Industrial Education (1914)," in *Middle Works*, vol. 8: 97.

31. John Dewey, "Splitting Up the School System (1915)," in *Middle Works*, vol. 8: 123, 126.

32. John Dewey, "A Policy of Industrial Education (1914)," in *Middle Works*, vol. 8: 96.

33. David Snedden, "Vocational Education (1915)," in Appendix 2 of *Middle Works*, vol. 8: 464.

34. John Dewey, "Education vs. Trade-Training: Reply to David Snedden (1915)," in *Middle Works*, vol. 8: 412–413.

35. John Dewey, "From Absolutism to Experimentalism (1930)," in *Later Works*, vol. 5: 156; John Dewey to Horace Kallen, 1 July 1916 (record 03236), in *Correspondence*, vol. 1.

36. Quoted in "Textual Commentary," in *Middle Works*, vol. 9: 397.

37. Dewey, *Democracy and Education*, 184, 191, 195, 208, 219.

38. Ibid., 274, 275, 309.

39. Ibid., 3, 4, 7, 15, 17.

40. Ibid., 36, 48.

41. Ibid., 207, 229, 338, 340.

42. Ibid., 224, 211, 225.

43. Ibid., 116, 73.

44. Ibid., 313–315.

45. Ibid., 110, 119, 119–120.

46. Ibid., 13, 13, 24, 30.

47. John Dewey to Elsie Clapp, 10–11 [month unknown] 1911 (record 02947), in *Correspondence*, vol. 1.

48. John Dewey to Evelyn Dewey, 10 February 1905 (record 01453), in *Correspondence*, vol. 1.

49. James Harvey Robinson, "John Dewey and His World," *Harvard Teachers Record*, 2 (1932): 14.

50. James Harvey Robinson, *New History: Essays Illustrating the Modern Historical Outlook* (New York: Macmillan, 1912), 22, 153.

51. Dewey, *Democracy and Education*, 208, 260.

52. Ibid., 214.

53. Ibid., 215.

54. Ibid., 36.

55. John Dewey, "Philosophy and Democracy (1918)," in *Middle Works*, vol. 11: 52–53.

56. "Confidential Report of Conditions among Poles in the United States (1918)," in *Middle Works*, vol. 11: 260.

57. "Second Preliminary Confidential Memorandum (1918)," in *Middle Works*, vol. 11: 258. For critiques of Dewey's treatment of the Polish issue see Clarence J. Karier, Paul Violas, and Joel Spring, eds., *Roots of Crisis: American Education in the Twentieth Century* (New York: Rand McNally, 1973), and Walter Feinberg, *Reason and Rhetoric: The Intellectual Foundations of 20th Century Liberal Educational Policy* (New York: Wiley, 1975).

58. John Dewey, "Autocracy under Cover (1918)," in *Middle Works*, vol. 11: 241–242, 245.

Chapter 5

1. Watkins, *White Architects of Black Education;* Menand, *Metaphysical Club;* Schafer, "W.E.B. Du Bois, German Social Thought, and the Racial Divide"; Ross, *Origins of American Social Science;* Richards, *Darwin and the Emergence of Evolutionary Theories;* Bowler, *Eclipse of Darwinism;* Gould, *Ontogeny and Phylogeny;* Stocking, *Race, Culture and Evolution.*

2. Quoted in Menand, *Metaphysical Club,* 116.

3. Quoted in Richards, *Darwin and the Emergence of Evolutionary Theories,* 596.

4. Joseph Moreau, *Schoolbook Nation: Conflicts Over American History Textbooks from the Civil War to the Present* (Ann Arbor: University of Michigan Press, 2003), 147–154.

5. Charles DeGarmo, "Social Aspects of Moral Education," in *Forgotten Heroes of American Education: The Great Tradition of Teaching Teachers,* ed. J. Wesley Null and Diane Ravitch (Greenwich, CT: Information Age, 2006), 293.

6. Schafer, "W.E.B. Du Bois, German Social Thought, and the Racial Divide," 927.

7. W.E.B. Du Bois, "The Conservation of the Races," in *W.E.B. Du Bois: Writings,* ed. Nathan Hughes (1897; New York: Viking Press, 1986), 825, 822.

8. Franz Boas, *The Mind of Primitive Man,* rev. 2nd ed. (1911; New York: Macmillan, 1938).

9. Franz Boas, "The History of Anthropology," in *The Shaping of American Anthropology, 1883–1911: A Franz Boas Reader,* ed. George Stocking, Jr. (1904; New York: Basic Books, 1974), 36.

10. See Menand, *Metaphysical Club,* 377–408.

11. John Dewey, "Address to National Negro Conference (1909)," in *Middle Works*, vol. 4: 156–157; and John Dewey, "Nationalizing Education (1916)," in *Middle Works*, vol. 10: 205.

12. Dewey and Tufts, *Ethics* (1908), in *Middle Works*, vol. 5: 23.

13. John Dewey to Clara Mitchell, 29 November 1895 (record 00272), in *Correspondence*, vol. 1.

14. Dewey, *Child and the Curriculum* and *The School and Society*, 19.

15. Runyon, "Teaching of Elementary History," 55.

16. Dewey and Tufts, *Ethics* (1908), in *Middle Works*, vol. 5: 25, 26.

17. For evidence of this assertion see Chapter 6, "The Dark Skinned Savage: The Image of Primitive Man in Evolutionary Anthropology," in Stocking, *Race Culture, and Evolution.*

18. Veblen, *Theory of the Leisure Class*, 240, 215, 218.

19. Quoted in Watkins, *White Architects of Black Education*, 73, 75.

20. Jones, *Social Studies*, 4

21. Jones, *Social Studies*, 5, 47.

22. On Tarde's influence see Ruth Leys, "Mead's Voices: Imitation as Foundation; or the Struggle against Mimesis," in *Modernist Impulses in the Human Sciences*, ed., Dorothy Ross, 213.

23. Dewey, *Democracy and Education*, 20

24. Ibid., 47.

25. Quoted in David Wallace Adams, *Education for Extinction: American Indians and the Boarding School Experience* (Lawrence: University Press of Kansas, 1995), 148.

26. John Dewey, "Evolution and Ethics" (1898), in *Early Works*, vol. 5: 50.

27. Ibid., 50.

28. Thomas and Kelsey quoted in Stocking, *Race, Culture, and Evolution*, 258.

29. On this important discovery see Gould, *Ontogeny and Phylogeny*, 203–204; Menand, *Metaphysical Club*, 382; and Bowler, "Darwinism and Modernism," in *Modernist Impulses in the Human Sciences*, ed. Dorothy Ross, 240.

30. William Bagley, "Optimism in Teaching," in *Forgotten Heroes of American Education: The Great Tradition of Teaching Teachers*, ed. J. Wesley Null and Diane Ravitch (Greenwich, CT: Information Age, 2006), 44.

31. Dewey, "Address to National Negro Conference (1909)," in *Middle Works*, vol. 4: 156–157.

32. Dewey, *Democracy and Education*, 74.

33. Dewey, "Contributions to *A Cyclopedia of Education* (1911)," in *Middle Works*, vol. 6: 406.

34. John Dewey, "The Philosophical Work of Herbert Spencer (1904)," in *Middle Works*, vol. 3: 196.

35. Quoted in Stocking, *Race, Culture, and Evolution*, 148.

36. Quoted in Menand, *Metaphysical Club*, 384.

37. Boas, "History of Anthropology," 36.

38. Boas, *Mind of Primitive Man*, 16.

39. Johnson, *Teaching of History*, 36–38.

40. William I. Thomas, *Source Book for Social Origins* (Chicago: University of Chicago Press, 1909), 169, 26.

41. Dewey, "Contributions to *A Cyclopedia of Education* (1911)," in *Middle Works*, vol. 6: 411.

42. W.E.B. Du Bois, "The Conservation of the Races," 822.

43. Quoted in Menand, *Metaphysical Club*, 395.

44. Du Bois quoted in Schafer, "W.E.B. Du Bois, German Social Thought, and the Racial Divide," 73.

45. Schafer, "W.E.B. Du Bois, German Social Thought, and the Racial Divide," 945.

46. William Bagley, "Education and Utility" and "Education and Our Democracy," in *Forgotten Heroes of American Education: The Great Tradition of Teaching Teachers*, ed. J. Wesley Null and Diane Ravitch (Greenwich, CT: Information Age, 2006), 71, 117.

47. Dewey, *Democracy and Education*, 93.

48. Ibid., 87.

49. White, *Social Thought in America*, 147.

50. U.S. Department of the Interior, Bureau of Education, *Americanization as a War*

Measure: Report of a Conference Called by the Secretary of the Interior, and Held in Washington, April 3, 1918 (Washington, DC: Government Printing Office, 1918), 61.

51. Royal Dixon, *Americanization* (New York: Macmillan, 1916), 179.

52. U.S. Department of the Interior, *America, Americanism, and Americanization* (Washington, DC: Government Printing Office, 1919), 17, 14.

53. Peter Roberts, *The Problem of Americanization* (New York: Macmillan, 1920), 30.

54. Dewey and Tufts, *Ethics* (1908), in *Middle Works*, vol. 5: 30.

55. Peter Roberts, *The Problem of Americanization* (New York: Macmillan, 1920), 35.

56. Ibid., 229, 234.

57. Milton Bennion, *Citizenship: An Introduction to Social Ethics* (Yonkers-on Hudson, NY: World Book Co., 1919), 23.

58. See Philip Van Ness Myers, *A Short History of Medieval and Modern Times* (New York: Ginn, 1906), 3–5.

59. Dixon, *Americanization*, 176.

60. Ibid., 192.

61. Ibid., 194.

62. Dewey, "Nationalizing Education (1916)," in *Middle Works*, vol. 10: 203, 204, 205, 206. Although my Dewey is slightly more conservative than the one presented in this essay, a good discussion of Dewey on the Americanization of immigrants is J. Christopher Eiesle, "John Dewey and the Immigrants," *History of Education Quarterly* 15 (Spring 1975): 67–85.

63. Peter Novick, *That Noble Dream: The Objectivity Question and the American Historical Profession* (New York: Cambridge University Press, 1988), 88.

64. Quoted in Menand, *Metaphysical Club*, 393.

65. John Dewey to Horace Kallen, 31 March 1915 (record 003222) and 22, 24, December 1895 in *Correspondence*, vol. 1.

66. Dewey, *Democracy and Education*, 86.

67. John and Evelyn Dewey, *Schools of To-Morrow* (1915), in *Middle Works*, vol. 8: 336.

Chapter 6

1. Quoted in Richards, *Darwin and the Emergence of Evolutionary Theories*, 506.

2. Quoted in O'Donnell, *The Origins of Behaviorism*, 183, 184.

3. See Hamilton Cravens and John C. Burnham, "Psychology and Evolutionary Naturalism in American Thought, 1890–1940," *American Quarterly* 23 (Dec 1971): 635–657.

4. Charles Ellwood, "The Theory of Imitation in Social Psychology," *American Journal of Sociology* 6 (May 1901): 721.

5. Quoted in Ruth Leys, "Mead's Voices: Imitation as Foundation; or the Struggle against Mimesis," in *Modernist Impulses in the Human Sciences*, ed. Dorothy Ross, 219.

6. John Dewey, "Contributions to *A Cyclopedia of Education* (1914)," in *Middle Works*, vol. 7: 236.

7. Dewey, *Democracy and Education*, 35.

8. Dewey, "Contributions to *A Cyclopedia of Education* (1914)," in *Middle Works*, vol. 7: 236.

9. John Dewey to William James, 15 March 1903 (record 00797), in *Correspondence*, vol. 1.

10. Quoted in Menand, *Metaphysical Club*, 378.

11. Dewey, *Democracy and Education*, 21, 82, 84–85.

12. Dewey, "Nationalizing Education (1916)," in *Middle Works*, vol. 10: 205, 204.

13. John Dewey, "American Education and Culture" (1916), in *Middle Works*, vol. 10: 198.

14. Dewey, *Democracy and Education*, 331.

15. Scudder Klyce to John Dewey, 4 April 1915 (record 03511), in *Correspondence*, vol. 1.

16. John Dewey to Scudder Klyce, 19 June 1915 (record 03540)), in *Correspondence*, vol. 1.

17. John Dewey, "The Need for Social Psychology (1917)," in *Middle Works*, vol. 10: 56, 58, 60, 59.

18. Ibid., 57.

19. John Dewey, "The Subject-Matter of Metaphysical Inquiry (1915)," in *Middle Works*, vol. 8: 11.

20. Ibid., 7.

21. John Dewey, "The Need for Recovery of Philosophy (1917)," in *Middle Works*, vol. 10: 11–12.

22. Dewey, *Democracy and Education*, 87, 90.

23. Dewey, "The Subject-Matter of Metaphysical Inquiry (1915)," in *Middle Works*, vol. 8: 11.

24. Jessica Ching-Sze Wang, *John Dewey in China: To Teach and To Learn* (Albany: State University of New York Press, 2007), 3–4.

25. Dewey and Tufts, *Ethics* (1908), in *Middle Works*, vol. 5: 35.

26. Alice Dewey to Dewey Children, 15 April 1919 (record 10751), in *Correspondence*, vol. 2.

27. John Dewey to Albert C. Barnes, 23 March 1919 (record 04083), in *Correspondence*, vol. 2.

28. John Dewey to Dewey Children, 27 March 1919 (record 10742), in *Correspondence*, vol. 2.

29. John Dewey to Albert C. Barnes, 23 March 1919 (record 04083), in *Correspondence*, vol. 2.

30. Alice Dewey to Dewey Children, 20 June 1919 (record 10763), in *Correspondence*, vol. 2.

31. Quoted in Wang, *John Dewey in China*, 76.

32. John Dewey, "American and Chinese Education," in *Middle Works*, vol. 13: 230, 232.

33. John Dewey, "Syllabus: Types of Philosophic Thought (1922)," in *Middle Works*, vol. 13: 356.

34. Ryan bases his assertion that Boas directly influenced Dewey on a interview done with Ernest Nagel that appears in Corliss Lamont (ed.), Dialogue on John Dewey (New York: Horizon, 1959), in which Nagel explains: "Dewey got a good deal from Boas; but if one can judge from what former students of Boas repeat, Boas got very little from Dewey. . . . I recently heard about a joint seminar that Boas and Dewey gave, which Dewey attended very faithfully. Boas did all the talking, while throughout the semester Dewey didn't say a word. Toward the end of the semester after a long exposition on some question by Boas, he turned to Dewey and asked, 'Professor Dewey, what do you think of this?' Dewey sat for a while lost in thought and finally said, 'Well, I don't really know.' And that, according to my informant, was Dewey's contribution to the seminar" (pp. 55–56). Ryan somehow translated this story into, "When Dewey attended Boas's seminar, it is said that he spoke only once and then to say he agreed with everything Boas said" (p. 167). Besides the fact that Ryan's account seems like a distortion of Nagel's actual story, the influence of Boas on Dewey is not confirmed by the correspondence they exchanged during these years, which seems like a more reliable source than the secondhand story related by Nagel.

35. Franz Boas to John Dewey, 29 March 1916 (record 02573), in *Correspondence*, vol. 2.

36. John Dewey to Robert Daniels, 29 December 1949 (record 14805), in *Correspondence*, vol. 3.

37. John Dewey to Seth Low, 16 June 1898 (record 01886), in *Correspondence*, vol. 1.

38. Ellwood, "The Theory of Imitation in Social Psychology," 735.

39. William I. Thomas, "The Mind of Woman and the Lower Races," *American Journal of Sociology* 12 (January 1907): 438, 438–439.

40. Ibid., 468–469.

41. William I. Thomas, "The Psychology of Race-Prejudice," *American Journal of Sociology* 9 (March 1904): 610.

42. William I. Thomas, "Race Psychology: Standpoint and Questionnaire, with Particular Reference to the Immigrant and the Negro," *American Journal of Sociology* 17 (May 1912): 726, 736.

43. Dewey, "Racial Prejudice and Friction" (1922), in *Middle Works,* vol. 13: 243, 246.

44. Ibid., 252.

45. Ibid., 253.

46. Ibid., 254.

47. Dewey, "Individuality, Equality, and Superiority (1922)," in *Middle Works,* vol. 13: 295.

48. John Dewey, "The School as Means of Developing a Social Consciousness and Social Ideals in Children (1923)," in *Middle Works,* vol. 15: 155.

49. John Dewey, "Education as Engineering" (1922), in *Middle Works,* vol. 13: 328.

50. John Dewey "Education as a Religion" (1922), in *Middle Works,* vol. 13: 318, 319, 321.

51. Education as Engineering" (1922), in *Middle Works,* vol. 13: 328.

52. John Dewey "Education as Politics" (1922), in *Middle Works,* vol. 13: 332, 333.

53. Dewey, *Democracy and Education,* 50.

54. Dewey, "Review of Katherine Elizabeth Dopp" (1903), in *Middle Works,* vol. 2: 308; Dewey, "The Need for Social Psychology" (1917), in *Middle Works,* vol. 10: 60.

Chapter 7

1. Dorothy Ross, *Origins of American Social Science,* 390–470.

2. John B. Watson, *Behaviorism* (Chicago: University of Chicago Press, 1924), 104.

3. Diana Selig, *Americans All: The Cultural Gifts Movement* (Cambridge, MA: Harvard University Press, 2008), 5.

4. John Dewey, "Human Nature and Conduct: An Introduction to Social Psychology (1922)," in *Middle Works,* vol. 14: 3.

5. Ibid., 19, 22, 72, 57, 74–75, 108, 109.

6. Ibid., 67

7. Ibid.

8. Ibid., 141, 144, 179, 179.

9. Ibid., 225, 222.

10. Ibid., 38.

11. John Dewey, "Report and Recommendation upon Turkish Education (1924)," in *Middle Works,* vol. 15: 276.

12. Ibid., 276.

13. Ibid., 280, 281, 289.

14. Ibid., 293, 283.

15. Robert M. Scotten to Charles Evans Hughes, 23 September 1924 (record 06414), in *Correspondence,* vol. 2.

16. Avni Basman to John Dewey, 30 October 1926 (record 04029), in *Correspondence,* vol. 2.

17. John Dewey, "Secularizing a Theocracy (1924)," in *Middle Works,* vol. 15: 133.

18. John Dewey, "Angora, The New (1924)," in *Middle Works,* vol. 15: 138.

19. Hu Shih to John Dewey, 11 October 1926 (record 04023), in *Correspondence,* vol. 2.

20. Ibid.

21. Dewey, *Human Nature and Conduct,* 202.

22. Dewey, "The School as Means of Developing a Social Consciousness and Social Ideals in Children (1923)," in *Middle Works,* vol. 15: 151, 152, 153, 155.

23. Ibid., 154, 155, 156.

24. John Dewey, "Social Purposes in Education (1923)," in *Middle Works,* vol. 15: 159, 163, 165, 168.

25. John Dewey, "Review of *Public Opinion* by Walter Lippman, New York: Harcourt, Brace and Co, 1922 (1922)," in *Middle Works,* vol. 13: 334, 333, 334.

26. John Dewey, "Mediocrity and Individuality (1922)," in *Middle Works,* vol. 13: 293, 292, 294.

27. John Dewey, "Individuality, Equality, and Superiority (1922)," in *Middle Works,* vol. 13: 295, 296, 300.

28. John Dewey, "Individuality in Education (1923)," in *Middle Works,* vol. 15: 178, 173, 175, 173.

29. Dewey, "Human Nature and Conduct: An Introduction to Social Psychology" (1922), in *Middle Works,* vol. 14: 229, 230.

30. John Dewey, *Experience and Education* (New York: Touchtone, 1938), 36, 42

Epilogue

1. Michael Eldridge, "Dewey on Race and Social Change," in *Pragmatism and the Problem of Race,* eds. Bill E. Lawson and Donald Koch (Bloomington: Indiana University Press, 2004), 11, 19.

2. See Sam F. Stack, Jr. "John Dewey and the Question of Race: The Fight for Odell Walker," *Education and Culture* 25 (2009), 17–35.

3. Eddie S. Glaude, Jr. *In a Shade of Blue: Pragmatism and the Politics of Black America.* (Chicago: University of Chicago Press, 2007), 1, 8.

4. Frank Margonis, "John Dewey's Racialized Visions of the Student and Classroom Community," *Educational Theory* 59 (Spring 2009): 17–39; Shannon Sullivan, "(Re) construction Zone," in *In Dewey's Wake: The Unfinished Work of Pragmatic Reconstruction,* ed. W. Gavin (Albany: State University of New York Press, 2003), 109–127.

5. For a more precise definition of "orders of consciousness" and how this genetic psychological theory, stripped of its racist and ethnocentric baggage, is applicable to the postmodern world, see Robert Kegan, *In Over Our Heads: The Mental Demands of Modern Life* (Cambridge, MA: Harvard, 1994).

Bibliography

Collected Papers in Print

Dewey, John. *The Correspondence of John Dewey, 1871–1952*. Edited by Larry Hickman. 3rd ed. 3 vols. Carbondale: Center for Dewey Studies, Southern Illinois University, 2005. CD-ROM.

Dewey, John. *John Dewey: The Early Works, 1882–1898. The Collected Works of John Dewey*. Edited by Jo Ann Boydston. 5 vols. Carbondale: Southern Illinois University Press, 1969–1975.

Dewey, John. *John Dewey: The Middle Works, 1899–1924. The Collected Works of John Dewey*. Edited by Jo Ann Boydston. 15 vols. Carbondale: Southern Illinois University Press, 1976–1983.

Dewey, John. *John Dewey: The Later Works, 1925–1953. The Collected Works of John Dewey*. Edited by Jo Ann Boydston. 17 vols. Carbondale: Southern Illinois University Press, 1981–1990.

Published Primary Works

Dewey, John. *The Child and the Curriculum* and *The School and Society*. 10th ed. Chicago: University of Chicago Press, 1969. Originally published 1902 and 1900, respectively.

———. *Democracy and Education: An Introduction to Philosophy of Education*. New York: Free Press, 1916.

———. *Experience and Education*. New York: Touchtone, 1938.

———. *How We Think*. Mineola, NY: Dover, 1997. Originally published 1910.

McLellan, James A., and John Dewey. *The Psychology of Number and Its Application to Methods of Teaching Arithmetic*. New York: Appleton, 1895.

Runyon, Laura. "A Day with the New Education." *Chautauquan: Organ of the Chautauqua Literacy and Science Circle* 30 (1900): 589–592.

———. "The Teaching of Elementary History in the Dewey School." Master's thesis, University of Chicago, 1906.

Published Secondary Works

Adams, David Wallace. *Education for Extinction: American Indians and the Boarding School Experience*. Lawrence: University Press of Kansas, 1995.

Adams, John, Sir. *The Herbartian Psychology Applied to Education*. New York: D. C. Heath, 1897.

Alilunas, Leo. "John Dewey's Pragmatic Idea about School History and the Early Application." *Social Studies* 41 (March 1950): 111–114.

Ankersmit, F. R. "Historicism: An Attempt at Synthesis." *History and Theory* 34 (Oct. 1995): 143–161.

Bagley, William. "Education and Our Democracy." In *Forgotten Heroes of American Education: The Great Tradition of Teaching Teachers,* edited by J. Wesley Null and Diane Ravitch, 113–117. Greenwich, CT: Information Age, 2006. Article originally published 1918.

———. "Education and Utility." In *Forgotten Heroes of American Education: The Great Tradition of Teaching Teachers,* edited by J. Wesley Null and Diane Ravitch, 59–72. Greenwich, CT: Information Age, 2006. Article originally published 1909.

———. "Optimism in Teaching." In *Forgotten Heroes of American Education: The Great Tradition of Teaching Teachers,* edited by J. Wesley Null and Diane Ravitch, 37–47. Greenwich, CT: Information Age, 2006. Article originally published 1908.

Baldwin, James Mark. *Social and Ethical Interpretations in Mental Development: A Study in Social Psychology.* New York: Macmillan, 1897.

Bennion, Milton. *Citizenship: An Introduction to Social Ethics.* Yonkers-on Hudson, NY: World Book Co., 1919.

Boas, Franz. "The History of Anthropology." In *The Shaping of American Anthropology, 1883– 1911: A Franz Boas Reader,* edited by George Stocking, Jr., 23–35. New York: Basic Books, 1974. Article originally published 1904.

———. *The Mind of Primitive Man.* 2nd ed, rev. New York: Macmillan, 1938. Originally published 1911.

Bourne, Randolph. *The Gary Schools.* New York: Houghton Mifflin, 1916.

Bowler, Peter. *The Eclipse of Darwinism: Anti-Darwinian Evolution Theories in the Decades around 1900.* Baltimore: Johns Hopkins Press, 1983.

Bredo, Eric. "Evolution, Psychology, and John Dewey's Critique of the Reflex Arc Concept." *The Elementary School Journal* 98 (May 1998): 447–466.

Chakrabarty, Dipesh. *Provincializing Europe: Postcolonial Thought and Historical Difference.* Princeton, NJ: Princeton University Press, 2000.

Church, Robert. "Educational Psychology and Social Reform in the Progressive Era." *History of Education Quarterly* 11 (Winter 1971): 390–405.

Commager, Henry Steel. *The American Mind: An Interpretation of American Thought and Character since the 1880s.* New Haven, CT: Yale University Press, 1950.

Coughlan, Neil. *Young John Dewey: An Essay in American Intellectual History.* Chicago: University of Chicago Press, 1975.

Cravens, Hamilton, and John C. Burnham. "Psychology and Evolutionary Naturalism in American Thought, 1890–1940." *American Quarterly* 23 (December 1971): 635–657.

Cremin, Lawrence. *American Education: The Metropolitan Experience, 1876–1980.* New York: Harper & Row, 1988.

———. *Transformation of the School: Progressivism in American Education, 1876–1957.* New York: Knopf, 1961.

DeGarmo, Charles. *The Essentials of Methods, A Discussion of the Essential Form of Right Methods of Teaching: Observation, Generalization, Application.* Boston: D. C. Heath, 1889.

———. "Social Aspects of Moral Education." In *Forgotten Heroes of American Education: The Great Tradition of Teaching Teachers,* edited by J. Wesley Null and Diane Ravitch, 273– 294. Greenwich, CT: Information Age, 2006. Article originally published 1907.

———. "Is Herbart's Theory Dangerous?" Letter to the Editor. *The Public-School Journal* 14 (May 1895): 514–515.

Denver Public Schools. *Social Science, Grades Seven, Eight, and Nine, Junior High School.* Course of Study Monograph, no. 3. Denver, CO: Denver Public Schools, 1924.

Dewey, Jane. "Biography of John Dewey." In *The Philosophy of John Dewey,* edited by Paul Arthur Schlipp, 1-45. New York: Tudor, 1951.

Dewey, John. "Why Reflective Thinking Must Be an Educational Aim." In *John Dewey on Education: Selected Writings,* edited by Reginald D. Archambault, 212–228. Chicago: University of Chicago Press, 1964.

Dewey, John. "Ethical Principles Underlying Education." In *The National Herbart Society for the Scientific Study of Teaching, Third Yearbook*, 7–34. Chicago: Herbart Society, 1897.

Diesterweg, Wilhelm. "Instruction in History." In *Methods of Teaching History*, 1–137. Pedagogical Library, vol. 1, edited by G. Stanley Hall. Boston: Ginn, Heath, 1883.

Dixon, Royal. *Americanization*. New York: Macmillan, 1916.

Dodd, Catherine Isabel. *Introduction to the Herbartian Principles of Teaching*. New York: Macmillan, 1898.

Dopp, Katherine Elizabeth. *The Tree-Dwellers: Age of Fear*. New York: Rand McNally Company, 1904.

Du Bois, W.E.B. "The Conservation of the Races." In *W.E.B. Du Bois: Writing*, edited by Nathan Hughes, 822–826. New York: Viking, 1986. Article originally published 1897.

Dykhuizen, George. *The Life and Mind of John Dewey*. Carbondale: University of Illinois Press, 1973.

Egan, Kieran. *Getting it Wrong from the Beginning: Our Progressive Inheritance from Herbert Spencer, John Dewey, and Jean Piaget*. New Haven: Yale University Press, 2002.

Eiesle, Christopher. "John Dewey and the Immigrants." *History of Education Quarterly* 15 (Spring 1975): 67–85.

Eldridge, Michael. "Dewey on Race and Social Change." In *Pragmatism and the Problem of Race*, edited by Bill E. Lawson and Donald Koch, 11–21. Bloomington: Indiana University Press, 2004.

Ellwood, Charles. "The Theory of Imitation in Social Psychology." *American Journal of Sociology* 6 (May 1901): 721–741.

Fallace, Thomas D. "Tracing John Dewey's Influence on Progressive Education, 1903–1951: Toward a Received Dewey." *Teachers College Record* (forthcoming).

Feinberg, Walter. *Reason and Rhetoric: The Intellectual Foundations of 20th Century Liberal Educational Policy*. New York: Wiley, 1975.

Gardner, Howard. *The Mind's New Science: A History of the Cognitive Revolution*. New York: Basic Books, 1987.

Glaude, Eddie S., Jr. *In a Shade of Blue: Pragmatism and the Politics of Black America*. Chicago: University of Chicago Press, 2007.

Gould, Stephen Jay. *Ontogeny and Phylogeny*. Cambridge, MA: Belknap, 1977.

Hall, G. Stanley. "Moral Education and Will Training." *The Pedagogical Seminary* (1892): 72–89.

———. "The Natural Activities of Children as Determining the Industries in Early Education II." *Journal of Proceedings and Addresses of the Forty-Third Annual Meeting of the National Education Association* (1904): 443–447.

———. "The New Psychology as Basis of Education." *The Forum* 17 (March–August 1894): 710–720.

Harris, William T. "Herbart's Doctrine of Interest." *Educational Review* 10 (June 1895): 71–80.

———. "Professor Dewey's Doctrine of Interest as Related to the Will." *Educational Review* 11 (May 1896): 486–493.

———. *Psychologic Foundations of Education: An Attempt to Show the Genesis of the Higher Faculties of the Mind*. New York: Appleton, 1902.

———. "Reply to DeGarmo's 'Is Herbart's Theory of Interest Dangerous?'" *Public-School Journal* 14 (June 1895): 575–576.

Hirsch, E. D. *Cultural Literacy: What Every American Needs to Know*. Boston: Houghton Mifflin, 1987.

Hobhouse, L. T. *Mind in Evolution*. London: Macmillan, 1901.

Hofstadter, Richard. *Anti-Intellectualism in American Life*. New York: Knopf, 1963.

Johnson, Henry. *Teaching of History in Elementary and Secondary Schools*. New York: Macmillan, 1916.

Jones, Thomas Jesse. *Social Studies in the Hampton Curriculum*. Hampton, VA: Hampton Institute Press, 1908.

Karier, Clarence J., Paul Violas, and Joel Spring, eds. *Roots of Crisis: American Education in the Twentieth Century*. New York: Rand McNally, 1973.

Kegan, Robert. *In Over Our Heads: The Mental Demands of Modern Life*. Cambridge, MA: Harvard University Press, 1994.

Kliebard, Herbert. *The Struggle for the American Curriculum, 1893–1958*. 2nd ed. New York: Routledge, 1995.

Kuhn, Thomas S. *The Essential Tension: Selected Studies in Scientific Tradition and Change*. Chicago: University of Chicago Press, 1977.

Lamont, Corliss, ed. *Dialogue on John Dewey*. New York: Horizon, 1959.

Leys, Ruth. "Mead's Voices: Imitation as Foundation; or the Struggle against Mimesis." In *Modernist Impulses in the Human Sciences 1870–1930*, edited by Dorothy Ross, 210-235. Baltimore: Johns Hopkins University Press, 1991.

Margonis, Frank. "John Dewey's Racialized Visions of the Student and Classroom Community." *Educational Theory* 59 (Spring 2009): 17–39.

Mayhew, Katherine Camp, and Alice Camp Edwards. *The Dewey School: The Laboratory School of the University of Chicago, 1896–1903*. New York: Appleton-Century, 1936.

McKee, James B. *Sociology and the Race Problem: Failure of a Perspective*. Urbana: University of Illinois Press, 1993.

McMurry, Charles. *The Elements of General Method: Based on Principles of Herbart*. New York: Macmillan, 1903.

McMurry, Dorothy. *Herbartian Contributions to History Instruction in American Elementary Schools*. New York: Bureau of Publications, Teachers College, Columbia University, 1946.

McMurry, Frank. "Interest: Some Objections to It." *Education Review* 6 (February 1896): 146–156.

Menand, Louis. *The Metaphysical Club: A Story of Ideas in America*. New York: Farrar, Straus, and Giroux, 2001.

Moreau, Joseph. *Schoolbook Nation: Conflicts over American History Textbooks from the Civil War to the Present*. Ann Arbor: University of Michigan Press, 2003.

Muzzey, David Saville. *An American History*. New York: Ginn, 1911.

Myers, Philip Van Ness. *A Short History of Medieval and Modern Times*. New York: Ginn, 1906.

Novick, Peter. *That Noble Dream: The Objectivity Question and the American Historical Profession*. New York: Cambridge University Press, 1988.

Null, J. Wesley, and Diane Ravitch, eds. *Forgotten Heroes of American Education: The Great Tradition of Teaching Teachers*. Greenwich, CT: Information Age, 2006.

O'Donnell, John M. *The Origins of Behaviorism: American Psychology, 1870–1920*. New York: New York University Press, 1985.

Parker, C. S. *A Textbook in History of Modern Elementary Education with Emphasis on School Practice and Relation to Social Conditions*. New York: Ginn, 1912.

Provenzoi, Eugene F. "History as Experiment: The Role of the Laboratory School in the Development of John Dewey's Philosophy of History." *The History Teacher* 12 (May 1979): 373–382.

Richards, Robert. *Darwin and the Emergence of Evolutionary Theories of Mind and Behavior*. Chicago: University of Chicago Press, 1987.

Richardson, Robert. *William James: In the Maelstrom of American Modernism*. New York: Houghton Mifflin, 2006.

Roberts, Peter. *The Problem of Americanization*. New York: Macmillan, 1920.

Robinson, James Harvey. "John Dewey and His World." *Harvard Teachers Record* 2 (1932): 6–16.

———. *New History: Essays Illustrating the Modern Historical Outlook*. New York: Macmillan, 1912.

Rockefeller, Steven. *John Dewey: Religious Faith and Democratic Humanism*. New York: Columbia University Press, 1991.

Rogers, Daniel. *Atlantic Crossings: Social Politics in a Progressive Age*. Cambridge, MA: Belknap, 1998.

Rorty, Richard. *Contingency, Irony, and Solidarity*. New York: Cambridge University Press, 1989.

Ross, Dorothy. *G. Stanley Hall: The Psychologist as Prophet*. Chicago: University of Chicago Press, 1972.

———, ed. *Modernist Impulses in the Human Sciences, 1870–1930*. Baltimore: Johns Hopkins Press, 1994.

———. *The Origins of American Social Science*. New York: Cambridge University Press, 1991.

Ryan, Alan. *John Dewey and the High Tide of American Liberalism*. New York: Norton, 1995.

Schafer, Axel R. "W.E.B. Du Bois, German Social Thought, and the Racial Divide in American Progressivism." *Journal of American History* 88 (December 2001): 925–949

Selig, Diana. *Americans All: The Cultural Gifts Movement*. Cambridge, MA: Harvard University Press, 2008.

Small, Albion. "Demands of Sociology upon Pedagogy." *Addresses and Proceedings: National Education Association of the United States* (1896): 174–184.

Snedden, David. "Teaching of History in Secondary Schools." *The History Teachers Magazine* 5 (November 1914): 277–282.

Stack, Sam F., Jr. "John Dewey and the Question of Race: The Fight for Odell Walker." *Education and Culture* 25 (2009): 17–35.

Stocking, George W., Jr. *Race, Culture and Evolution: Essays in the History of Anthropology*. Chicago: University of Chicago Press, 1968.

———. *Victorian Anthropology*. New York: Free Press, 1987.

Strickland, Charles. "The Child, the Community, and Clio: The Uses of Cultural History in Elementary School Experiments of the Eighteen-Nineties." *History of Education Quarterly* 7 (Winter 1967): 474–492.

Sullivan, Shannon. "(Re)construction Zone." In *In Dewey's Wake: The Unfinished Work of Pragmatic Reconstruction*, edited by W. Gavin, 109–127. Albany: State University of New York Press, 2003.

Tanner, Laurel N. *Dewey's Laboratory School: Lessons for Today*. New York: Teachers College Press, 1997.

———. "The Meaning of Curriculum in Dewey's Laboratory School, 1986–1904." *Journal of Curriculum Studies* 23 (1991): 101–117.

Thomas, William I. "The Gaming Instinct." *American Journal of Sociology* 6 (July–May 1901): 750–763.

———. "The Mind of Woman and the Lower Races." *American Journal of Sociology* 12 (January 1907): 435–469.

———. "The Psychology of Race-Prejudice." *American Journal of Sociology* 9 (March 1904): 593–610.

———. "Race Psychology: Standpoint and Questionnaire, with Particular Reference to the Immigrant and the Negro." *American Journal of Sociology* 17 (May 1912): 725–775.

———. *Source Book for Social Origins*. Chicago: University of Chicago Press, 1909.

Thorndike, Edward, and R. S. Woodworth. "The Influence of Improvement in One Mental Function upon the Efficiency of Other Functions." *Psychological Review* (May 1901): 247–260.

Tucker, Henry. "The Doctrine of Interest in the Social Sciences in the High School." *The History Teacher's Magazine* 3 (March 1912): 50–53.

U.S. Department of the Interior. *America, Americanism, and Americanization*. Washington, DC: Government Printing Office, 1919.

U.S. Department of the Interior, Bureau of Education. *Americanization as a War Measure: Report of a Conference Called by the Secretary of the Interior, and Held in Washington, April 3, 1918*. Washington, DC: Government Printing Office, 1918.

Van Liew, C. C. "Culture Epoch Theory." Letter to the Journal. *The Public-School Journal* (June 1896): 546.

———. "The Educational Theory of Cultural Epochs: Viewed Historically and Critically." *The Yearbook of the Herbart Society for the Scientific Study of Teaching*. Chicago: Herbart Society, 1895.

Veblen, Thorstein. *The Theory of the Leisure Class: An Economic Study of Institutions*. New York: Macmillan, 1899.

Wang, Jessica Ching-Sze. *John Dewey in China: To Teach and to Learn*. Albany: State University of New York Press, 2007.

Ward, Lester F. *The Psychic Factors of Civilization*. 2nd ed. New York: Ginn, 1906.

Watkins, William. *The White Architects of Black Education: Ideology and Power in America, 1865–1954*. New York: Teachers College Press, 2001.

Watson, John B. *Behaviorism*. Chicago: University of Chicago Press, 1924.

West, Cornell. *The American Evasion of Philosophy: A Genealogy of Pragmatism*. Madison: University of Wisconsin Press, 1989.

Westbrook, Robert. *John Dewey and American Democracy*. Ithaca, NY: Cornell University Press, 1991.

White, Morton. *Social Thought in America: The Revolt against Formalism*. New York: Oxford University Press, 1947.

Wilson, W. E. "The Doctrine of Interest." *Educational Review* 11 (March 1896): 254–263.

INDEX

About the Author

Thomas D. Fallace is an assistant professor of social studies education at William Paterson University of New Jersey. He earned a Ph.D. in education, an M.A. in history, and an M.Ed., all from the University of Virginia, after receiving a B.A. in history from Washington and Lee University. His research interests include history and social sciences education, Holocaust education, the history of education, and the philosophy and influence of John Dewey. In addition to several articles, he is the author of *The Emergence of Holocaust Education in American Schools* (2008).